Exam Ref 70-535
Architecting Microsoft
Azure Solutions

Haishi Bai
Dan Stolts
Santiago Fernández Muñoz

Exam Ref 70-535 Architecting Microsoft Azure Solutions

Published with the authorization of Microsoft Corporation by:
Pearson Education, Inc.

Copyright © 2018 by Pearson Education

ISBN-13: 978-1-5093-0468-4
ISBN-10: 1-5093-0468-1

Library of Congress Control Number: 2018939074
1 18

Trademarks

Warning and Disclaimer

Special Sales

For information about buying this title in bulk quantities, or for special sales opportunities (which may include electronic versions; custom cover designs; and content particular to your business, training goals, marketing focus, or branding interests), please contact our corporate sales department at corpsales@pearsoned.com or (800) 382-3419.

For government sales inquiries, please contact governmentsales@pearsoned.com.

For questions about sales outside the U.S., please contact intlcs@pearson.com.

Editor-in-Chief	Greg Wiegand
Senior Acquisitions Editor	Laura Norman
Development Editor	Troy Mott
Managing Editor	Sandra Schroeder
Senior Project Editor	Tracey Croom
Editorial Production	Backstop Media
Copy Editor	Christina Rudloff
Indexer	Julie Grady
Proofreader	Liv Bainbridge
Technical Editor	Jason Haley
Cover Designer	Twist Creative, Seattle

I would like to dedicate this book to editors, technical reviewers and co-authors. It's been a long and collaborative process to get the book out. I appreciate your dedication, professionalism and persistence to complete the quest.

—HAISHI BAI

I would like to dedicate this book to my son Brad. His love, encouragement, drive and motivation gave me the strength to get to the finish line.

—DAN STOLTS

I would like to dedicate this book to my wife Rocio, for supporting me all the time I spent on this and other projects and being the most important reason on my life to be a better person.

—SANTIAGO FERNÁNDEZ MUÑOZ

Contents at a glance

Contents

Acknowledgments

DAN STOLTS: I'd like to thank the following people: Brad Stolts, Leslie Stolts, Kathy Vieira, John Ross, and Ronald Thibeau.

SANTIAGO FERNÁNDEZ MUÑOZ: I'd like to thank my mentor and, much more important, my friend Rafa, for always helping and advising me on the right path. He always makes me think twice, helping me make the correct questions that have helped me to become the person that I am today. Thank you Rafa!

About the authors

HAISHI BAI, principal software engineer at Microsoft, focuses on the Microsoft Azure compute platform, including IaaS, PaaS, networking, and scalable computing services. Ever since he wrote his first program on an Apple II when he was 12, Haishi has been a passionate programmer. He later became a professional software engineer and architect. During his 21 years of professional life, he's faced various technical challenges and a broad range of project types that have given him rich experiences in designing innovative solutions to solve difficult problems. Haishi is the author of a few cloud computing books, and he's an active contributor to a few open-source projects. He also runs a technical blog(*http://blog.haishibai.com*) with millions of viewers. His twitter handle is @HaishiBai2010.

DAN STOLTS "ITProGuru" is a proven leader in business and technology with over 30 years of experience. He is a technology expert and leader who is a master of systems management, DevOps, and security. He is Chief Technology Strategist for Microsoft, owns Bay State Integrated Technology, Inc. and is a published author. Reach him on his primary blog *http://itproguru. com* or twitter @ITProGuru. He is a proven leader of teams, people and projects. He is proficient in many datacenter technologies (Windows Server, System Center, Virtualization, Cloud, SQL, etc.) and holds many certifications including MCT, MCITP, MCSE, TS, etc. Dan is currently specializing in DevOps and cloud technologies. Dan is and has been a very active member of the user group community. He is an enthusiastic advocate of technology and is passionate about helping others. See more at LinkedIn *https://www.linkedin.com/in/danstolts* or on his blog *http://itproguru.com/about.*

SANTIAGO FERNÁNDEZ MUÑOZ started his career as a trainee in a training center in Seville where he started working with Unix and Windows systems. He followed his passion and taught other people, but it was not what he wanted to do with the rest of his life, so he moved to other companies where he started to work with bigger and bigger projects, with more people and countries involved. He's been working as an Infrastructure Solution Architect for the last six years. He has always been passionate about Microsoft technologies, starting with Windows Server 2003 through to Windows Server 2016 and Azure. He is focused on the automation of cloud infrastructure and continuous integration and delivery for software development.

Introduction

This book teaches you how to design and architect secure, highly-available, performant, monitored and resilient solutions on Azure. This book guides you through leveraging functional, operational and deployment requirements to deploy best in class solutions running in Azure or a hybrid environment. DevOps, automation, monitoring and hands-off management are all key foundations of the highly resilient systems you will be able to design after understanding the material covered.

This book covers every major topic area found on the exam, but it does not cover every exam question. Only the Microsoft exam team has access to the exam questions, and Microsoft regularly adds new questions to the exam, making it impossible to cover specific questions. You should consider this book a supplement to your relevant real-world experience and other study materials. If you encounter a topic in this book that you do not feel completely comfortable with, use the "Need more review?" links you'll find in the text to find more information and take the time to research and study the topic. Great information is available on Azure Documentation, *https://docs.microsoft.com/en-us/azure/*, MSDN, TechNet, and in blogs and forums.

Organization of this book

This book is organized by the "Skills measured" list published for the exam. The "Skills measured" list is available for each exam on the Microsoft Learning website: *http://aka.ms/examlist*. Each chapter in this book corresponds to a major topic area in the list, and the technical tasks in each topic area determine a chapter's organization. If an exam covers six major topic areas, for example, the book will contain six chapters.

Microsoft certifications

Microsoft certifications distinguish you by proving your command of a broad set of skills and experience with current Microsoft products and technologies. The exams and corresponding certifications are developed to validate your mastery of critical competencies as you design and develop, or implement and support, solutions with Microsoft products and technologies both on-premises and in the cloud. Certification brings a variety of benefits to the individual and to employers and organizations.

> **MORE INFO**   **ALL MICROSOFT CERTIFICATIONS**
>
> For information about Microsoft certifications, including a full list of available certifications, go to *http://www.microsoft.com/learning*.

Check back often to see what is new!

Microsoft Virtual Academy

Build your knowledge of Microsoft technologies with free expert-led online training from Microsoft Virtual Academy (MVA). MVA offers a comprehensive library of videos, live events, and more to help you learn the latest technologies and prepare for certification exams. You'll find what you need here:

http://www.microsoftvirtualacademy.com

Quick access to online references

Throughout this book are addresses to webpages that the author has recommended you visit for more information. Some of these addresses (also known as URLs) can be painstaking to type into a web browser, so we've compiled all of them into a single list that readers of the print edition can refer to while they read.

Download the list at *https://aka.ms/examref535/downloads*

The URLs are organized by chapter and heading. Every time you come across a URL in the book, find the hyperlink in the list to go directly to the webpage.

Errata, updates, & book support

We've made every effort to ensure the accuracy of this book and its companion content. You can access updates to this book—in the form of a list of submitted errata and their related corrections—at:

https://aka.ms/examref535/errata

If you discover an error that is not already listed, please submit it to us at the same page.

If you need additional support, email Microsoft Press Book Support at *mspinput@microsoft.com*.

Please note that product support for Microsoft software and hardware is not offered through the previous addresses. For help with Microsoft software or hardware, go to *http://support.microsoft.com*.

Stay in touch

Let's keep the conversation going! We're on Twitter: *http://twitter.com/MicrosoftPress*.

Important: How to use this book to study for the exam

Certification exams validate your on-the-job experience and product knowledge. To gauge your readiness to take an exam, use this Exam Ref to help you check your understanding of the skills tested by the exam. Determine the topics you know well and the areas in which you need more experience. To help you refresh your skills in specific areas, we have also provided "Need more review?" pointers, which direct you to more in-depth information outside the book.

The Exam Ref is not a substitute for hands-on experience. This book is not designed to teach you new skills.

We recommend that you round out your exam preparation by using a combination of available study materials and courses. Learn more about available classroom training at *http://www.microsoft.com/learning*. Microsoft Official Practice Tests are available for many exams at *http://aka.ms/practicetests*. You can also find free online courses and live events from Microsoft Virtual Academy at *http://www.microsoftvirtualacademy.com*.

This book is organized by the "Skills measured" list published for the exam. The "Skills measured" list for each exam is available on the Microsoft Learning website: *http://aka.ms/examlist*.

Note that this Exam Ref is based on this publicly available information and the author's experience. To safeguard the integrity of the exam, authors do not have access to the exam questions.

CHAPTER 1

Design compute infrastructure

What is the cloud? Among all of the possible definitions, you can capture the essence of the cloud with this simple explanation: "The cloud is a huge pool of resources that supports a variety of services."

The foundation of the cloud is a large pool of storage, compute, and networking resources. A key value proposition of the cloud is that you can acquire any amount of these resources at any time, from anywhere, without needing to worry about managing any underlying infrastructures. And when you are done with these resources, you can return them to the cloud just as easily to avoid the unnecessary cost to keep them around.

> **IMPORTANT**
>
> **Have you read page xix?**
>
> It contains valuable information regarding the skills you need to pass the exam.

You can run services on top of these resources. Some of the services give you access to the infrastructure, such as virtual machines (VMs) and virtual networks—these services are called Infrastructure as a Service (IaaS). Some of the services provide support for building your own services in the cloud—these services are called Platform as a Service (PaaS). On top of IaaS and PaaS run Software as a Service (SaaS), which handle all kinds of workloads in the cloud.

This first chapter gives you the knowledge you need to design many different types of compute resources using different technologies such as virtual machines, serverless computing, microservices, web applications, and finally compute-intensive workloads.

Skills in this chapter:

- Skill 1.1: Design solutions using virtual machines
- Skill 1.2: Design solutions for serverless computing
- Skill 1.3: Design microservices-based solutions
- Skill 1.4: Design web applications
- Skill 1.5: Create compute-intensive applications

Skill 1.1: Design solutions using virtual machines

You can run both Windows and Linux VMs on Azure to host your workloads. You can provision a new VM easily on Azure at any time so that you can get your workload up and running without spending the time and money to purchase and maintain any hardware. After the VM is created, you are responsible for maintenance tasks such as configuring and applying software patches.

To provide the maximum flexibility in workload hosting, Azure provides a rich image gallery with both Windows-based and Linux-based images. It also provides several different series of VMs with different amounts of memory and processor power to best fit your workloads. Furthermore, Azure supports virtual extensions with which you can customize the standard images for your project needs. DevOps is a process by which companies streamline all aspects of the business. The primary driver of DevOps in business is communications and processes between development (Dev) and Operations (Ops). The biggest and most pressing component to streamline is the development pipeline (CI/CD pipeline). DevOps provides for cutting out waste through automation, so a key driver of DevOps is automation. Azure supports many tools and processes and allows for streamlining DevOps processes. While learning about compute and other areas in this book, recognize the massive opportunity available to automate any and every step of the technology you learn about. As an example, Azure can provision resources using ARM templates, deploy with code, and constantly monitor with Azure Monitor, Application Insights, and more. High availability (HA) can be achieved to limit downtime and waste associated with downtime. This is provided through designing highly resilient workloads running on Azure. Every aspect of DevOps challenges can be answered by tools and processes developed in or for Azure.

> **This skill covers the following topics:**
> - Design VM deployments by leveraging Availability sets, Fault Domains, and Update Domains in Azure
> - Use web app for containers
> - Design VM scale sets
> - Design for compute-intensive tasks using Azure Batch
> - Define a migration strategy from cloud services
> - Recommend use of Azure Backup and Azure Site Recovery

Design VM deployments by leveraging Availability sets, Fault Domains, and Update Domains in Azure

Cloud datacenters are made up of commodity hardware. With hundreds or even thousands of servers running at any given time, hardware failures are unavoidable. To help you to cope with such failures, Azure introduces three architectural constructs: *Availability sets, Fault Domains* and *Update Domains*. They work together to ensure flexibility and availability of services during failures and planned downtime such as patching.

- **Fault Domain**   This is a group of resources that can fail at the same time. For example, a group of servers on the same rack belong to the same Fault Domain because they share the same power supply, cooling, and network routing systems. When any of these shared devices fail, all servers on the same rack are affected.

- **Availability set**   This is a grouping of resources created to force multiple instances of a service to span multiple Fault Domains. This ensures resources remain available if anything in a single Fault Domain goes down.

- **Update domain**   An Update Domain is a logical group of resources that can be simultaneously updated during system upgrades. When Azure updates a service, it doesn't bring down all instances at the same time. Instead, it performs a rolling update via an Update Domain walk. Service instances in different Update Domains are brought down group by group for updates.

Availability sets, Fault Domains, and Update Domains help you guarantee your service has at least one running instance at any given time during hardware failures and software updates.

A *Fault Domain* is a construct to define the physical layer of a service or deployment. It includes everything that makes up a Single Point of Failure (SPoF) for a system. This includes things such as hosts, switches, racks, and power. There is no assurance or guarantee that a Fault Domain will remain up. In fact, the very nature and definition of a Fault Domain implies that it is either up or down. You do not have the ability to set or change a particular Fault Domain. However, there is a way to force servers and services into different Fault Domains. This is done through an *Availability set*.

An Availability set is a logical grouping of like services that forces components into multiple Fault Domains. If there is only one component in an Availability set, the Availability set serves no purpose. The value of an Availability set is realized as additional component services are added to it. These additional services are automatically split between Fault Domains. An Availability set is designed to protect against underlying hardware or service outages. An additional value of an Availability set is that when you have duplicate services within it, Microsoft provides a Service Level Agreement (SLA) that guarantees availability to the service will be maintained (see Figure 1-1).

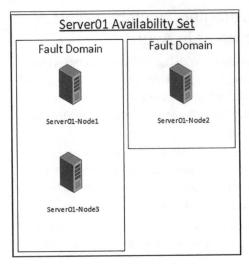

FIGURE 1-1 Fault Domains in an Availability set

For multiple services in an Availability set, you will always have at least two Fault Domains. An Availability set provides redundancy to your application or services. It is recommended that you group two or more virtual machines in an Availability set. This configuration ensures that during a planned or unplanned maintenance event, at least one virtual machine will be available and meet the 99.95% Azure SLA. The Availability set of a virtual machine can't be changed after it is created. Virtual machines that are not in an Availability set and do not have at least two machines deployed in that Availability set do not have an SLA.

An *Update Domain* determines which machines and the sequence that patches are applied to the underlying OS. When you deploy multiple instances of a service, the process managed by an *Update Domain*. An Update Domain (also referred to as an Upgrade Domain) is a logical grouping of role services that defines separation between services. It is different from an Availability set in that it has no impact on Fault Domain allocation. It is an additional grouping that you can use to limit underlying upgrades and outages to services caused by application or underlying service patches.

You can have a maximum of 20 Update Domains per role service; the default is set to five per service. When a new service role is deployed, it is automatically assigned an Update Domain. The assignment ensures that the fewest number of servers or services are impacted by a system patch. Update Domains are logically separated across Fault Domains; however, there are usually more Update Domains than there are Fault Domains, so there will be multiple services on a single Fault Domain. Also, if the number of Update Domains is less than the number of services, you will have multiple services in a single Update Domain. As an example, if you have three services with Update Domain 0, 1, or 2 applied to them, only one will be brought down at the same time for updates. However, both Update Domains 0 and 2 might be on the same Fault Domain, so if there is a failure, multiple services could go down but others would still be running.

As seen in Table 1-1, if you have 11 servers or services, each additional service you add would alternate Fault Domains. If you have the default value of 5 Update Domains defined, each of the first 5 servers would go into different Update Domains. In this scenario, during an update Srv0, Srv5 and Srv10 would all be updated at the same time. In the case of a Fault Domain failure, there would always be services running. Even during an update of Update Domain 0 if Fault Domain 0 goes down, Srv1, Srv3, Srv7, Srv9 and Srv11 would all be running. Even if you only had the first three services and there was a failure of Fault Domain 0 during Update Domain 0 update, Srv1 would continue running.

TABLE 1–1 Service Update Domain and Fault Domain layout

Name	Update Domain	Fault Domain
Srv0	0	0
Srv1	1	1
Srv2	2	0
Srv3	3	1
Srv4	4	0
Srv5	**0**	**1**
Srv6	1	0
Srv7	2	1
Srv8	3	0
Srv9	4	1
Srv10	0	0
Srv11	1	1

When patches or upgrades/updates are applied, they are applied within a single Update Domain. When that Update Domain is finished, Azure moves on to the next one, and so on until all systems updates are completed. As patches are applied, there is a possibility—indeed a likelihood—of service outage for the services in that Update Domain due to services being stopped or servers being rebooted. The more Update Domains you have, the less of a burden or probability of failure during an update. However, the more Update Domains you have, the longer it will take to perform the updates because they are done sequentially. Learn more about updates from *https://docs.microsoft.com/en-us/azure/cloud-services/cloud-services-update-azure-service*.

Fault Domains, Availability sets, and Update Domains all work together to maximize the availability of services during hardware failure and patching, as shown in Figure 1-2.

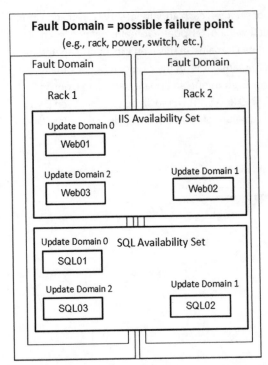

FIGURE 1-2 Fault Domains, Availability sets, and Update Domains

If we were to build this out further, let's suppose that we had eight services in an Availability set. If we kept the default of five Update Domains, in two of them we would only have one service; in the other three, we would have two. This means that when patches are applied to those three Update Domains, two services would be unavailable at the same time. To avoid this, you can increase the number of Update Domains. Having multiple service outages for updates at the same time across a large set of services is not generally a problem, because the more services you have, the lower the probability of failure. Additionally, if you are auto-scaling services and the additional services are needed at the time of the update, additional services can be made available to handle the load while the update is underway (see Figure 1-3).

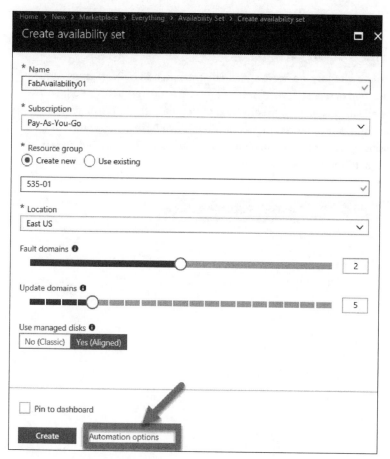

FIGURE 1-3 Create Availability set Screenshot

Availability sets are created in the Azure portal by clicking **+ Create A Resource** > typing **availability set** > clicking **Create**. Provide a name for the Availability set, select the subscription, select or create the resource group, select the location, and then define the number of Fault Domains and the number of Update Domains. Notice in Figure 1-3 you can click an Automation options button to get the scripts for the creation. Click the Create button.

Virtual Machine Deployments

A virtual machine can be created in the Azure portal by creating a resource. Click **+ Create a resource** > click **Compute** and then click the type of virtual machine you want to create. Notice that there are many different types of virtual machines including different operating systems and applications already installed on various operating systems. There are also other compute options that will be covered later in this chapter. We will create a virtual machine running Windows Server 2016 Datacenter to explain the design elements behind the available choices.

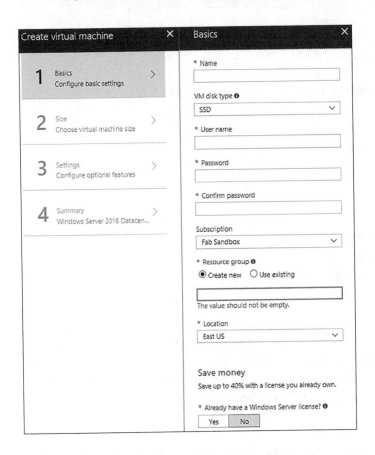

FIGURE 1-4 Create Virtual Machine Screenshot in Azure Portal

Click **Windows Server** > click **Windows Server 2016 Datacenter**. For the deployment model, you always want to use Resource Manager unless you are building a machine that is part of a legacy system that is already up and running in Classic Azure. Click **Create**. This will open up a new wizard blade to fill out the options for a virtual machine.

- **Name** The name is simply the name of the virtual machine. It cannot contain non-ASCII or special characters (spaces not allowed either) and must have at least one alpha character. See Figure 1-4.

- **VM disk type** SSD is the premium disk offering and is backed by solid-state drives. SSD offers consistent, low-latency performance. Solid-state drives offer great performance and are ideal for I/O-intensive applications and production workloads. Standard disks (HDD) are backed by magnetic drives and are preferable for applications where data is accessed infrequently.

> **NOTE ABOUT TEMPORARY DISKS**
>
> Each VM will include a temporary disk, which is considered volatile. Both OS drives and data drives are virtual hard drives (VHDs) stored in Azure Blob storage. Their data is automatically duplicated three times for reliability. However, the temporary drives reside on the hosting servers. If the host fails, your VM will be moved to a healthy host, but not the temporary drive. In this case, you'll lose all temporary data. By default, the temporary drive is mounted as drive D on a Windows system, and /dev/sdb1 on a Linux system.

- **Username** The username is the administrative username that will be created on the new server. It is the name you will use to log in to the server.

- **Password and Confirm Password** This is the password to be used to authenticate to the server. The password must have three of the following: one lowercase character, one uppercase character, one number, and one special character, but this is not '/' or '-'. It must be between 12 and 123 characters in length.

- **Subscription** This is the subscription the machine will be built on.

- **Resource group** You can create a resource group on the fly or use an existing resource group.

- **Location** Location allows you to decide which datacenter region the virtual machine will be created in.

- **License** Notice now you can also bring your own license. If you already have a license, you can save money by not having to include the license fees in the cost of the server.

After clicking **Create OK** on the basic page, the Size blade will be displayed. This is where you decide what size VM you will need. By default, you are only provided with a few Recommended options. There is no intelligence behind these recommendations, so to see more options click the **View All** link on the page. On the top of the blade, the first question is what kind of disk you would like to have. You can also select the number of CPUs and the amount of memory. These options will automatically filter the server options for you. You cannot select the exact number of processors and memory separately, because Azure packages machines based on CPU and processors, so you will be given options that fit the requirements of the filter. As an example, if you put in SSD, 8 vCPUs, and 64GB memory, you will be provided with machines that range in price from under $700 (E8S_V3) to many thousands of dollars (DS14_V2). See Table 1–2 for a list of Azure virtual machines, including their sizes and description.

TABLE 1–2 Virtual machine sizing in Azure

TYPE	SIZES	DESCRIPTION
General Purpose	B, Dsv3, Dv3, DSv2, Dv2, DS, D, Av2, A0-7	Balanced CPU-to-memory ratio. Ideal for testing and development, small to medium databases, and low to medium traffic web servers. DS adds high-performance IO for persisted data.
Compute Optimized	Fsv2, Fs, F	High CPU-to-memory ratio. Good for medium traffic web servers, network appliances, batch processes, and application servers.
Memory Optimized	Esv3, Ev3, M, GS, G, DSv2, DS, Dv2, D	High memory-to-CPU ratio. Great for relational database servers, medium to large caches, and in-memory analytics.
Storage Optimized	Ls	High disk throughput and IO. Ideal for Big Data, SQL, and NoSQL databases.
GPU	NV, NC, NCv2, ND	Specialized virtual machines targeted for heavy graphic rendering and video editing. Available with single or multiple GPUs.
High Performance Compute	H, A8-11	Fastest and most powerful CPU virtual machines with optional high-throughput network interfaces (RDMA).

> **NOTE** VIRTUAL MACHINE USE CASES
>
> To get additional information on the sizes of virtual machines and the use cases for them, check out: *https://docs.microsoft.com/en-us/azure/virtual-machines/windows/sizes*.

The Settings blade will be displayed after selecting the size of the virtual machine. Notice the first setting on the blade is Availability set, which is under the heading High Availability. This is where you attach or create an Availability set. The Availability set must be in the same location and resource group as the VMs that will be in the Availability set. Additional options on the Settings blade include Subnet, Public IP address, Network Security Group, Accelerated networking, Extensions, Auto-shutdown, Monitoring, Guest OS Diagnostics, Diagnostics Storage Account, and Backup.

When building a VM in an Availability set, you can provide an instance count of one. However, you need to scale up the Availability set to at least two instances in order for the Availability set to do the job of making sure the system is always running. The instances need to be configured with a network load balancer so traffic to the systems is managed. This way, if one server goes down for maintenance, the other will be up and taking requests. For a template that sets up multiple VMs in an Availability set with a load balancer and NAT configured, see *https://azure.microsoft.com/en-us/resources/templates/201-multi-vm-lb-zones/*.

EXAM TIP

Scaling out is a growth architecture or method that focuses on horizontal growth, adding additional new resources instead of increasing the capacity of current resources. Scaling out requires additional up-front technology to split the incoming requests between the available resources. In Azure, this is generally done by increasing the number of instances of a resource.

EXAM TIP

Scaling up is a growth architecture or method that focuses on vertical growth, increasing the size of an existing resource. It is increasing the capacity of current resources. This is done by increasing processor size, processor count, memory size, disk size, or other internal resources on a machine. In Azure, this is generally done with increasing the size of the deployed virtual machine (e.g. changing a D3_v2 to a DS9_v2).

When you scale-out an application, the workload needs to be distributed among the participating instances. This is done by load balancing. The virtual machine or application workload is distributed among the participating instances by the Azure public-facing load-balancer in this case. More on load balancing in Chapter 3.

EXAM TIP

Azure Hybrid Benefit for Windows Server, for customers with Software Assurance, allows you to use your on-premises Windows Server licenses and run Windows virtual machines on Azure at a reduced cost. You can use Azure Hybrid Benefit for Windows Server to deploy new virtual machines from any Azure-supported platform, Windows Server image, or Windows custom images: *https://docs.microsoft.com/en-us/azure/virtual-machines/windows/hybrid-use-benefit-licensing*.

Managing Images

There are several sources for Azure VM: Azure VM gallery and custom images. You can use these images as foundations to create, deploy, and replicate your application run-time environments consistently for different purposes such as testing, staging, and production. To learn more about images, see the following:

- **VM gallery** The Azure VM gallery offers hundreds of VM images from Microsoft, partners, and the community at large. You can find recent Windows and Linux OS images as well as images with specific applications, such as SQL Server, Oracle Database, and SAP HANA. Visual Studio subscribers or customers with an Enterprise Agreement also have exclusive access to some other images such as Windows 10 Enterprise. For a complete list of the market place images, go to: *http://azure.microsoft.com/en-us/marketplace/virtual-machines/*.

- **Template Images**   There are also many template (JSON) images available from various people and sites including the Azure Quickstart Templates (*https://azure.microsoft.com/en-us/resources/templates/*) that can be leveraged to deploy as is or modify and then deploy. There is also a tool, Packer, which allows you to create identical machines on multiple platforms for leveraging a single source configuration. Packer is lightweight, runs on every major operating system, and is highly performant, creating machine images for multiple platforms in parallel (*https://docs.microsoft.com/en-us/azure/virtual-machines/windows/build-image-with-packer*).

- **Custom images**   You can capture images of your VMs and then reuse these images as templates to deploy more VMs. You can also upload your own images that were created on-premises or on another platform (*https://docs.microsoft.com/en-us/azure/virtual-machines/windows/prepare-for-upload-vhd-image*).

Custom Images

You can capture two types of images: generalized or specialized.

A generalized image doesn't contain computer or user-specific settings. These images are ideal for use as standard templates to roll out preconfigured VMs to different customers or users. Before you can capture a generalized image, you need to run the System Preparation (Sysprep) tool in Windows or use the **waagent –deprovision** command in Linux. All of the operating system (OS) images you see in the VM gallery are generalized. Before you can capture a generalized image, you need to shut down the VM. After the VM is captured as an image, the original VM is automatically deleted.

Specialized images, conversely, retain all user settings. You can think of specialized images as snapshots of your VMs. These images are ideal for creating checkpoints of an environment so that it can be restored to a previously known good state. You don't need to shut down a VM before you capture specialized images. Also, the original VM is unaffected after the images are captured. If a VM is running when an image is captured, the image is in a crash-consistent state. If application consistency or cross-drive capture is needed, it's recommended to shut down the VM before capturing the image.

You can use your own custom images to create new VMs just as you would use standard images. When a new VM is created, the original VHD files are copied so the originals are not affected. You can see step-by-step instructions on how to generalize a virtual machine in Azure so it can be used as an image at *https://docs.microsoft.com/en-us/azure/virtual-machines/windows/capture-image-resource*.

VM extension

When you provision a new VM, a light-weight Azure Virtual Machine Agent (VM Agent) is installed on the VM by default. VM Agent is responsible for installing, configuring, and managing Azure VM Extensions (VM Extensions). VM Extensions are first-party or third-party components that you can dynamically apply to VMs. These extensions make it possible for you to dynamically customize VMs to satisfy your application, configuration, and compliance needs.

For example, you can deploy the McAfee Endpoint Security extension to your VMs by enabling the *McAfeeEndpointSecurity* extension.

You can use the Azure PowerShell cmdlet *Get-AzureVMAvailableExtension* to list currently available extensions.

> **NOTE** **VM AGENT OPT-OUT**
>
> When creating a VM, you can choose not to install the VM agent. You can install the VM Agent to an existing VM; however, when a VM agent is installed, removing it is not a supported scenario. You can, of course, physically remove the agent, but the exact behavior after removal is undocumented.

Custom Script Extension and DSC

Custom Script Extension downloads and runs scripts you've prepared on an Azure Blob storage container, GitHub, or another accessible URL. You can upload Azure PowerShell scripts or Linux Shell scripts, along with any required files, to a storage container or accessible location, and then instruct Custom Script Extension to download and run the scripts. See *https://github.com/ Azure/azure-linux-extensions/tree/master/CustomScript* for code snippets showing an example Azure CLI command to use with the Custom Script Extension for Linux (CustomScriptForLinux).

Using scripts to manage VM states overcomes the shortcomings of managing them with images. Scripts are easier to change, and you can apply them faster. An added benefit is that you can trace all changes easily by using source repositories.

However, writing a script to build up a VM toward a target state is not easy. For each of the requirement components, you'll need to check if the component already exists and if it is configured in the desired way. You'll also need to deal with the details of acquiring, installing, and configuring various components to support your workloads. Windows PowerShell Desired State Configuration (DSC) takes a different approach. Instead of describing steps of how the VM state should be built up, you simply describe what the desired final state is with DSC. Then, DSC ensures that the final state is reached. The following is a sample DSC script that verifies the target VM has IIS with ASP.NET 4.5 installed:

```
Configuration DemoWebsite
{
param ($MachineName)
Node $MachineName
{
#Install the IIS Role
WindowsFeature IIS
{
Ensure = "Present"
Name = "Web-Server"
}
#Install ASP.NET 4.5
WindowsFeature ASP
{
```

```
Ensure = "Present"
Name = "Web-Asp-Net45"
}
}
}
```

State management at scale

For larger deployments, you often need to ensure consistent states across a large number of VMs. You also need to periodically check VM states so they don't drift from the desired parameters. An automated state management solution such as Chef and Puppet can save you from having to carry out such repetitive and error-prone tasks.

For both Chef and Puppet, you write "cookbooks" that you can then apply to a large number of VMs. Each cookbook contains a number of "recipes" or "modules" for various tasks, such as installing software packages, making configuration changes, and copying files. They both facilitate community contributions (Puppet Forge and Chef Supermarket) so that you can accomplish common configuration tasks easily. For example, to get a Puppet module that installs and configures Redis, you can use Puppet to pull down the corresponding module from Puppet Forge:

```
puppet module install evenup-redis
```

Both Chef and Puppet install agents on your VMs. These agents monitor your VM states and periodically check with a central server to download and apply updated cookbooks. Azure provides VM extensions that bootstrap Chef or Puppet agents on your VMs. Furthermore, Azure also provides VM images that assist you in provisioning Chef and Puppet servers. Chef also supports a hosted server at *https://manage.chef.io*.

Managing VM states is only part of the problem of managing application run-time environments in the cloud. Your applications often depend on external services. How do you ensure that these external services remain in desired states? The solution is Azure Automation. With Automation, you can monitor events in VMs as well as external services such as Azure App Service Web Apps, Azure Storage, and Azure SQL Server. Then, workflows can be triggered in response to these events.

Automation's cookbooks, called *runbooks*, are implemented as Azure PowerShell Workflows. To help you author these runbooks, Azure has created an Azure Automation Runbook Gallery at *http://aka.ms/ScriptCenterGallery* where you can download and share reusable runbooks. You can browse the gallery by navigating to **Automation Accounts** > **Runbooks** > **Browse Gallery**.

Azure Custom Script Extension allows for running a script on a virtual machine, which can be used for forcing a configuration on that virtual machine.

Capturing infrastructure as code

Traditionally, development and operations are two distinct departments for an Independent Software Vendor (ISV). Developers concern themselves with writing applications, and the folks in operations are concerned with keeping the applications running. However, for an application to function correctly, there are always explicit or implicit requirements regarding how the supporting infrastructure is configured. Unfortunately, such requirements are often lost during communication, which leads to many problems such as service outages due to misconfigurations, frictions between development and operations, and difficulties in re-creating and diagnosing issues. All of these problems are unacceptable in an Agile environment.

In an Agile ISV, the boundary between development and operations is shifting. The developers are required to provide consistently deployable applications instead of just application code; thus, the deployment process can be automated to roll out fixes and upgrades quickly. This shift changed the definition of an application. An application is no longer just code. Instead, an application is made up of both application code and explicit, executable description of its infrastructural requirements. This is known as infrastructure code or *infrastructure as code (IaC)*. The name has two meanings. First, "infrastructure" indicates that it's not business logics, but instructions to configure the application runtime. Second, "code" indicates that it's not subject to human interpretation but can be consistently applied by an automation system.

Infrastructure code is explicit and traceable, and it makes an application consistently deployable. Consistently deployable applications are one of the key enabling technologies in the DevOps movement. The essence of DevOps is to reduce friction so that software lifecycles can run smoother and faster, allowing continuous improvements and innovations. Consistently deployable applications can be automatically deployed and upgraded regularly across multiple environments. This means faster and more frequent deployments, reduced confusion across different teams, and increased agility in the overall engineering process.

Azure Resource Manager Template

Azure Resource Templates are JSON files that capture infrastructure as code. You can capture all of the Azure resources your application needs in a single JSON document that you can consistently deploy to different environments. All resources defined in an Azure Resource Template are provisioned within a Resource Group, which is a logical group for managing related Azure resources.

> **NOTE SUPPORTING ALL AZURE RESOURCE TYPES**
>
> Azure Resource Manager Templates support changes over time. As each Azure resource type is implemented as a Resource Provider that can be plugged into Azure Resource Manager, the service that governs resource creation, and those services become available in Azure Resource Manager Templates.

You can write an Azure Resource Template from scratch using any text editor. You can also download a template from an Azure template gallery, such as Azure Quickstart Templates at *https://azure.microsoft.com/en-us/resources/templates*. At the top of the template file, an Azure Resource Template contains a schema declaration; see Figure 1-5. This consists of a content version number and a "resources" group, which contains resource definitions.

```
"$schema": "https://schema.management.azure.com/schemas/2015-01-01/deploymentTemplate.json#",
"contentVersion": "1.0.0.0",
"parameters": {},
"variables": {},
"resources": []
```

FIGURE 1-5 Sample Azure Template

Optionally, you can also define parameters, variables, tags, and outputs. A complete introduction of the template language is beyond the scope of this book. However, creating a Resource Group is as easy as running a few PowerShell commands to log in, set up your environment and create the resource group:

```
Login-AzureRmAccount       # Login to Azure
Select-AzureRmSubscription -SubscriptionName <yourSubscriptionName>  # Select
your subscription
# Create the new ResourceGroupName
New-AzureRmResourceGroup -Name ExampleResourceGroup -Location "South Central US"
```

Supply the resource group name to the command along with other required parameters and then validate if your template is ready to be deployed.

To deploy a template, use the *New-AzureRmResourceGroupDeployment* cmdlet:

```
New-AzureRmResourceGroupDeployment -Name ExampleDeployment –ResourceGroupName
 ExampleResourceGroup `
  -TemplateFile c:\MyTemplates\storage.json -storageAccountType Standard_GRS
```

An Azure Resource Template captures the entire topology of all Azure resources required by your application. And, you can deploy it with a single Azure PowerShell command. This capacity greatly simplifies resource management of complex applications, especially service-oriented architecture (SOA) applications that often have many dependencies on hosted services.

Use Web App for Containers

Web application service for containers allows you to easily deploy and run containerized Web Apps that scale as needed. Web App for Containers allows you to run your app on a fast always-on infrastructure, relieving you from the burden of managing the underlying infrastructure. It leverages built-in auto-scaling and load balancing and allows you to streamline CI/CD pipeline with Docker Hub, Azure Container Registry, GitHub, and more. We will discuss Web Apps in detail later, for now we will dive into running Web Apps for Containers. Containers take advantage of all the great advantages of Web Apps. They allow you to get your apps in front of users faster, increase developer productivity, ship updates faster, achieve global scale on demand, get actionable insights and analytics, take advantage of hybrid consistency, run on enterprise-grade services and perhaps most importantly provide almost limitless portability at significantly reduced costs compared to virtual machines.

Web App is a fully managed compute platform that is optimized for hosting websites and web applications. Customers can use App Service on Linux to host Web Apps natively on Linux for supported application stacks. Web App for Containers is designed natively to run Linux-based apps. The Linux-based containers are referred to as "Azure App Service on Linux." It supports a number of built-in images in order to increase developer productivity. If the runtime your application requires is not supported in the built-in images, there are instructions on how to build your own Docker image to deploy to Web App for Containers: *https://docs.microsoft.com/en-us/azure/app-service/containers/tutorial-custom-docker-image*.

Currently Web Apps for containers supports Node.js, PHP, .NET Core and Ruby. See *https://docs.microsoft.com/en-us/azure/app-service/containers/app-service-linux-intro* for supported versions, updates and limitations. Current limitations on capabilities with this platform include:

- App service for containers only works with basic or standard service plans; there are no free or shared options.

- You cannot create Web App for Containers in an App Service plan already hosting non-Linux Web Apps.

- When creating Web App for Containers in a resource group containing non-Linux Web Apps, you must create an App Service plan in a different region than the existing App Service plan.

It is possible and well documented on how to expand the current capabilities of the platform with available tools. As an example you can use Azure Toolkit for IntelliJ to publish your Java app with IntelliJ to an Azure App Service: *https://docs.microsoft.com/en-us/java/azure/intellij/azure-toolkit-for-intellij-hello-world-web-app-linux*.

Containers allow very easy portability between Azure, on-premises, and other cloud or hosting providers. They also follow the key tenants of DevOps. By building your application in a container, the container can be built and deployed as code allowing for complete automation through every step in the CI/CD pipeline. This means you can have complete confidence that the application will deploy and run every time with no human intervention. For additional information and step-by-step tutorials on App Service for containers, see: *https://docs.microsoft.com/en-us/azure/app-service/containers*.

Design VM scale sets

A virtual machine gives you the capability to build, deploy and run a set of identical virtual machines. With all VMs configured the same, scale sets are designed to support true autoscale, and no pre-provisioning of VMs is required. This allows you to build large-scale services that target big compute, large data, and containerized workloads. For applications that need to scale compute resources out and in, scale operations are implicitly balanced across fault and Update Domains. For a further introduction to scale sets, refer to the Azure documentation located at *https://docs.microsoft.com/en-us/azure/virtual-machine-scale-sets/*. You can create a scale set in the Azure portal by selecting new and typing scale on the search bar. The virtual machine scale set is listed in the results. From there, you can fill in the required fields to customize and deploy your scale set. You also have options to set up basic autoscale rules based on CPU usage in the portal. To manage your scale set, you can use the Azure portal, Azure PowerShell cmdlets, or the Azure CLI 2.0.

Figure 1-6 shows a Create virtual machine scale set screenshot. Notice that both autoscaling and load balancer are available when you create the scale set in the management portal.

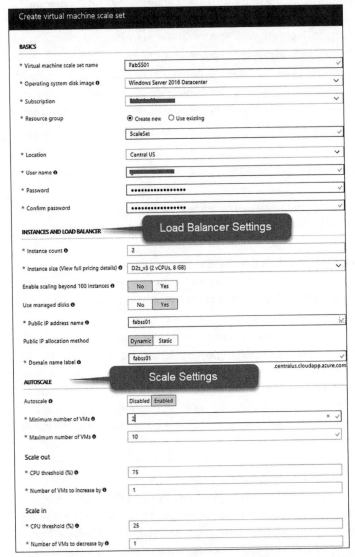

FIGURE 1-6 Create Virtual Machine Scale Set with Multiple Instances and Autoscale

Generally, scale sets are useful for deploying highly available infrastructure where a set of machines have similar configurations. However, some features are only available in scale sets while other features are only available in VMs. In order to make an informed decision about when to use each technology, you should first take a look at some of the commonly used features that are available in scale sets but not VMs.

SCALE SET-SPECIFIC FEATURES

- Once you specify the scale set configuration, you can update the "capacity" property to deploy more VMs in parallel. This is much simpler than writing a script to orchestrate deploying many individual VMs in parallel.
- You can use Azure Autoscale to automatically scale a scale set, but not individual VMs.
- You can reimage scale set VMs but not individual VMs.
- You can overprovision scale set VMs for increased reliability and quicker deployment times. You cannot do this with individual VMs unless you write custom code to do this.
- You can specify an upgrade policy to make it easy to roll out upgrades across VMs in your scale set. With individual VMs, you must orchestrate updates yourself.

VM-SPECIFIC FEATURES

Some features are currently only available in VMs:

- You can attach data disks to specific individual VMs, but attached data disks are configured for all VMs in a scale set.
- You can attach non-empty data disks to individual VMs but not VMs in a scale set.
- You can snapshot an individual VM but not a VM in a scale set.
- You can capture an image from an individual VM but not from a VM in a scale set.
- You can migrate an individual VM from native disks to managed disks, but you cannot do this for VMs in a scale set.
- You can assign IPv6 public IP addresses to individual VM NICs but cannot do so for VMs in a scale set. You can assign IPv6 public IP addresses to load balancers in front of either individual VMs or scale set VMs.

SCALE SETS WITH AZURE MANAGED DISKS

Scale sets can be created with Azure Managed Disks instead of traditional Azure storage accounts. Managed Disks provide the following benefits:

- You do not have to pre-create a set of Azure storage accounts for the scale set VMs.
- You can define attached data disks for the VMs in your scale set.
- Scale sets can be configured to support up to 1,000 VMs in a set.

If you have an existing template, you can also update the template to use Managed Disks.

USER-MANAGED STORAGE

- A scale set that is not defined with Azure Managed Disks relies on user-created storage accounts to store the OS disks of the VMs in the set. A ratio of 20 VMs per storage account or less is recommended to achieve maximum IO and also take advantage of overprovisioning (see below). It is also recommended that you spread the beginning characters of the storage account names across the alphabet. Doing so helps spread load across different internal systems.

OVERPROVISIONING

- Scale sets currently default to "overprovisioning" VMs. With overprovisioning turned on, the scale set actually spins up more VMs than you asked for and then deletes the extra VMs once the requested number of VMs are successfully provisioned. Overprovisioning improves provisioning success rates and reduces deployment time. You are not billed for the extra VMs, and they do not count toward your quota limits.

- While overprovisioning does improve provisioning success rates, it can cause confusing behavior for an application that is not designed to handle extra VMs appearing and then disappearing. To turn overprovisioning off, ensure you have the following string in your template: "overprovision": "false". See *https://docs.microsoft.com/en-us/rest/api/virtualmachinescalesets/create-or-update-a-set*.

- If your scale set uses user-managed storage and you turn off overprovisioning, you can have more than 20 VMs per storage account, but it is not recommended to go above 40 for IO performance reasons.

LIMITS

- A scale set built on a Marketplace image (also known as a platform image) and configured to use Azure Managed Disks supports a capacity of up to 1,000 VMs. If you configure your scale set to support more than 100 VMs, not all scenarios work the same (for example load balancing). See *https://docs.microsoft.com/en-us/azure/virtual-machine-scale-sets/virtual-machine-scale-sets-placement-groups*.

- A scale set configured with user-managed storage accounts is currently limited to 100 VMs (and 5 storage accounts are recommended for this scale).

- A scale set built on a custom image (one built by you) can have a capacity of up to 300 VMs when configured with Azure Managed disks. If the scale set is configured with user-managed storage accounts, it must create all OS disk VHDs within one storage account. As a result, the maximum recommended number of VMs in a scale set built on a custom image and user-managed storage is 20. If you turn off overprovisioning, you can go up to 40.

EXAM TIP

Marketplace images with Azure Managed Disks support a capacity of up to 1,000 VMs. User-managed storage account are limited to 100 VMs. A custom image scale set on Azure Managed Disks can have a capacity of 300 VMs. Custom images on user-managed storage capacity has a recommended limit of 20 VMs.

For more VMs than these limits allow, you need to deploy multiple scale sets. For updates and additional information on design considerations for VM scale sets see: *https://docs.microsoft. com/en-us/azure/virtual-machine-scale-sets/virtual-machine-scale-sets-design-overview.*

Design for compute-intensive tasks using Azure Batch

The Azure cloud provides you with the capability to efficiently run compute-intensive Linux and Windows workloads, from parallel batch jobs to traditional HPC solutions. You can run your HPC and batch workloads on Azure infrastructure, with your choice of compute services, grid managers, Marketplace solutions, and vendor-hosted (SaaS) applications. Azure provides flexible solutions to distribute work and scale to thousands of VMs or cores and then scale down when you need fewer resources.

Azure Batch is a platform service for running large-scale parallel and high-performance computing (HPC) applications efficiently in the cloud. Azure Batch schedules compute-intensive work to run on a managed pool of virtual machines and can automatically scale computes resources to meet the needs of your jobs. SaaS providers or developers can use the Batch SDKs and tools to integrate HPC applications or container workloads with Azure, stage data to Azure, and build job execution pipelines.

Azure Batch allows you to run applications, long-running scripts, or heavy compute scripts without creating or managing the underlying infrastructure. Batch is a managed Azure service that is used for batch processing or batch computing—running a large volume of similar tasks for a desired result. Batch computing is most commonly used by organizations that regularly process, transform, and analyze large volumes of data.

Batch works well with intrinsically parallel (also known as "embarrassingly parallel") applications and workloads. Intrinsically parallel workloads are those that are easily split into multiple tasks that perform work simultaneously on many computers. For the differences between Batch and other HPC solution options in Azure, see HPC, Batch, and Big Compute solutions at *https://docs.microsoft.com/en-us/azure/virtual-machines/linux/high-performance-computing.*

As the name suggests, the purpose of *Big Compute* is to perform a lot of computational tasks in a distributed yet coordinated fashion. Typical Big Compute workloads include simulation (such as fluid-dynamics simulation), analysis (such as genome search), modeling (such as risk modeling), and so on. These often require a large number of compute hours.

Microsoft Azure provides both hardware and software resources with which you can run large-scale batch jobs in parallel in the cloud. Instead of managing expensive infrastructure yourself at your own datacenters, you can dynamically request compute resources at any time, perform compute tasks on them, and then release them to avoid extra costs. To learn more about batch and MPI applications, see *https://docs.microsoft.com/en-us/azure/batch/ batch-mpi.*

Azure Batch Service is a great solution If you don't want the trouble of managing a compute cluster yourself. Using Batch, you can schedule and manage large-scale parallel workloads on Azure-managed compute resources without the need to manage any infrastructure details.

Batch is designed to run a large number of parallel tasks on a set of allocated compute resources. Because all compute resources are managed for you by Azure, you simply prepare the input data as well as the processing program, and then Azure takes cares of the rest for you. There is no additional charge for using Batch. You only pay for the underlying resources consumed, such as the virtual machines, storage, and networking.

You have two ways to programmatically interact with Batch: Pool application packages, which are deployed to every node in the pool, and Task application packages, which are deployed only to compute nodes scheduled to run a task. Within Azure Batch, an application refers to a set of versioned binaries that can be automatically downloaded to the compute nodes in your pool. An application package refers to a specific set of those binaries and represents a given version of the application.

Learn more about developing solutions using the Batch REST API or the Batch .NET Library by leveraging packages at: *https://docs.microsoft.com/en-us/azure/batch/batch-application-packages*.

- **Batch account**   To interact with Batch, you need a Batch account, which you can create via the Azure management portal. All Batch service requests must be authenticated with a Batch account and its associated security key.

- **ComputeNode**   A ComputeNode is a dedicated VM that is allocated to run your tasks. A collection of nodes form a pool. You don't directly manage the underlying infrastructure, but you can control the characteristics of these pools by using the Batch API. For example, you can specify the number, size, operating system, as well as scaling rules of notes in a resource pool.

- **Job Schedule, Jobs and Tasks**   Job Schedule is the scheduler and executor of the jobs. A job contains the details of the job including how the tasks are run on the ComputeNode pool. A job consists of a number of tasks.

- **Input File**   An input file is the input data that a task processes. You need to upload input data files to Azure Storage, and then Batch will transfer them to nodes for processing.

- **Monitor**   Monitor is a process that can be queried for the progress of the job and its tasks.

- **Task Output**   This results in data created and uploaded to Azure Storage as a task once completed.

- **Output Files**   They contain data output files after a job completes.

Define a migration strategy from cloud services

There are now cloud services that can assist or enable you to migrate to Azure. First, and most importantly, you should be aware of the Azure Migration Center (*https://azure.microsoft.com/en-us/migrate*), where you can simplify your cloud migration with proven tools, guidance, and partners. Whether you are transferring data, migrating infrastructure, or modernizing apps, Azure offers you the agility, security, reliability, global scale, and cost efficiencies you need, helping you:

- Lower your total cost of ownership (TCO) by right-sizing your infrastructure and taking advantage of the economies of scale and hybrid benefits.

- Take advantage of a secure, reliable, and global infrastructure.

- Accelerate your Azure migration with step-by-step guidance and technical resources that are customized to your workloads.

Azure Migrate

Azure Migrate makes your migration faster and easier with workflows that lead you through the migration process for your workloads and databases. Azure Migrate makes it easy to assess on-premises workloads for migration to Azure. It helps you with discovering and assessing VM and database workloads.

DISCOVERY

- Non-intrusive discovery of virtual machines (VMs)
- Ability to visualize VM dependencies to easily identify multi-tier applications
- Support for vCenter Server 5.5, 6.0, and 6.5

ASSESSMENTS

- Azure readiness: Is a VM suitable for running in Azure?
- Right-sizing: What's the best Azure VM size based on utilization history?
- Cost estimates: How much would be the recurring cost of running the VM in Azure?

The Azure Migrate service assesses on-premises workloads for migration to Azure. The service assesses migration suitability and performance-based sizing and provides cost estimations for running your on-premises machines in Azure. If you're contemplating lift-and-shift migrations or are in the early assessment stages of migration, this service is for you. After the assessment, you can use services such as Azure Site Recovery and Azure Database Migration to migrate the machines to Azure.

Get started by creating a new migration project. The migration project holds metadata of your on-premises VMs and enables you to assess their migration suitability. From the **Portal**, click **+New**, and type **Migrate**. You will see there are many services available to assist you with various workload migrations including Azure Migrate and Azure Database Migration Service from Microsoft.

1. Create an Azure Migrate project.

2. Azure Migrate uses an on-premises VM called the collector appliance to discover information about your on-premises machines. To create the appliance, you download a setup file in Open Virtualization Appliance (.ova) format and import it as a VM on your on-premises vCenter Server (Figure 1-7).

3. You connect to the VM using console connection in vCenter Server, specify a new password for the VM while connecting, and then run the collector application in the VM to initiate discovery.

4. The collector collects VM metadata using VMware PowerCLI cmdlets. Discovery is agentless and doesn't install anything on VMware hosts or VMs. The collected metadata includes VM information (cores, memory, disks, disk sizes, and network adapters). It also collects performance data for VMs, including CPU and memory usage, disk IOPS, disk throughput (MBps), and network output (MBps).

5. The metadata is pushed to the Azure Migrate project. You can view it in the Azure portal.

6. For the purposes of assessment, you gather the discovered VMs into groups. For example, you might group VMs that run the same application. You can group VMs in the Azure Migrate portal or use tagging in vCenter Server. Additionally, you can use dependency visualization to view dependencies of a specific machine or for all machines in a group and refine the group.

7. Once your group is formed, you create an assessment for the group.

8. After the assessment finishes, you can view it in the portal, or download it in Excel format.

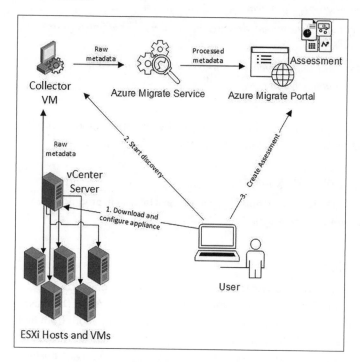

FIGURE 1-7 Azure Migration Workflow

After you've assessed on-premises machines for migration with the Azure Migrate service, you can use Azure Site Recovery to migrate VMs or Azure Database migration to migrate databases.

Azure Site Recovery

You can use Azure Site Recovery to migrate to Azure, as follows:

1. Prepare Azure resources, including an Azure subscription, an Azure virtual network, and a storage account.

2. Prepare your on-premises physical servers, Hyper-V, and VMware servers for migration. Verify VMware support requirements for Site Recovery, prepare servers for discovery, and prepare to install the Site Recovery Mobility service on VMs that you want to migrate.

3. Set up migration. Set up a Recovery Services vault, configure source and target migration settings, set up a replication policy, and enable replication. You can run a disaster recovery drill to check that migration of a VM to Azure is working correctly.

4. Run a failover to migrate on-premises machines to Azure.

NOTE **SETUP SOURCE ENVIRONMENT FOR REPLICATION TO AZURE RECOVERY SERVICES VAULT**

VMware: *https://docs.microsoft.com/en-us/azure/site-recovery/tutorial-vmware-to-azure#set-up-the-source-environment*

Physical: *https://docs.microsoft.com/en-us/azure/site-recovery/tutorial-physical-to-azure#set-up-the-source-environment*

Hyper-V: *https://docs.microsoft.com/en-us/azure/site-recovery/tutorial-hyper-v-to-azure#set-up-the-source-environment*

See step-by-step instructions or learn more in the Site Recovery migration tutorial: *https://docs.microsoft.com/en-us/azure/site-recovery/tutorial-migrate-on-premises-to-azure*.

NOTE DON'T CANCEL A FAILOVER IN PROGRESS

Before failover is started, VM replication is stopped. If you cancel a failover in progress, failover stops, but the VM won't replicate again.

Azure Database Migration

If on-premises machines are running a database such as SQL Server, MySQL, or Oracle, you can use the Azure Database Migration Service to migrate them to Azure. The Azure Database Migration Service is a fully managed service designed to enable seamless migrations from multiple database sources to Azure Data platforms with minimal downtime. For detailed steps see *https://docs.microsoft.com/en-us/azure/dms/quickstart-create-data-migration-service-portal*. The Data Migration Assistant (DMA) is leveraged as part of Azure Database Migration.

Data Migration Assistant (DMA) enables you to upgrade to a modern data platform by detecting compatibility issues that can impact database functionality in your new version of SQL Server and Azure SQL Database. DMA recommends performance and reliability improvements for your target environment and allows you to move your schema, data, and uncontained objects from your source server to your target server. To migrate SQL Server to Azure SQL DB see *https://docs.microsoft.com/en-us/azure/dms/tutorial-sql-server-to-azure-sql*. Learn more about Azure Database Migration at: *https://docs.microsoft.com/en-us/azure/dms/dms-overview*.

Recommended use of Azure Backup and Azure Site Recovery

Azure Backup and Azure Site Recovery can be used together to offer unparalleled data and system backup. Azure is a great platform for adding redundancy to your on-premises systems. There are circumstances in your business continuity and disaster recovery (BC/DR) plan for which you do not need high availability. In these cases, you might simply want to have another copy of the data and services available should there be a problem. Here are some questions that you need to consider when planning.

- What is an acceptable amount of data loss? How many minutes, hours, or days of data can your business afford to lose in case of a disaster? The answer to this will determine your *Recovery Point Objective*.

- How long are you prepared to be down before the data and services are back online after a disaster? This is known as *Recovery Time Objective*.

Let's look at a few key terms you will need to understand.

- **Recovery Point Objective (RPO)**   RPO is the target maximum length of time that data loss can occur during a disaster—how many seconds, minutes, hours, or days you can afford to lose data. This can be, and usually is, different for different types of data. From a planning standpoint, this is the amount of data (in time) that can be lost due to a disaster.

- **Recovery Time Objective (RTO)**   This is the amount of time that systems can be unavailable in the event of a disaster before unacceptable business loss occurs. From a planning standpoint, systems must be restored to functional levels within the RTO.

- **Data Loss**   Data loss is data that has been collected by systems but is not recoverable after a disaster. This could be in the form of lost data that was not saved or data that was saved but is now corrupt and no longer usable.

- **Disaster**   This is any event that causes system outages or data loss. It is generally a term that is used only in extreme cases such as natural disasters, but from a systems standpoint, any outage or data loss can be considered a disaster. This should also include accidental deletion of data.

EXAM TIP

RPO is the amount of data that can be lost (in time)—it is the amount of time between backup, replication, or synchronization. It answers the question, "What is an acceptable amount of data loss?" It is usually *much* smaller than RTO.

RTO is how long it takes to restore services after a disaster. It answers the question, "How long will it take to get this service back up?"

Using the RPO and RTO, you can determine how much money and effort you should put into your BC/DR plan and your systems. It will impact and dictate costs, so calculate what the real numbers are based on the business; this is not just a stab in the dark. How much money does the company lose when systems are unavailable? How much money is lost when data is lost? It is only after you ascertain these answers that you can properly establish the RPO and RTO. If your RPO is short (minutes), you need to design high availability for services. If your RTO is short, you will likely need to use multiple geographies and synchronize your data so that the systems can be brought up quickly.

AZURE SITE RECOVERY

Disaster recovery and business continuity is the primary use case for Azure Site Recovery. You can configure disaster recovery of your VMs and hosts in the same datacenter, other datacenters or Azure. You can use Hyper-V Replica and Site Recovery for on-premises to on-premises protection. Using Hyper-V Replica in a single datacenter gives you the ability to bring a VM on a crashed host back online very quickly by activating a replica of that VM on another host. This does not require the use of Site Recovery or System Center.

Replicating to Azure can offer an additional layer of protection for single-datacenter environments. Replicating to Azure as the replica datacenter can give customers almost instant offsite recovery capabilities without expensive hardware purchases. When replicating to Azure, you can use Availability sets, which can give high-availability workloads the uptime SLA they need.

If there is more than one datacenter, you can replicate between datacenters, increasing the protection available over that of a single datacenter. This capability will offer protection from not only the host failing, but also an entire site outage. In a dual-datacenter scenario, all data can be stored on-premises. A hybrid approach is also viable, in which you can replicate some VMs to another datacenter while replicating others to Azure.

You can use Site Recovery as a migration mechanism to move workloads from one datacenter to another or from on-premises datacenters to Azure. In fact, Site Recovery is particularly advantageous for migration, especially considering Site Recovery has built-in capabilities for testing deployments before the final move.

When there are multiple sites involved in the disaster recovery or migration plan, you need Site Recovery. And using Site Recovery in a datacenter has tremendous cost benefits, too; with Azure, you are charged a small fee for each instance that is configured and synchronized as well as the storage, but you are not charged for the Azure VM itself until it actually fails-over.

AZURE BACKUP

There are many things that you should expect to get out of your properly designed backup solution. Here are some of them:

- **Flexible capability** This is the ability to back up various workloads, applications, servers, disks, files, and folders. Flexibility includes different levels of details for different types of data or data stored in different locations.

- **Resilient, non-disruptive, on-demand, and scheduled** You should be able to run backups without any interruptions in accessing any of the underlying data. You should be able to schedule and run backups without any human interaction. There are also times when you might want to trigger a manual on-demand snapshot of your data; thus, the system should provide that, as well.

- **Scalable and secure offsite storage** Storage needs within any company can and almost always do change regularly. Because of this, the backup storage capability should be able to scale as the volume of data to be backed up increases. This data should also be accessible outside the datacenter so that if there is a regional or datacenter disaster, the data can be retrieved outside the disaster zone. The data needs to be able to be encrypted while in transit as well as while it's at rest. The backup of the data should conserve retention space as well as transfer bandwidth.

- **Meet RPO and RTO**   Backup should, regardless of circumstances, be able to meet RPO. You should be able to recover the systems and data within the time allocated by the RPO, recognizing that different data or data types might have different RPOs. It should also allow for recovery of data and systems within the RTO designed for the data.

- **Simple data recovery**   The real reason for backup is to have the ability to restore data and systems. Backup solutions should easily be able to recover data, manually or automatically, and provide the ability to restore to the same location or a different location. It should provide the ability to restore entire systems of very small subsets such as individual files.

- **Simple management and monitoring**   You must be able to check the status of the backup and have the ability to easily modify or act on the status of the backup solution.

- **End-user capabilities**   In many cases, you might want to offer users the ability to recover their own files without having to open a ticket or place a call to the help desk. It might also be beneficial to provide costing so that individual departments can be charged for the IT servers that are being provided.

Microsoft backup solutions give you all of these capabilities, and while some require Data Protection Manager, most do not. However, even the basic features that are available with Azure Backup are greatly enhanced by using Data Protection Manager.

Backup encrypts and protects your backups in offsite cloud storage with Azure. This gives you scalable and secure offsite storage that complies with your RPO. You can manage cloud backups within Windows Server Backup, which means that you can use very familiar tools and benefit from simple scheduling, the ability to run on demand, and use management and monitoring capabilities. Backup minimizes network bandwidth use, provides flexible data retention policies, and provides a cost-effective data protection solution that can be geo-replicated with ease. There is no bandwidth cost to move data into (ingress) Azure. You pay for the instance plus the storage consumed. Your data is encrypted before it leaves your premises, and remains encrypted in Azure, and only you have the key. You can use this key to recover to the server that made the backup or to any server to which you have provided the key. Incremental backups provide multiple versions of data for point-in-time recovery. Plus, you can recover just what you need with file-level recovery.

For VMs running in Azure, you can perform a snapshot of the blob to capture the drives kept in Blob storage in Azure. This works for both Windows and Linux machines. However, to get the system state, the VM must be stopped or shut down. To perform this task, use the Azure PowerShell Export-AzureVM and Import-AzureVM cmdlets. To register VMs for backup and manage jobs right from the management portal, you must first discover them. A better option for backing up VMs is to use the Azure Backup Agent.

The Azure Backup Agent is supported on Windows clients (version 7 or above) and servers 2008 SP2 or above. One restriction is that data must be on an online local fixed disk, which must be an NTFS-formatted volume. Read-only volumes, network share volumes, and removable drives are not supported.

This gives you the detailed capabilities most customers need.

> **NOTE** **RECOVERY VAULT REGION**
>
> When you create a recovery vault for Backup, use a different region than that of the servers and services you will be backing up. This will provide a level of protection against a regional disaster such as the failure of an Azure datacenter or hurricane that can take out an entire region, including your on-premises datacenter.

A step-by-step tutorial for backing up of a virtual machine can be found at *https://docs. microsoft.com/en-us/azure/backup/tutorial-backup-windows-server-to-azure*. The high-level steps to set up the backup of a virtual machine are:

1. Create and configure Recovery Services.
2. Download the Agent.
3. Download Vault Credentials from Azure.
4. The install & register agent installation requires .NET Framework 4.5 and Windows PowerShell.
5. Upload Vault Credentials to the virtual machine.
6. Configure backup and retention.
7. Launch Microsoft Azure **Backup**.
8. Set Microsoft Azure Backup properties.
9. Schedule Backup select files, specify a schedule, and specify retention.
10. Choose the initial backup type Automatically Over The Network Or Offline.
11. Test Restore.

EXAM TIP

Whether backing up a file server, virtual machine, SQL database or other workload, you need to ensure that a recovery point has all of the required data to restore the backup copy.

You can monitor the job status and job history from both the backup agent application and from the management portal in the Recovery Services section. Azure Backup provides:

- A list of all protected items in the Protected Items section blade.
- Overview along with success and failure counts of jobs in the Overview blade.
- Azure Backup provides application-consistent backups.
- Restoring application consistent data to reduce the restoration time, allowing you to quickly return to a running state.
- Up to 9999 recovery points per protected instance.

- Ability to back up Azure virtual machines to a Recovery Services vault with Azure IaaS VM Backup; see *https://docs.microsoft.com/en-us/azure/backup/backup-azure-arm-vms*.
- See Table 1-3 for feature list by component.

TABLE 1-3 Azure Backup Options

Component	Benefits	Protected
Azure Backup (MARS) agent	Back up files and folders on physical or virtual Windows OS (VMs can be on-premises or in Azure) No separate backup server required.	Files, Folders, System State
System Center DPM	Application-aware snapshots (VSS) Full flexibility for when to take backups Recovery granularity (all) Can use Recovery Services vault Linux support on Hyper-V and VMware VMs Back up and restore VMware VMs using DPM 2012 R2	Files, Folders, Volumes, VMs, Applications, Workloads
Azure Backup Server	App-aware snapshots (VSS) Full flexibility for when to take backups Recovery granularity (all) Can use Recovery Services vault Linux support on Hyper-V and VMware VMs Back up and restore VMware VMs Does not require a System Center license	Files, Folders, Volumes, VMs, Applications, Workloads
Azure IaaS VM Backup	Native backups for Windows/Linux No specific agent installation required Fabric-level backup with no backup infrastructure needed	VMs, All disks (using PowerShell)

EXAM TIP

If you choose Offline for your initial backup, you can save your backup or replication data to empty 2.5-inch or 3.5-inch SATA II, SATA III or SSD hard drives that can then be shipped to Microsoft to import into your storage account. You select the staging location, import job name, Azure publish settings file, Azure subscription ID, Azure storage account, and Azure storage container. Microsoft needs all of this to gain access to your account and storage, placing the files where you want them.

NOTE BACKUP SIZE LIMITS

Backup imposes per-volume size limits on backup data sources. Windows 7, Windows Server 2008 and Windows Server 2008 R2 are limited to 1,700 GB. Windows 8 and Windows Server 2012 or later have a maximum size of 54,400 GB per data source. The limit does not apply to IaaS VM backup. Limits are expected to grow to support disks up to 4TB, which is currently in preview. For additional information see: *https://docs.microsoft.com/en-us/azure/backup/backup-azure-backup-faq* and *https://docs.microsoft.com/en-us/azure/azure-subscription-service-limits#backup-limits*.

Learn more about Azure backup at *https://docs.microsoft.com/en-us/azure/backup/backup-introduction-to-azure-backup*. Learn how to use Azure PowerShell to perform tasks in Backup at *https://docs.microsoft.com/en-us/azure/backup/backup-azure-vms-automation*.

Skill 1.2: Design solutions for serverless computing

Compute is not only provided by virtual machines. There are many new technologies that provide compute without setting up and configuring virtual machines. These other methods leverage virtual machines in the background, but the complexity and management are abstracted so you can just use them as a service. Serverless computing is the abstraction of servers, infrastructure, and operating systems. When you build serverless apps, you don't need to provision and manage servers, so you can take your mind off infrastructure concerns. Serverless computing is driven by the reaction to events and triggers happening in near-real-time—in the cloud. As a fully managed service, server management and capacity planning are invisible to the developer, and billing is based just on resources consumed or the actual time your code is running. (*https://azure.microsoft.com/en-us/overview/serverless-computing/*).

This section covers the following topics:

- Use Azure Functions to implement event-driven actions
- Design for serverless computing using Azure Container Instances
- Design application solutions by using Azure Logic Apps, Azure Functions, or both
- Determine when to use API management service in a cloud-only virtual network

Use Azure Functions to implement event-driven actions

Azure Functions are a solution for easily running small pieces of code, or "functions," in the cloud. Functions can make development more productive, and you can use your development language of choice, such as PowerShell, C#, F#, Node.js, Java, or PHP and more (*https://docs.microsoft.com/en-us/azure/azure-functions/supported-languages*). Pay only for the time your code runs and trust Azure to scale as needed. Azure Functions let you develop serverless applications on Microsoft Azure: *https://docs.microsoft.com/en-us/azure/azure-functions*.

Azure Functions support triggers, which are ways to start the execution of your code, and bindings, which are ways to simplify coding for input and output data. For a detailed description of the triggers and bindings that Azure Functions provides, see the Azure Functions triggers and bindings developer reference: *https://docs.microsoft.com/en-us/azure/ azure-functions/functions-triggers-bindings*. A trigger defines how a function is invoked, and it must have exactly one trigger. Triggers have associated data, which is usually the payload that triggered the function. Input and output bindings provide a declarative way to connect to data from within your code. Similar to triggers, you specify connection strings and other properties in your function configuration. Bindings are optional, and a function can have multiple input and output bindings. Using triggers and bindings, you can write code that is more generic and does not hardcode the details of the services with which it interacts. Data coming from services simply becomes input values for your function code. To output data to another service (such as creating a new row in Azure Table Storage), use the return value of the method. Or, if you need to output multiple values, use a helper object. Triggers and bindings have a name property, which is an identifier you use in your code to access the binding. You can configure triggers and bindings in the Integrate tab in the Azure Functions portal. Under the covers, the UI modifies a file called function.json file in the function directory. You can edit this file by changing to the Advanced editor.

To create a function app, click **+ Create A Resource**; click **Compute**, and then click **Function App** (Figure 1-8).

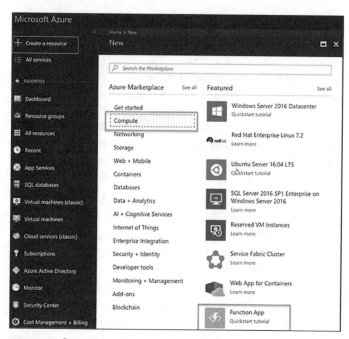

FIGURE 1-8 Create Azure Function App through the portal

On the settings blade, configure the App name, Subscription, Resource Group, OS, Hosting Plan, Location, Storage and Application Insights, and then click **Create**. See Table 1-4 for sample values and setting descriptions.

TABLE 1-4 Azure Function Sample Values and Descriptions

Setting	Sample value	Description
App name	FabFunctionsStorage01	Globally unique name identifying your function app. Valid characters are a-z, 0-9, and -
Subscription	Fab Sandbox	Select the subscription under which this new function app will be created.
Resource Group	FabFunctionsStorage01	Select or create a Resource Group for this function app.
OS	Windows	Select if this function will run on Linux or Windows.
Hosting Plan	Consumption Plan	Consumption plan lets you pay-per-execution and dynamically allocates resources based on your app's load. App Service Plans let you use a predefined capacity allocation with predictable costs and scale.
Location	Central US	Choose a location close to you or other services that will be using the function. This is the datacenter region where the service will be deployed.
Storage	fabfunctionssto8da6	Create or select an existing storage account. Names must be between 3 and 24 characters in length and may contain numbers and lowercase letters only. You can also use an existing account.
Application Insights	Off	Deep monitoring of the application. If you select on, you must also enter a location for the application insights data.

EXAM TIP

Hosting Plans: with consumption you pay for what you use (per execution). With the App service you pay for what you believe you need, giving you a predictable cost plan.

Once you have created the function, go to Function Apps in the Navigation Bar or click on **All Services**, type **Function App**, and click on **Function Apps**. Note, if you click on the star on the right of the Function Apps, you can add it to your favorites, which will display Function App in the left navigation pane. Now that you have a new Function App, let's create a function. To show the use of Azure Functions to implement event-driven actions, create a Blob storage trigger. When a file is added to a blob store, it will have the function write out to a log file.

Expand the function app and click **+** to the right of Functions (hover to show the **+**). For this function, choose the scenario as **Timer** and the language as **CSharp**, and then click on **Custom function**. A number of templates will be available. You can type in blob to the search field to make it easy to find the Blob trigger. Select Blob trigger, select the language C#, and give the trigger a name such as BlobTriggerCSharp1. For the Azure Blob Storage trigger, we have to supply a path. This is the folder within the storage account that the trigger will monitor. Keep the defaults:

- Path: samples-workitems/{name}

- Storage Account connection: AzureWebJobsDashboard

Then click **Create**. You will quickly see the Blob trigger successfully created. In your function click **Integrate**. You will see the trigger and the options set for it. Click the **+** next to Documentation to expand. Since we have created the storage when creating the function and trigger, you will see that the Account Name, Account Keys and Connection String are already set. If you continue to scroll down, you will see example paths that may come in handy. The key values could also be grabbed from the storage account access keys.

Now it's time to create the container that we are monitoring. You can use storage explorer or the Azure Portal, but I prefer Storage Explorer; see *http://storageexplorer.com/*. After installing Storage Explorer, run the new program Microsoft Azure Storage Explorer. The Connect to Azure Storage dialog box will be displayed. Select **Use A Storage Account Name And Key**, then click **Sign In**. Enter your Azure credentials to continue authentication. When authenticated, you will be in Azure Storage Explorer with a list of all your subscriptions. You can expand each subscription to see and explore the storage accounts.

If you only have access to a storage key or want to authenticate with a storage key instead of Azure credentials, you will need to connect in a different way.

1. Run the **Microsoft Azure Storage Explorer** tool, click the connect icon (power plug) on the left, choose Use a storage account name and key, and click Next.

2. Login to Azure from a browser. Navigate to **All Services** > **Storage Accounts** > **Access Keys**. Copy and paste both the Storage account name and either of the two keys into Storage Explorer and then click Next.

3. On the connection Summary screen click Connect.

4. Under your storage account right-click **Blob Containers** and select **Create Blob Container.** Type the name of the container to monitor, which is *samples-workitems*. Now that the container is created, drop a file in the container and confirm that the function is triggering.

Click on the **samples-workitems** container; click **Upload**, then **Upload Files.** In the Upload files dialog box, click the Files field. Browse to a file on your local computer, such as an image file, select it and click **Open** and then **Upload**. Go back to your function Monitor and verify that the blob has been read; see Figure 1-9.

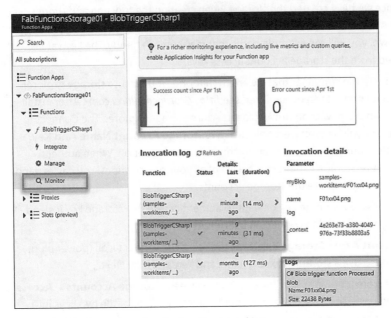

FIGURE 1-9 Monitor and confirm the function is working

EXAM TIP

When your function app runs in the default Consumption plan, there may be a delay of up to several minutes between the blob being added or updated and the function being triggered. If you need low latency in your blob triggered functions, consider running your function app in an App Service plan.

There are many other event-driven technologies that you can explore. See the Azure Functions Documentation at *https://docs.microsoft.com/en-us/azure/azure-functions/* to learn how to use more of the functions capabilities.

Design for serverless computing using Azure Container Instances

Azure Container Instances allow you to develop apps fast without managing virtual machines or having to learn new tools—it's just your application, in a container, running in the cloud. Container Instances can be grouped within a container group to unlock additional capabilities. Multi-container groups are useful in cases where you want to divide up a single functional task into a small number of container images, which can be delivered by different teams and have separate resource requirements. As an example, you may want to have a container group that has your application in one container and the monitoring, logging, archiving, or other capability for the application in another. See how to deploy a multi-container group at *https://docs. microsoft.com/en-us/azure/container-instances/container-instances-multi-container-group*.

When deploying to Azure Container Instances you can deploy from a public registry like Docker Hub, or you can create a private registry using Azure Container Registry. You can store all images you use, public or custom, in a private store assuring that only you have access to your images. Choose the options that fit your needs. See more step-by-step at: *https://docs. microsoft.com/en-us/azure/container-instances/container-instances-tutorial-prepare-app*.

When designing for serverless compute with Azure Container Instances start with where you will put the images. Azure Container Registry is a great choice. You then should standardize on images, store those images on your own registry, and vet the images. Images that you download off the web or from a public registry can have unknown information in them. It is a best practice to understand everything in your container.

You should not only have a registry for your containers, but also a code repository (Microsoft VSTS has a great one) to store container configuration files (DOCKERFILE). These code and configuration files can be leveraged to fully deploy containers. You should also set up a deployment mechanism for containers. Again, you can leverage VSTS for this but there are plenty of other tools too. There should be a strategy and processes in place to manage the different aspects of the container. To determine a strategy answer some questions:

- Who will manage and confirm port openings, IP addresses, and other traditional IT networking and security tasks?

- Once the container is deployed, how will it be monitored? You can use Azure to monitor the containers and the services running in the container.

- What alerts will be sent and to whom?

- What auto-corrective actions will be put into place and who will manage them?

- What orchestrator will be used? Azure Service Fabric is a good choice.

- What are the application requirements of the services running in the container and how will they scale out?

- Do you need to run a cluster environment? If so, which one? Azure Service Fabric is a good choice.

- Finally, what is the process for updating the application, patching the framework and rolling out hotfixes?

Tasks in a containerized environment are usually managed very differently than in a VM environment. Generally, when you patch or update a container, you do it by redeploying the container with all the patch in it or with the latest framework included. All of this should be part of the overall design for your container-based server infrastructure.

Design Application Solutions by using Azure Logic Apps, Azure Functions, or both

Application Solutions for serverless compute can be done with Azure Logic apps or Azure Functions. These services are useful when "gluing" together disparate systems. They can define input, actions, conditions, and output. You can run them on a schedule or trigger. They enable you to run a script or a piece of code in response to various events, such as new Storage Blobs or a WebHook request. Comparing them is not a question of "Which service is the best?" but one of "Which service is best suited for this situation?" Often, a combination of these services is the best way to rapidly build a scalable, full-featured integration solution.

Azure Functions are code-first integration services. Azure Functions allow you to easily run small pieces of code, or "functions," in the cloud. Functions can be triggered (a way to start execution) in a number of different ways: HTTP (REST), Timer, Blob, Event, Queue, webhooks, and more. For a detailed description of the triggers and bindings that Azure Functions provide, see Azure Functions triggers and bindings developer reference: *https://docs.microsoft.com/en-us/azure/azure-functions/functions-triggers-bindings*. There are several sample use cases for functions:

- You want to run code snippets for other Azure services or third-party apps.
- You want to manage your integration code separately from your App Service apps.
- You want to call your code snippets from a Logic app.

Logic Apps are *configuration-first* integration services. Azure Logic Apps provide a way to simplify and implement scalable integrations and workflows in the cloud. It provides a visual designer (Logic App Designer) to model and automate your process as a series of steps known as a workflow. There are many connectors across the cloud and on-premises to quickly integrate services and protocols. A logic app begins with a trigger (like "When an account is added to Dynamics CRM") and after firing can begin many combinations of actions, conversions, and condition logic. Logic apps are for advanced integration scenarios, including those required by DevOps capabilities. Logic Apps is a fully managed iPaaS (integration Platform as a Service), so developers don't have to worry about building hosting, scalability, availability, and management. Logic Apps will scale up automatically to meet demand, and here are some sample use cases:

- Move files uploaded to an FTP server into Azure Storage
- Process and route orders across on-premises and cloud systems

- Monitor all tweets about a certain topic, analyze the sentiment, and create alerts and tasks for items needing follow-up

Both functions and Logic Apps are designed for developers and IT operations. Logic Apps and functions can enable advanced integrations (for example, B2B processes) where enterprise-level DevOps and security practices are required. You can call a function in a logic app, and a logic app in a function. The integration between Logic Apps, and functions continues to improve over time. You can build something in one service and use it in the other service. In short, they work well together, or on their own.

The fundamental difference between functions and Logic Apps has to do with how they are created, classified and updated. Functions (code-first integration) are code-based apps where you have to write code to execute an action. Logic apps (configuration-first integration) are GUI-based workflow apps that can build many different connections together and execute that workflow. You can use code in workflows, including calls to code in functions.

Logic Apps and functions have the ability to connect to cloud services as well as on-premises services, and both can connect to networks (although in different ways) in Azure and on-premises. Logic Apps connectors allow for a very streamlined and automated way to not only connect to more services without code but to organize those connections into a workflow.

For workflow types of tasks, the preferred service is Logic App. For tasks that just need to execute one thing at a time functions are usually the right choice. As an example, a bit over a year ago, I had a customer that wanted to move their VDI infrastructure into Azure. At that time, there was not a VDI solution available in Azure (Citrix now has a solution). We were able to move all of the VDI capabilities they needed into Azure using functions. There was a function to:

- Start a VM
- Stop a VM
- Deallocate a VM
- Create an email report of how long VMs were running
- Check for idle VMs
- Deploy a new VM

All of these tasks can easily be triggered and performed by functions. There is no need for workflow in this scenario so functions work alone.

If you wanted to create an app that executes various tasks in a sequence, then Logic Apps are the best solution. An example of this is when a record is updated in a database performs actions:

- Transform the data
- Register in data repository
- Post to slack or other system

In cases where you need advanced capability or integration to a system that does not have a connector, the best solution is to use Logic Apps with functions. Logic Apps manage the workflow, while functions do the more advanced connections or tasks that Logic Apps cannot perform. The greatest value of serverless compute is obtained when you use multiple technologies together to solve complex business challenges.

Determine when to use API Management service

API Management provides a mechanism to publish APIs to external, partner, and employee developers securely and at scale. API Management allows you to publish, manage, secure, and analyze your APIs in minutes. When API Management deploys in internal virtual network mode, all of the service endpoints (gateway, developer portal, publisher portal, direct management, and Git) are only visible inside a virtual network that you control the access to. None of the service endpoints are registered on the public DNS server. Azure Virtual Networks (VNETs) allow you to place any of your Azure resources in a non-Internet routable network that you control access to. These networks can then be connected to your on-premises networks using various VPN technologies. Consuming a cloud virtual network securely extends your capabilities to include cloud services in your on-premises solutions.

Using API Management in internal mode, you can achieve the following scenarios:

- Make APIs hosted in your private datacenter securely accessible by third parties outside of it by using site-to-site or Azure ExpressRoute VPN connections.
- Enable hybrid cloud scenarios by exposing your cloud-based APIs and on-premises APIs through a common gateway.
- Manage your APIs hosted in multiple geographic locations by using a single gateway endpoint.

See step-by-step details: *https://docs.microsoft.com/en-us/azure/api-management/api-management-using-with-internal-vnet*.

Combining API Management provisioned in an internal VNET with the Application Gateway frontend enables the following scenarios:

- Use the same API Management resource for consumption by both internal consumers and external consumers.
- Use a single API Management resource and have a subset of APIs defined in API Management available for external consumers.
- Provide a turn-key way to switch access to API Management from the public Internet on and off.

See step-by-step details: *https://docs.microsoft.com/en-us/azure/api-management/api-management-howto-integrate-internal-vnet-appgateway*.

Skill 1.3: Design microservices-based solutions

Microservices-based solutions are small loosely coupled solutions that break large complex tasks into small easy to manage ones that can be deployed and that scale independently. With microservices-based solutions there are often many technologies that are used to perform a single task. Instead of having one service do many tasks, you have many services performing one simple task. This structure means you can choose the best solution or technology for the individual tasks.

> **This section covers the following topics:**
> - Determine when a container-based solution is appropriate
> - Determine when container-orchestration is appropriate
> - Determine when Azure Service Fabric (ASF) is appropriate
> - Determine when Azure Functions is appropriate
> - Determine when to use API Management service
> - Determine when the Web API is appropriate
> - Determine which platform is appropriate for container orchestration
> - Consider migrating existing assets versus cloud native deployment
> - Design lifecycle management strategies

Determine when a container-based solution is appropriate

In the past few years, container technologies such as Docker have gained great popularity in the industry. Container technologies make it possible for you to consistently deploy applications by packaging them and all of their required resources together as a self-contained unit. You can build a container manually, or it can be fully described by metadata and scripts. This way, you can manage containers as source code. You can check them in to a repository, manage their versions, and reconcile their differences just like managing source code. In addition, containers have some other characteristics that make them a favorable choice for hosting workloads in the cloud, which are described in the sections that follow.

Compared to VMs, containers are much more light weight because containers use process isolation and file system virtualization to provide process-level isolations among containers. Containers running on the same VM share the same system core so that the system core is not packaged as part of the container. Because starting a new container instance is essentially the same as starting a new process, you can start containers quickly—usually in time frames less than a second. The fast start time makes containers ideal for the cases such as dynamic scaling and fast failover.

Because container instances are just processes, you can run a large number of container instances on a single physical server or VM. This means that by using containers, you can achieve much higher compute density in comparison to using VMs. A higher compute density means that you can provide cheaper and more agile compute services to your customers. For example, you can use a small number of VMs to host a large number of occasionally accessed websites, thus keeping prices competitive. And you can schedule a larger number of time-insensitive batch jobs.

Another major benefit of using containers is that the workloads running in them are not bound to specific physical servers or VMs. Traditionally, after a workload is deployed, it's tied to the server where it's deployed. If the workload is to be moved to another server, the new one needs to be repurposed for the new workload, which usually means the entire server needs to be rebuilt to play its new role in the datacenter. With containers, servers are no longer assigned with specific roles. Instead, they form a cluster of CPUs, memory, and disks within which workloads can roam almost freely. This is a fundamental transformation in how the data-center is viewed and managed.

The ease and speed of deploying containers in Azure Container Instances provides a compelling platform for executing run-once tasks like build, test, and image rendering in a container instance. With a configurable restart policy, you can specify that your containers are stopped when their processes have completed. Because container instances are billed by the second, you're charged only for the compute resources used while the container is executing and running your task. In this scenario and in others, persisted data can often be a challenge. Since the machine is terminated and disposed after it finishes the job, you will need to store data outside the container. There are many ways to persist data outside of a container, including SQL, blob stores, table storage, file storage or other. See mounting an Azure file share with Azure Container Instances for an example: *https://docs.microsoft.com/en-us/azure/container-instances/container-instances-mounting-azure-files-volume*.

One of the largest values of containerized compute is the massive number of preconfigured container images that are ready to be used. Expanding on container image hubs are application clone sources and code repositories such as GitHub that have containers (as code) ready to deploy. Many of these have step-by-step instructions and often even a 1-click deploy option to deploy directly to Azure Container Instances. Regardless of application needs, framework, or other application connectivity requirements, applications can be run in containers. The operating system, programming language, runtime environment, and framework are options in your container deployment. So choose Node.js, .NET Framework, or others, and quickly and easily have the application running in Azure Container Instances. As you design for serverless compute using Azure Container Instance, consider what technologies you want to leverage, what source you will build on, if you will use a registry and what registry, and how you will deploy and manage your containers.

You should select containers when you are implementing DevOps practices (containers provide Infrastructure as Code), creating apps with a micro-services architecture, or running apps that don't fit Web App, API App, functions or other thin and serverless deployment options. Another great use case is if you want to maintain 100% compatibility across on-premises, Azure, or other cloud providers. Containers run the same regardless of platform so you do not have to be concerned with vendor lock-in.

Determine when container-orchestration is appropriate

Because of their small size and application orientation, containers are well suited for agile delivery environments and microservice-based architectures and DevOps processes. The task of automating and managing a large number of containers and how they interact is known as orchestration. Popular container orchestrators include Kubernetes, Mesosphere DC/OS, and Docker Swarm, all of which are available in the Azure Container Service. Azure also has an orchestrator, Azure Service Fabric, but more on that later. Orchestrated containers form the foundation of container-based PaaS offerings by providing services such as coordinated deployments, load balancing, and automated failover.

Orchestrated containers provide an ideal hosting environment for applications that use a microservices architecture. You can package each service instance in its own corresponding container. You can join multiple containers together to form a replica set for the service. You can automate container cluster provisioning by using a combination of Azure Resource Manager Template, VM Extensions, Custom Script Extension, and scripts. The template describes the cluster topology, and VM extensions perform on-machine configurations. Finally, automated scripts in containers themselves can perform container-based configurations.

Azure Container Services provide all of the scheduling and management capabilities required to run a single container. Azure also handles critical tasks like health monitoring and maintenance for you. Additional orchestration is provided by orchestrator platforms that manage multi-container tasks on top of Azure Container Service.

Because all of the underlying infrastructure for Container Instances is managed by Azure, an orchestrator platform does not need to concern itself with finding an appropriate host machine on which to run a single container. The elasticity of the cloud ensures that one is always available. Instead, the orchestrator can focus on the tasks that simplify the development of multi-container architectures, including scaling and coordinated upgrades. Because they start quickly and bill by the second, an environment based exclusively on Azure Container Instances offers the fastest way to get started and to deal with highly variable workloads.

Orchestration is not needed in cases where you are just running single standalone apps in a container. You can even have many of them and not need an orchestrator. Although, even in this scenario, you may want to have an orchestrator monitoring your container and restarting it in case it crashes or is not servicing clients (self-healing). As the number of containers increase, or the complexity of the application increases, so does the need for an orchestrator. The orchestrator significantly reduces the burden on IT and development personnel while eliminating user error. If you have an app that requires horizontal scaling an orchestration engine can perform that job with no interaction from administrators. If your app has multiple tiers that need to be scaled at different times or based on different criteria, the orchestrator is your solution. If you want to load balance multiple containers across a single DNS name, perform container migrations or deployments so that the orchestrator can help. The easiest way to look at orchestration is this: if you need to do something based on multiple containers, the orchestrator does it.

Determine when Azure Service Fabric (ASF) is appropriate

Azure Service Fabric is a distributed systems platform that makes it easy to package, deploy, and manage scalable and reliable microservices and containers. You can create clusters for Service Fabric in many environments, including Azure or on premises, on Windows Server, or on Linux. You can even create clusters on other public clouds. If you are deploying and managing containers, Service Fabric can provide orchestration for the container infrastructure. Azure Service Fabric provides an ultra-fast, highly available, scalable application fabric. Service Fabric a perfect solution for orchestrating and deploying microservices in containers across a cluster of machines.

Determine when Azure Functions is appropriate

Azure functions are most appropriate if you want to run snippets of code. You can run these snippets from a variety of languages and execute via a REST API call. Functions are appropriate anytime you want to use serverless infrastructure to run code snippets, integrate with third-party apps, or run Azure apps like Azure Logic Apps.

Determine when to use the API Management service

Think of API Management as an API store. Use the API Management service anytime you want to standardize on how and when your developers use APIs. API Management services allow you to strip out the complexity of what the code behind a particular API is, and just leverage it as a set of code that can be leveraged into apps. You will want to use API Management when you need a central repository for API Management, or when you want to have an easy way to add, test, roll out or roll back API access for internal or external users.

Each API contains a reference to the back-end service that implements the API, and its operations map to the operations implemented by the back-end service. This means that if documenting and organizing APIs and API calls that multiple developers will use, much advantage can be gained. In addition to managing your own APIs, you can manage third-party APIs that are used by your developers. If you currently do not have a great model for managing and streamlining the use of APIs, use API Management.

You can gate access with API keys, limiting vulnerability and applying advanced security policies. It does not matter where the API is running, it could be on-premises, in the cloud, from partners or third-party providers. If you want to share APIs outside your organization, you can easily encapsulate the code and have these external partners open the API that can be exposed for them.

Use the API management service when you want to deploy an easy to use and fully authenticated portal for developers to use to request access to APIs. Use the service when you want to fully document APIs, their connection and call details, and other important information that can be easily provided to developers.

Use API Management when you want to monitor any aspect of the API including availability, performance, deep insights, requests, and response. Learn more at: *https://docs.microsoft.com/en-us/azure/api-management/api-management-key-concepts*.

Determine when Web API is appropriate

Web API defines the resources, relationships, and navigation schemes accessible to client applications. Use Web API when you want to expose using REST actions of a web app. Some of these actions may include GET, POST, PUT, DELETE, or any other functions including custom functions. Web API is appropriate when you need these capabilities and you want to maintain responsiveness, scalability and availability across the requests.

Use the Web API when you want to directly monitor your API. This includes availability, performance, usage data, and deep applications insights. Monitoring can also track information about requests, responses and more.

Best Practices for Web API: *https://docs.microsoft.com/en-us/azure/architecture/best-practices/api-implementation*.

> **MORE INFO CUSTOM WEB API**
>
> You can learn about the custom Web APIs using SQL Server at: *http://azure.microsoft.com/en-us/documentation/articles/web-sites-dotnet-rest-service-aspnet-api-sql-database/*.

Determine which platform is appropriate for container orchestration

There are a number of platforms you can use for container orchestration. As mentioned earlier, popular container open source orchestrators include Kubernetes, Mesosphere DC/OS, and Docker Swarm. Azure also has Azure Service Fabric, which is an orchestrator. Orchestration includes:

- **Scheduling**   Given a container image and a resource request, find a suitable machine on which to run the container.
- **Affinity/Anti-affinity**   Specify that a set of containers should run nearby each other (for performance) or sufficiently far apart (for availability).
- **Health monitoring**   Watch for container failures, and automatically reschedule them.
- **Failover**   Keep track of what is running on each machine and reschedule containers from failed machines to healthy nodes.

- **Scaling**   Add or remove container instances to match demand, either manually or automatically.

- **Networking**   Provide an overlay network for coordinating containers to communicate across multiple host machines.

- **Service discovery**   Enable containers to locate each other automatically even as they move between host machines and change IP addresses.

- **Coordinated application upgrades**   Manage container upgrades to avoid application down time and enable rollback if something goes wrong.

At a high level, each platform offers the above list of orchestration capabilities. Setup and configuration are often a differentiator among orchestrators. As an example, when running in the Azure cloud, most of the hard work of setup is done for you through scripts and resource templates. The first point on selecting an orchestrator is skills and familiarity. If you do not already have skills and familiarity with a tool and you are deploying on Azure, Azure Service Fabric is the best solution. If you are already using an orchestrator on-premises or in other clouds, continuing with that orchestrator will save learning time and minimize frustrations of learning a new tool.

Kubernetes is an open source platform. It has much maturity in Linux, but less maturity in Windows. Kubernetes provides more capabilities for managing different cluster scenarios and has a large open source community that shares ideas and practices. It is the best solution when you are already using Kubernetes or have a need for clustering capabilities not covered by others.

Docker Swarm is an open source product from the company Docker. Swarm is growing in popularity and is generally easier to set up and configure than others. Docker Swarm benefits from the fact that it is built on and for Docker. Docker Swarm has some interesting features such as rolling updates and desired state reconciliation. It is the best solution if you are already using Docker and Docker Swarm or want to stick to the same company for orchestration that are using for containers.

Mesosphere Enterprise DC/OS runs containers and distributed applications. Mesosphere has a scheduler integrated with DC/OS (Marathon). In addition to running orchestration of containers it provides data services automation to run distributed services like Spark, Kafka, Cassandra, or Hadoop file systems. Like Kubernetes, Mesosphere is very mature in Linux, but less mature in Windows. Use Mesosphere DC/OS if you are already running this infrastructure or want to take advantage of the additional data services automation.

Azure Service Fabric runs on Azure, on-premises, and on any other cloud. When you do not already have a preference for orchestration, Azure Service Fabric is a good choice. Use this if you want to manage containers and other Azure services. It provides a new perspective on what an orchestrator should do through Service Manager programming models, such as stateful services and reliable actors.

Read more about container orchestration at: *https://docs.microsoft.com/en-us/dotnet/ standard/microservices-architecture/architect-microservice-container-applications/scalable-available-multi-container-microservice-applications.*

Consider migrating existing assets versus cloud native deployment

There is much to understand when considering whether to migrate existing assets to the cloud or changing them to be cloud native apps. Time, cost and migration objective will obviously play a part, but you must also consider aspects of application architecture such as: application management, application security, application compatibility, integration complexity, and even database compatibility.

If you need to migrate and time is of the essence, such as the need to close down a datacenter by a certain date, you may make a decision to lift and shift assets to the cloud as is. If time is not critical, you can get much more value from migrating to a native cloud deployment. When migrating assets to the cloud, you are not taking advantage of most of the inherent benefits of the cloud. Some of these benefits include cost savings (improved ROI), security advantages, adopt and develop best practices, improve efficiencies, maximize returns, scalability, and high availability.

Migrating an existing virtual machine that is running one or more apps is easy to do. You simply move the virtual machine from your hardware to the hardware running in Azure. By doing so, you will gain many of the benefits of the cloud. However, these applications are not usually cloud aware, which means you cannot just enable some capabilities that are automatic in a cloud native application. Let's take networking and security as an example. In this scenario, you are shifting the network from your on-premises environment into the cloud. This network that may have been designed decades ago is now running in the cloud with no additional protections. You will still have the inherent security of the very robust and automated network security and infrastructure as well as monitoring and management. However, by going native, applications often have dedicated networks that completely isolate what happens in the app from all other applications and services. From a security standpoint you will gain some obscurity (over on-premises) by getting an external IP address. This is not sequential with your other services, so there is some value, but the value could be much greater. It begs the question of why are servers and services not on isolated networks on-premises? Sometimes they are using vLAN or other like technologies. However, in a physical environment segregating networks is very expensive, an enormous amount of work to manage. In the cloud network isolation and segregation is free and automatic. In the cloud all the networks are virtual networks, and all of the switching is managed by software instead of IT hardware.

All of the benefits and application architecture components listed above will ultimately play a role in which is best for each scenario. There are many considerations when choosing an architecture. The best solution will depend on many factors including:

- Complexity of the applications or systems
- Connections to other internal and external services and resources
- Variations of configuration needs
- Costs associated with each application or workload
- Time constraints for having services available in the cloud

When making the decision to move an application, you not only have to consider the application needs but also how it integrates with any services it touches. When considering if migrating assets or changing deployment to cloud native, there is no single right answer that covers every situation or even most situations. Rather, it is a risk versus reward proposition. It is recommended that each application and workload be evaluated separately instead of making the decision based on one application. If you have hundreds of applications, you can group the applications that are similar and make the decision on the group, but recognize that the more you understand the workload, the more likely you are to have a better and more valued solution in the long run. Let's take a look at some common scenarios. In both cases, using containers can greatly improve flexibility by making it simple to move to other platforms or providers. Application authentication can also be a consideration. Native cloud applications are generally re-architected to authenticate using Azure Active Directory, while on-premises applications generally use either local or Active Directory Authentication. Some DevOps practices can be applied when migrating assets, but far more can be applied converting to a native cloud application.

Scenarios for migrating assets (lift and shift)

Migrating assets means taking those assets like virtual machines and running them in the cloud. This is often referred to as "lift and shift." These workloads generally run on cloud IaaS offerings such as virtual machines, virtual machine scale sets, or similar. This migration strategy is generally the fastest to perform and least likely to introduce issues. Moving virtual machines also give you more flexibility in moving to a different cloud provider later. This strategy should be used if native cloud application deployment is not an option for some reason. Use this approach when:

- Time is critical; applications are running in stand-alone virtual machines
- High complexity applications with many integration points
- Application language or framework not compatible with native cloud deployment
- Time to migrate is the most critical or only factor
- Many dissimilar applications and application platforms
- Scale-up ability is a primary driver
- Oracle Database

Scenarios for Switching to Native Cloud Application Deployment

Native cloud application deployment means refactoring the application or workload to run natively in the cloud. This refactoring is sometimes very easy, but it can also sometimes be very hard. Some of the changes to refactor include authentication changes, stateful to stateless and making or receiving REST calls instead of direct calls through some other communication protocol or technology. Leveraging containers can often shortcut or delay the need for some of this refactoring.

I have worked with projects where we migrated many applications in a single day. I have also seen projects that would take over a year to refactor. Native cloud applications are applications that run on cloud PaaS offerings such as Azure Container Instance, Azure SQL Database, Web Apps or similar. Refactoring or switching to native cloud application deployment is the recommended approach because it is generally the highest value, the most flexible, and the most secure. Use switching to native cloud application deployment when:

- You have a large number of applications that have similar or identical architecture. In this scenario, you can often script the migration of one, then run for all. These apps can likely be natively deployed faster than migrating assets.

- Application is a standard compatible language and framework. Examples: .NET, Java, Node.js, PHP, and Python on Windows or .NET Core, Node.js, PHP or Ruby on Linux.

- Security is a high priority.

- Scale-out capability is a primary driver.

- Cost or RIO is a high priority.

- Automation, DevOps, and Agility is important.

- Stateless applications.

- SQL Database.

See: *https://docs.microsoft.com/en-us/dotnet/standard/modernize-with-azure-and-containers/#introduction.*

Design lifecycle management strategies

Lifecycle management strategies are strategies and policies that you put into place to give consistent and predictable guidelines to be followed for the availability and support throughout the life of an application. Since DevOps teaches automation and reduction of waste in every step and every practice, these key tenants should be a major part of designing lifecycle management strategies. Lifecycle management strategies should include every aspect of the application, system, or process at every stage from inception to termination. It should include advancing with technology, testing, deployment, updating, testing, performance, usability, security, scalability, monitoring, continuous innovation, integration and daily maintenance. Let's use an example of designing a new product to be brought to market. As we design this process we will incorporate the lifecycle management strategies and also show how DevOps plays such a vital role in this process.

DevOps

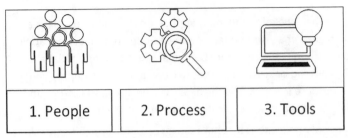

FIGURE 1-10 DevOps Core Tenants: People, Process, Tools

DevOps is the union of people process and tools to enable continuous delivery of value to end users (Figure 1-10). When referencing people, often people only think of developers (Dev) and infrastructure engineers (Ops). However, the people discussion is so much broader. DevOps seeks to get everyone working toward a single shared goal. An example goal might be to: "Deliver a great product that inspires our customers to become raving fans." By having every person in every department that touches or impacts a project to share a common goal it allows the team to break down barriers and silos. It helps create a mindset of "systems thinking" by emphasizing the value to the business rather than to the individual or department. Processes are created to reduce waste and deliver a repeatable and reliable application that meets the requirements of the application. These processes include "amplifying feedback loops" at every step. Finally, tools are evaluated and brought in to help streamline the processes and cut even more waste while also ensuring reliable repeatability in the process. People, process and tools combined allow for "a culture of continual experimentation and learning." Agile software development and DevOps have much in common. DevOps could even be considered a natural progression of agile development.

PEOPLE

The people for this project include developers, infrastructure engineer, architects, security (all aspects/departments), quality assurance, user acceptance testing, application owner and team, sales, marketing, helpdesk support, company leadership and anyone else who will engage with the team, the application or customers regarding the application. Yes, that is a lot of people. The amount of interaction with these people is different depending on the project.

Consider if you can exclude a group like sales or marketing from the team collaboration until after the product is released. What would be the outcome? You would have an application in production that the sales team does not understand and no marketing materials ready to start promoting it. What about the help desk? You would have no one trained to support the applications when customers contacted the company with an issue. What about the Active Directory Security team? You will have an application ready to deploy but no service user with the proper rights to run in production. This happens. Even worse, the SLA for creating the service account with the right permissions was four weeks. The application was ready for production but could not be deployed because all the people who needed to be part of the project were not actually part of the project. This leads to four weeks of wasted time before the customer can get their hands on the product.

In addition to having the right people, everyone needs to have the right focus and understand how they should work together as part of the team. Some examples of roles and responsibilities include:

- **Security**   Incorporate security necessities into every aspect of the business; enable others to automate compliance.
- **Development**   Quickly build, deploy, and update a product that our customers love. Enable other groups by building what they need to support you.
- **IS/IT**   Build infrastructure as code; enable others by helping to eliminate waste throughout the technology landscape.
- **Management**   Enable the teams by giving them flexibility, guidance, and support to do what is needed; remove obstacles.
- **Senior Management**   Embrace cultural change; drive transformation in the organization.

In these examples, notice that all responsibilities must do their job and support others. Let's drill down into senior management just for a moment. Do you really need senior management? If the question is can you do without it, the answer is yes. However, by having this support it is much easier to knock down barriers, reduce SLAs and get other people on the program. In any DevOps discussion it is a high priority to get this support.

> ***NOTE*** **THE THREE WAYS BY GENE KIM**
>
> The book "The Phoenix Project: A Novel About IT, DevOps, and Helping Your Business Win" written by Gen Kim, this novel has become the standard for how businesses should think about DevOps. In this book Gene talks about The Three Ways:
>
> 1. **The First Way**   Systems Thinking emphasizes the performance of the entire system
> 2. **The Second Way**   Amplify Feedback Loops
> 3. **The Third Way**   Culture of Continual Experimentation and Learning
>
> If you want to fully understand DevOps and how important it can be to an organization, this is a must-read book. See *http://itrevolution.com/the-three-ways-principles-underpinning-devops/* for more details.

PROCESS

Process is the way things are done and the guidelines created to ensure success. In DevOps, it is important to understand that processes can have shortcuts applied to them, usually with little or no opposition. However, doing things because that is how they have always been done is simply the wrong answer. DevOps is more about simplifying the processes and eliminating waste. Often waste is identified by long SLAs, long applications or forms that have to be filled out to get another department to do something that is needed for your project. DevOps teaches that these should be removed, usually by automation. There are many types of waste:

- **Manual Motions/Handoffs** Overhead, coordination, handoff, or other inefficiencies surrounding the setup and execution of work.

- **Waiting** Delays in starting or completing the next value-adding step for a unit of work.

- **Partially Done** Work output that isn't in a complete, usable state (from the customer perspective). Often needs input/action from others or further work. Increases defects, tasks switching and waiting.

- **Task Switching** Context switching from partially done work to other work creates waste due to high expense of context switching and greater likelihood of errors.

- **Extra process** Non-value-adding steps or processes that are required (formally or informally) as part of the standard flow of work.

- **Extra Features** Features, usually added during implementation, that are not required by or justified by current business needs. Doesn't remove limitations on the business or create customer value.

- **Heroics** Unreasonable burden or extraordinary effort required of someone to successfully complete work or satisfy the customer.

DevOps eliminates or reduces these wastes through automation and creation of processes and guidelines for all to follow. Automation can eliminate much, perhaps even most waste. In most cases this automation can be streamlined by looking at practices and leveraging tools that can help you deploy those practices as part of your solution. These practices should be used as part of your DevOps processes and your lifecycle management strategies. See Table 1-5 for DevOps practices and lifecycle management strategies.

TABLE 1–5 DevOps Practices and Lifecycle Management Strategies

DevOps Fundamentals	More Lifecycle Management Strategies
Infrastructure as Code (IaC)	Requirements Management
Continuous Integration (CI)	Governance / Compliance
Continuous Deployment (CD)	Maintenance and Auto-Healing
Automated Testing	Change management
Release Management	Hypothesis Driven Development
Configuration Management	Testing in Production – partial user base
Automated Recovery (Rollback & Roll-Forward)	Fault Injection
Advanced Monitoring	Usage Monitoring/Telemetry
Capacity Management	A/B Testing (aka canary testing)
Self-Service Environments	Feature Flags

TOOLS

We are not going to go deep on tools. The key points here are it is better to use the right tool for the job to help you eliminate waste. As an example, it would not be a good idea to develop your own tool for the job when there are likely other tools on the market that can do the same thing. Developing in-house tools will likely result in more delays and not contribute to the business objective because it will take focus off the customer needs while you are developing and maintaining those tools.

There are some incredible tools available that can help you in a significant way streamline processes. A couple of the best tools include Visual Studio Team Services (VSTS) and Visual Studio, which helps you in almost every practice and lifecycle area. It does much of the work of automating and integrates a high percentage of the capabilities needed into a highly integrated solution. Coupling these tools with Azure can cut months off of development cycles and improve management of the application lifecycle.

There are plenty of non-Microsoft tools that work well to help you on your DevOps journey as you build out your lifecycle management strategies. Some of these tools might include Chef, Puppet, Docker, Kubernetes, Jenkins, Git, and many more. There are literally thousands of tools that can help. If you already have a set of tools that you use, you can continue to use them, if they are functional and can still be used as you streamline your efforts.

If the tools you are currently using cause more work or waste, it is time to look at others that may be able to do the job better. Often using the right tools can cut waste significantly, so even if your existing tools work, it may be a good idea to find out what is possible with other tools so you have visibility into efficiencies that can be gained by using better tools.

PUTTING IT ALL TOGETHER – LIFECYCLE STRATEGY

Remember, your lifecycle strategy should include everything from inception to decommissioning the application. The lifecycle (and DevOps) often start with ideation. That is, an idea or customer problem that should be solved. Then it progresses through the people, process, tools, and so on. As the application progresses, it is progressing through the pipeline, which is broken down into many stages. Stages and steps are terms often used to mean the same thing. In other cases, steps are subsets of stages. As we look at a sample pipeline this will become clear. All work is done in a repeatable and automated fashion. The code is stored in a central repository (repo) that all working on the project have access and contribute rights. Check-in to the repository is done when it is ready for automated testing. Usually this is daily, often more frequently.

Plan out the solution, do the costing, and other analysis, requirements gathering, compliance and governance considerations, auditing needs as well as project management and staffing. Determine the update and maintenance windows as well as the release cycles. Determine people that will be working on the project, and what tools will be used in the process. Build out tasks, sprints, story boards and other tools who will be needed to manage the application project. Most important in the ideation and planning stages are funding. This is where the business understands the risks and rewards and decides to fund the project. Ideation and planning is sometimes split into two different stages and managed separately. The complexity of the project, as well as many other aspects of the project defined here, will ultimately determine what pipeline steps/stages are needed.

Create (if not already done) the development pipeline that will be used to automatically send the application through various stages of the pipeline adding checkpoints as needed. This is a key tenant of DevOps and is an important part of lifecycle management because this is how the application will advance through each stage of each release cycle of the application lifecycle. The development pipeline should be automated everywhere. As code is developed it is sent through the various stages of the deployment pipeline. Automatically progressing code is called continuous integration/continues deployment (CI/CD). Some stages might include, development, infrastructure/operations, test, quality assurance, integration pre-production and production or others. Because we are always looking at the entire system as the application, we also need to account for customer experience and feedback loops at every step in the development pipeline. A sample pipeline is shown in Figure 1-11.

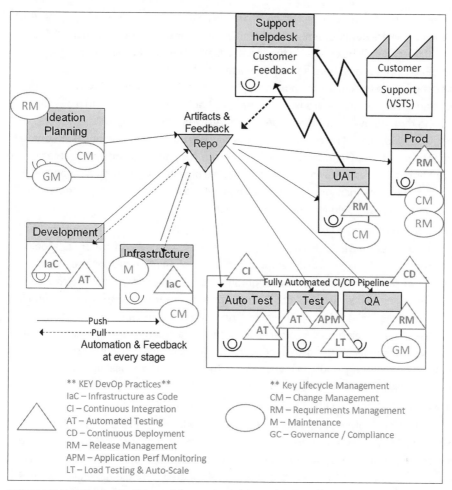

FIGURE 1-11 DevOps Application workflow, connectivity and CI/CD pipeline with DevOps practices and lifecycle management identified.

In Figure 1-11 you can see that flow of the application all runs through the code repository. Any changes that are made are pushed into the repo. As deployments are made, they are pulled, usually automatically, from the repo.

When an application runs through the pipeline, it can transfer as is (move the virtual machine or container) or it can be rebuilt at each stage. Rebuilding at each stage is the preferred or best practice for running applications through a pipeline. This ensures that nothing is in the image except those things that are explicitly called required. As an example, when you go from Dev to Test, you would deploy all components to test using scripted code. You create the container, deploy all frameworks or supporting code needed, and deploy the website all with code. In doing this, there is no chance that a developer did something in the container without tracking. If they did, then the error would be found in Test rather than down the road when moving into production.

Application development is broken down into sprints. Sprints are small chunks of time, usually 2 to 4 weeks, where development is done on the application. It is determined in advance what parts of the code will be created in the sprint. Usually three or more sprints are planned in advance. Each sprint should have an output of a minimal viable product (MVP). That is, the development tasks are broken down and assigned based on these small windows in time. At the conclusion of each sprint the product of the sprint should be fully tested and ready to stand alone, moving through the pipeline (test, QA, and often even production). This is known as agile or iterative development. Not developing in this way is referred to as traditional or waterfall development. Once a sprint if finished, there is a sign-off. The code and systems created as part of the sprint are simply deployed to the next stage in the pipeline. Application development often encompasses more than just developers. This is where architects, database administrators and other specialists would engage on the project.

Systems infrastructure, also known as operations, builds out the infrastructure needed using infrastructure as code (IaC). In Azure this is the JSON Resource Template. These should include everything the app needs in development. As development on the app progresses the infrastructure templates and custom configuration scripts, if needed, should be created to make sure everything needed in production is also done. As the application moves through the various stages of the pipeline, the infrastructure scripts and templates are being tested with the code since all of it is being used to create each stage. Infrastructure also has many roles and responsibilities in the pipeline. Bringing in networking, Active Directory, or other security experts, architects, monitoring, ongoing management, help desk, high-availability, performance monitoring, auditing, maintenance, backup and the like will all be scheduled, configured, implemented, automated and confirmed as part of the deliverable.

Automated testing is often programed by the same developers who are writing the code. As code is written, so are test scripts to test the code. The test scripts are checked into the code repository as artifacts just like code. These automated scripts are generally fired automatically every time there is a check-in to the code repository. Automated testing is generally not done by a person; it is fully automatic. However, developers, managers, testers and others review the results regularly. In addition to the automated tests that are created by the developers, most projects will have automated testing from third party tools. All of this can be fully automated and integrated into the development pipeline. Feedback is when a test fails, and developers will fix issues that are found and resubmit.

Additional testing is done by developers and others (architects, ops, managers, etc). This testing is done for components that are in sprints that have concluded. This deeper testing will often include integration testing. Sometimes integration testing with other systems is broken down into a separate stage called integration testing. Feedback is generally sent directly back to the development team, often through a ticketing system.

Quality assurance is another level of testing that tests everything. The QA team will review the testing logs, confirm usability, and generally make sure the application (or application subset) is ready to have external users see it. Feedback is generally given directly to the development team through a ticketing system.

User acceptance testing (UAT) is a stage were the non-development or project team tests the application. Often UAT testing will even bring in customers and other outside the organization to help test applications. Feedback is often provided directly to the development team for internal testers while tickets through the help desk are created for customer feedback. Developers are responsible for watching the queue for tickets or they will be automatically alerted when there is an issue.

Production or pre-production covers all testing and the code that is ready to be deployed to the general public. It will progress to the next stage like everything else, and the code will simply be deployed to the new destination. Sometimes there is a separate stage for pre-production, and sometimes it is all bundled with production. The application is ready to be deployed. When deploying the application to production, you are not overwriting the existing environment. Instead, you are setting up the new environment (just like you did in every other stage) and then just changing public pointers to the new location. By using this technology, it is easy and painless to roll back to the prior release if necessary. By now, change management, auditing, and all other obstacles have been triggered and completed. Often, once an application lands in production, there will be additional testing in production just to make sure everything is working as it did in development. This is often referred to is a sniff test or smoke test. Feedback comes in through helpdesk calls and tickets logged.

In DevOps the feedback loop is vital. In each stage of the application pipeline there is a process for feedback. When not following DevOps or Agile processes, once an application is in production, it sometimes needs to go back to the first steps (planning) to figure out where the bug that was caught in production would fit into the sprint task list. However, in more advanced deployment pipelines, these requests go right back to the development team. A quick decision is made if this issue is a bug that needs to be fixed right away or a feature request. If a bug, it would go back through the pipeline starting at dev and a fix would be quickly rolled out. This quick turnaround in delivering a hotfix is a best practice. Additionally, as feature requests come in, some may be inserted into the current sprint (or more likely the next sprint). This continuous innovation is a compelling advantage of DevOps practices.

Next, the application is monitored, maintained, and audited. Tickets are issued and the application progresses on this path of constantly innovating until the lifecycle nears its end. There is not time to go into more detail on all of the areas listed in Figure. 1-10. This should give you a base knowledge of the application lifecycle. Various departments are brought into the process because the timing is logical. As an example, sales and marketing would be brought in once enough of the application is known to start developing these plans.

Skill 1.4: Design web applications

There are many design considerations for web applications. In this skill we will describe various web application technologies as well as the back-end services and constructs that are required to implement them.

> **This section covers the following topics:**
> - Design Azure App Service Web Apps
> - Design custom web APIs
> - Secure Web API
> - Design Web Apps for scalability and performance
> - Design for high availability using Azure Web Apps in multiple regions
> - Determine which app service plan to use
> - Design Web Apps for business continuity
> - Determine when to use Azure App Service Environment (ASE)
> - Design for API apps
> - Determine when to use Web Apps on Linux
> - Determine when to use a CDN
> - Determine when to use a cache, including Azure Redis cache

Design Azure App Service Web Apps

Websites or Web Apps and Web Services are the identities that an individual or company presents to the rest of the world. The pervasiveness of technology in general and advances in the web in particular have made sophisticated users out of nearly everyone. People now reflexively use web resources to gather information, whether it's to learn about a company and its products or services or simply to connect with friends via social media. At the same time, users' expectations regarding performance and design have become more exacting. Today, a slow website is something that most people will not tolerate, and they will quickly move on to another site without hesitation. This means that websites must be designed to support features such as scalability as well as maintenance features such as backup and restore.

First, the application needs to be reliable, which means that it can consistently provide functionalities as designed. Second, the application needs to be available, such that it can continuously deliver services to its consumers. Third, the application needs to be scalable; that is, it can easily adapt for workload changes, either planned or unexpected.

Helping developers create and host high-quality service has been a primary focus of Azure as a cloud platform. Azure affords you opportunities to improve the QoS of your application via various tools and services. However, this doesn't mean your applications on Azure will be automatically available, reliable, and scalable. A successful Software as a Service (SaaS) solution is based on a healthy partnership between the developer and Azure. You need to design your application with the cloud in mind in order to take full advantage of the benefits that Azure provides.

You can define availability as a ratio between the system available time and total subscribed time. For example, a service that remains available for 9 out of 10 hours has an availability of 90 percent. Service availability is often backed by a Service Level Agreement (SLA), which guarantees the level of service availability. Most Azure services are backed by SLAs. Table 1-6 summarizes SLAs for some of the Azure services.

> *NOTE* **THE CHANGING NATURE OF SLAS**
>
> The data in Table 1-6 is an abbreviated sample for illustration only. Azure services, and their associated SLAs, may change over time. For more information, refer to: *http://azure.microsoft.com/en-us/support/legal/sla/*.

TABLE 1–6   SLAs for some of the Azure services

Service	SLA	Comment
Active Directory	99.9%	Applies to Basic and Premium services
API Management	99.9%	Applies to Standard tier
Automation	99.9%	Jobs will start within 30 minutes of their planned start time
Backup	99.9%	Availability of backup and restore functionality
BizTalk API Apps	99.9%	Connectivity to Basic, Standard, and Premium tiers
Cache	99.9%	Connectivity between cache endpoints and Azure's internal gateway
CDN	99.9%	Respond to client requests and deliver contents without error
Cloud Services˙	99.95%	Requires two or more instances in different fault and upgrade domains
Virtual Machines	99.95%	Requires two or more instances in the same Availability set
Virtual Network	99.9%	Gateway availability

A key technique to improve service availability is to use redundancy, which means to deploy multiple instances of a service so that when one or several instances fail, there are still healthy instances to provide continuous service. Be aware, however, that redundancy incurs additional cost. Before you set up an availability goal for your own application, you need to evaluate the availability requirements and decide how much redundancy you need to build into your deployments. When you've determined that level, you can begin to consider different strategies to improve service availability. First, you'll go over a couple of basic strategies for a single component or a single service. Then, you'll discover some strategies that apply to multicomponent systems.

Single-component availability

Single-instance availability is achieved by using multiple service instances. Many Azure services have built-in redundancy for high availability. For instance, if you use Azure SQL Database, the database instance is backed by multiple secondary instances to ensure availability.

Generally speaking, the two most common deployment strategies are homogeneous instances and primary–secondary instances.

HOMOGENEOUS INSTANCES

All instances are identical in a multi-instance deployment. They often have similar processing power, and they are joined behind a load balancer, which distributes workloads evenly to them.

These instances are often autonomous, as well, which means that they don't have dependencies on one another. Autonomous ensures that a failing instance won't have a ripple effect that might take down all instances. In other words, when some of the instances fail, the level of service might degrade due to reduced capacity, but the completeness of functionality is unimpaired.

A practical challenge of using homogeneous instances is session state management. Because services' requests are distributed by the load balancer, requests within a user session are likely to be routed to different instances. There are a couple of ways to deal with this challenge:

- **Session affinity**   All requests of a session will be routed to the same instance. You can achieve this by some routing mechanisms such as a gateway or cookie-based session affinity. Session affinity is also referred as *sticky sessions*.

- **External state store**   All session states are externalized and saved in a separate data store that is independent from the service instances. Using this design, requests can be freely distributed among instances. But, it comes with a performance penalty because of the overheads of accessing the external state store. When the states are externalized, the instances become *stateless*.

> **NOTE STATELESS VERSUS STATE-FUL**
>
> Using stateless instances is definitely not the only way to design scalable applications. In many cases, stateful instances have preferable characteristics in terms of simplicity and performance, and there are fascinating programming models such as the Actor pattern to help you to write scalable, distributed applications. Further discussion on the Actor pattern is beyond the scope of this book.

> **NOTE FAULT DOMAINS AND UPDATE DOMAINS**
>
> Fault Domains and Update Domains apply to Web Apps in the same way that they apply to virtual machines, which we covered earlier.

PRIMARY–SECONDARY INSTANCES

A primary–secondary deployment designates a primary instance that handles all incoming requests, with one or more secondary instances as active backups. When the primary instance fails, a secondary instance is promoted to primary to handle requests. The original primary instance is repaired and brought back online as a new secondary. If the original primary is unrecoverable, you can provision a new instance as a new secondary to restore the number of instances to the desired level.

You can predetermine primary selection. In this case, each instance is assigned a priority level. When an instance fails, the instance with the next highest priority level is elected as the primary. Another scheme of primary selection is to use a dynamic voting process among running instances.

TRANSIENT ERRORS

Transient errors are caused by some temporal conditions such as network fluctuation, service overload, and request throttling. Transient errors are quite elusive; they happen randomly and can't be reliably re-created. A typical way to handle transient error is to retry a couple of times. Many Azure SDK clients have built-in transit-error handling so that your code won't be cluttered by retry logics.

When your applications have dependencies on external services, you need to plan for throttling. You should clearly understand quotas imposed by these services and ensure that you don't exceed such limits. On the other hand, when you provide your services to the public, you might want to implement throttling yourself so that you can sustain enough resources for fair service consumption.

> **NOTE TRANSIT-FAULT HANDLING APPLICATION BLOCK**
>
> Microsoft Patterns and Practices provides a transient fault handling application block that helps you to cope with transient errors.

Loose coupling

When a service fails, all services with direct dependencies on the service are affected. Because of such dependencies, a single error can generate a chain of failures that ripple through multiple layers of the system. Loosely coupled components don't have direct dependencies on one another. Loose coupling has many benefits, such as dynamic scaling and load leveling. More important, loose coupling facilitates different components having separate lifecycles. You can maintain, host, and update the components independently without affecting other components. Architectures such as Service Oriented Architecture (SOA), microservices, and Message-Based Integrations all advocate for loose coupling among system components. With loose coupling, a failing component won't produce the ripple effect on the entire system.

Loosely coupled components are often integrated by using a reliable messaging system, such as an Azure Service Bus queue. In terms of reliability, the messaging system serves as an intercomponent buffer that helps to contain errors.

Health monitoring

It's very important to monitor a long-running application continuously to ensure that it's functioning normally, at a sustained performance level. Some problems such as resource leakage and bugs under stress only reveal themselves after the system has been running for a period of time. Having an efficient, reliable, and secure telemetry collection system is a necessity for most modern web applications.

A health-monitoring system can also help you to analyze the usage patterns of your application. It can assist in monitoring and analyzing how customers are accessing your service so that you can focus on the areas that are of greatest concern to your customers.

Azure supports various diagnostics, tracing, and monitoring solutions such as Azure Diagnostics and Application Insights.

Azure Application Insights is a hosted service that helps you to detect issues, solve problems, and analyze usage patterns of your applications, including .NET, .NET Core, Java, Node.js, and applications.

System-level availability

A more complex system is made up of multiple components. For example, an *n*-tiered application might have a presentation layer, a business layer, and a database layer. To make the overall system available, you must make each component of the system available. The following is a general rule of system availability:

A system is less available than its least available component.

This rule states that when designing a system, you need to ensure that *all* components are available, because any unavailable components will bring down the availability of the entire system.

AVOID SINGLE POINT OF FAILURE

A Single Point of Failure (SPoF) refers to a component that renders the entire system unavailable if it fails. For example, if an entire system relies on a single database instance to function, the database instance is a SPoF of the system.

You should aim to eliminate SPoFs from your system design. Although centralized components might be easy to design and implement, they bring a high risk to your system's availability. As a matter of fact, you can avoid many centralized components by using some innovative design. For example, you can replace a centralized job dispatcher with a job queue. With a job queue, jobs are published to the queue, and multiple job processors compete for jobs by reading jobs from the queue. Because Azure queue services such as Service Bus queue has ensured availability, such design is much more robust than a job dispatcher at application level.

ALTERNATIVE SERVICES

As the aforementioned rule-of-thumb states, a system is less available than its least available component. This rule assumes that there is a single dependency chain among components. You can overcome the constraints of this rule by introducing branches in dependency relationships. If you know a component is naturally unavailable, you should introduce alternative services so that when the component is inoperative, the system can continue to function by using alternative services. For example, when designing a notification system, you might want to implement multiple channels to ensure that a message is delivered, even when the preferred channel is unavailable.

CROSS-REGION DEPLOYMENTS

Although rare, region-wide outages do happen as a result of catastrophic events such as hurricanes and earthquakes. For mission-critical systems, it's advisable to have key services deployed across multiple geographic regions so that the system remains available.

Azure Traffic Manager provides automatic failover capabilities for critical applications. You can configure Traffic Manager to route your customers to a primary site, but redirect them to a backup site if the primary site continuously fails to answer health probe signals. Your customers don't need to remember different addresses of the various deployments. They simply access the service through endpoints provided by Traffic Manager. All health probes and traffic routing occur behind the scene. Furthermore, you also can associate custom domains to Traffic Manager endpoints to provide your customers friendlier service addresses.

Deployment slots

One feature that is available in the Azure Portal is that you can set the connection strings and app settings to be *sticky* with the slot for which they are defined. This way, a test site can use a connection string that points to a test database instead of the live database. When the test site is swapped into production, it will use the connection string that is set up to be used only in production. By default, the sticky feature is turned off in the connection strings and app settings, so you need to turn it on. This makes it possible for you to use the settings that are in the web.config file when testing on-premises and then use the one in the website configuration in Azure when it is uploaded to Web Apps. You can add deployment slots to web applications by using the Management Portal, using a RESTful API call, or by using an Azure PowerShell cmdlet. You can remove a deployment slot by using the same methods.

> **MORE INFO STAGING ENVIRONMENTS FOR WEB APPS**
>
> You can learn more about staging environments for Web Apps at: *http://azure.microsoft. com/en-us/documentation/articles/web-sites-staged-publishing/.*

> **MORE INFO WEB APPS**
>
> See the Azure App Service documentation: *https://docs.microsoft.com/en-us/azure/app- service/app-service-web-overview for a wealth of additional information on Web Apps.*

Design custom web APIs

Web Apps provides turn-key CORS support for RESTful API scenarios, and simplifies mobile app scenarios by enabling authentication, offline data sync, push notifications, and more. The Web API provides a powerful platform for exposing services and data through HTTP REST calls. These calls can come from any number of different applications or platforms including: browsers, mobile devices, traditional application, IoT devices, or any other device or service that can reach the HTTP endpoint. The operation that a web service exposes is the web API.

Platform independence is a primary design goal of the web service. Implementation of the API conforms to standards that enable a client application and web service to agree on which data formats to use. This data is then exchanged between the client and the web service. In this model, there is no requirement or expectation of how the service stores or manipulates the data, only that it returns the expected data in the agreed upon format. There is no need to retain any affinity between a client application making a series of requests and the specific web servers handling those requests. This enables highly scalable solutions.

Service evolution is another primary design goal of the web service. The service should be able to be updated to fix, add or remove features and capabilities without any impact to services that call the Web API. Existing client applications should be able to continue to operate as expected while the upgrade is taking place.

> **NOTE REPRESENTATIONAL STATE TRANSFER (REST)**
>
> REST is an architectural style for building distributed systems based on hypermedia. A primary advantage of the REST model is that it is based on open standards and does not bind the implementation of the model or the client applications that access it to any specific implementation. For example, a REST web service can be implemented by using the Microsoft ASP.NET Web API, and client applications can be developed by using any language and toolset that can generate HTTP requests and parse HTTP responses. REST is actually independent of any underlying protocol and is not necessarily tied to HTTP. However, most common implementations of systems that are based on REST use HTTP as the application protocol for sending and receiving requests. This book (and exam) focuses on mapping REST principles to systems designed to operate using HTTP. The URIs exposed by a REST web service should be based on nouns (the data to which the web API provides access) and not verbs (what an application can do with the data). For example:
>
> - http://adventure-works.com/orders // Good;
> - http://adventure-works.com/create-order // Avoid.
>
> See *https://docs.microsoft.com/en-us/azure/architecture/best-practices/api-design* for more on REST.

Simplicity and consistency are keys to designing a successful web API. These traits make it easier to build client applications that need to consume the API. Some of the common exposed functions of a REST API are:

- **GET**   To retrieve a copy of the resource at the specified URI. The body of the response message contains the details of the requested resource.

- **POST**   To create a new resource at the specified URI. The body of the request message provides the details of the new resource. Note that POST can also be used to trigger operations that don't actually create resources.

- **PUT**   To replace or update the resource at the specified URI. The body of the request message specifies the resource to be modified and the values to be applied.

- **DELETE**   To remove the resource at the specified URI.

Many more functions are often available, and custom functions are often available.

REST APIs are designed around resources, which are any kind of object, data, or service that can be accessed by the client. A resource has an identifier, which is a URI that uniquely identifies that resource. For example, the URI for a particular customer order might be:

```
http://adventure-works.com/orders/1
```

Clients interact with a service by exchanging representations of resources. Many web APIs use JSON as the exchange format. For example, a GET request to the URI listed above might return this response body:

```
{"orderId":1,"orderValue":99.90,"productId":1,"quantity":1}
```

REST APIs use a stateless request model. HTTP requests should be independent and may occur in any order, so keeping transient state information between requests is not feasible. The only place where information is stored is in the resources themselves, and each request should be an atomic operation. This constraint enables web services to be highly scalable, because there is no need to retain any affinity between clients and specific servers. Any server can handle any request from any client. That said, other factors can limit scalability. For example, many web services write to a backend data store, which may be hard to scale out.

REST APIs are driven by hypermedia links that are contained in the representation. For example, the following shows a JSON representation of an order. It contains links to get or update the customer associated with the order.

```
{    "orderID":3,
    "productID":2,
    "quantity":4,
    "orderValue":16.60,
    "links": [
        {"rel":"product","href":"http://adventure-works.com/customers/3",
"action":"GET" },
        {"rel":"product","href":"http://adventure-works.com/customers/3",
"action":"PUT" }
    ]
}
```

The URIs should be oriented around the data. The URL or location is used to refine actions of the function. Below are some GET examples:

- ../customers - retrieve all customers

- ../customers/8 - retrieve information for customer #8
- ../customers/8/orders - retrieve all orders for customer #8
- ../customers/8/orders/27 - retrieve order #27 from customer #8

These functions are executed by the Web API service to return data through a response to the request. Another method that is better for more complex data manipulation is to enable navigation to related resources using the Hypertext as the Engine of Application State (HATEOAS) approach. The details of HATEOAS are beyond the scope of this book, but should be considered when the depth of the API exceeds collection/item/collection or if the organization and call for data is not a simple hierarchical and standardized approach.

Performance should be considered in designing your Web API. Forcing many requests to get all the data a client may need degrades the value of the API to the client and also overloads the number of requests that come into the web service. To avoid this, you can implement single calls to pull larger sets of data that can then be manipulated by the client. This also has a performance hit on the web service as the service is pulling large amounts of data, packaging it, and then responding with the large data set. There is not right or wrong answer for all scenarios. When designing, consider the client data collection needs in conjunction with client performance for multiple requests, the client overhead of multiple requests, as well as the service overhead and performance of the number of requests and the size of the request. Expected frequency and size will help you define the requirements of the service.

Versioning a RESTful web APIs allows the capability of clients to use different versions of the API. This is a practice that allows the capability of the client to continue to use the API with the functionality that they have used in a prior version. This way if changes are made to the API, the API web service can continue to service the requests based on the syntax or expected results of the API for which it was built. Here are some versioning options to consider when designing your Web API:

- **No versioning**   A simple approach may be to always send API return sets in the same format, simply adding new or extra data to the end of the set. This new or extra data will likely be ignored by the older clients. However, this often causes issues as structures or capabilities are dropped or outputs rearranged. If the data the client is expecting is no longer being provided or organized differently, the client application could break.

- **URI versioning**   Returning the results based on the version passed in the URI. The older client will send the information in a particular format that is recognized by the Web API, and results are returned that this version expects. New or changed schema can add a version number to the URI for each resource. This allows for returning of data that is compatible with the version that has been requested. This is a great approach since it does not break remote clients allowing for older clients to continue to use the API without change.

- **Query string versioning**   You can specify the version of the resource by using a parameter within the query string appended to the HTTP request, such as *http://adventure-works.com/customers/3?version=2*. The version parameter should default to a meaningful value such as 1 if it is omitted by older client applications. This approach has the semantic advantage that the same resource is always retrieved from the same URI, but it depends on the code that handles the request to parse the query string and send back the appropriate HTTP response. This approach also suffers from the same complications for implementing HATEOAS as the URI versioning mechanism.

- **Header versioning** Rather than appending the version number as a query string parameter, you can implement a custom header that indicates the version of the resource. This approach requires that the client application adds the appropriate header to any requests, although the code handling the client request can use a default value (version 1) if the version header is omitted. The following example uses a custom header named Custom-Header. The value of this header indicates the version of web API as shown below:

```
GET http://adventure-works.com/customers/3 HTTP/1.1
...
Custom-Header: api-version=1
...
```

Other design elements to consider for your Web API include: autoscaling, background jobs, caching, content delivery networks, data partitioning, and large or binary data such as pictures, monitoring and diagnostics. For more information on Web API see: *https://docs.microsoft.com/en-us/azure/architecture/best-practices/api-design*.

> *NOTE* **OPEN API INITIATIVE**
>
> The Open API Initiative was created by an industry consortium to standardize REST API descriptions across vendors. As part of this initiative, the Swagger 2.0 specification was renamed the OpenAPI Specification (OAS) and brought under the Open API Initiative. Some points to consider:
>
> - The OpenAPI Specification comes with a set of opinionated guidelines on how a REST API should be designed. That has advantages for interoperability but requires more care when designing your API to conform to the specification.
>
> - OpenAPI promotes a contract-first approach, rather than an implementation-first approach. Contract-first means you design the API contract (the interface) first and then write code that implements the contract.
>
> - Tools like Swagger can generate client libraries or documentation from API contracts. For example, see ASP.NET Web API Help Pages using Swagger at *https://docs.microsoft.com/en-us/aspnet/core/tutorials/web-api-help-pages-using-swagger*.

Secure Web API

Web API apps provide great value to businesses for internal and externally exposing access to data. There are times when you want to secure your API app so authentication happens prior to connecting to the API. This can be done by leveraging Azure Active Directory (AAD) authentication for the applications. Protecting the application can also happen when using Azure API Management. In either case, Azure Active Directory can protect the backend using OAuth 2.0. For instructions on how to protect API Backend with Azure Active Directory see: *https://docs. microsoft.com/en-us/azure/api-management/api-management-howto-protect-backend-with-aad*. The high-level steps are as follows:

- Create a Web API service and change Authentication to Microsoft Azure organizational account
- Configure Microsoft Azure Web App with public name, service plan, resource group, etc.
- Grant permissions to the AAD backend service application
- Make note of the APP ID URI and Import the API into API Management
- Register the application as an AAD application
- Configure an API Management OAuth 2.0 authorization server
- Add AAD Endpoints
- Configure single sign-on
- Configure a desktop application to call the API
- Configure and validate JSON Web Tokens (JWT) validation policy to pre-authorize requests

You may also configure authentication with client-side certificates; see: *https://docs.microsoft.com/en-us/azure/api-management/api-management-howto-mutual-certificates-for-clients*.

Design Web Apps for scalability and performance

When a website is slow or unresponsive, people are quick to think that it is unavailable or is just a poorly constructed site, and they will move on to another one. So, performance is an important issue that you need to address and keep in mind when designing the web application. Azure Web Apps provides options to scale and debug a website to help developers find issues that can cause slow performance. Azure has multiple ways to host websites and to support moving existing websites or generating a new one. Web Apps also supports any type of web development language and not just websites developed with Microsoft Visual Studio. Azure Web Apps was built to be used for any type of website and to support the operation of the site. In order to make sure you are getting the performance you need out of your applications you can monitor the apps and auto-scale as additional resources are needed.

Scaling your apps out will both solve the problem of scalability and performance. Scaling out is adding additional instances of the same size and load balancing between them. As most applications also connect to backend storage, the best way to make sure the backend is not a bottleneck is to use technology such as Azure SQL database, which will allow you to scale out the data layer.

Middle-tier application layers can also be scaled out to increase scalability and performance by setting up an internal load balancer in front of the tier and scaling out those application tiers as well.

More companies are doing business globally and need to have their website support scaling globally. App Service Web Apps supports scaling globally to help decrease load times for accessing a website, which translates to a better experience for users.

One option to scale a website globally is to use a Content Delivery Network (CDN). This will cache the static content of a website to other regions around the world, placing the website physically closer to the various locations from which people are trying to access it. You can configure the CDN with the domain name itself and have it point to a web application as its *origin domain*. When requests then come into the CDN for the website, it ensures that the site is copied over to a region closest to the user. There are very few settings for the CDN. You can add a custom domain name to the website, and you can enable HTTPS and query string forwarding.

CDN improves site performance in two ways: First, it provides faster response time by serving contents from locations closest to the end user, and second, it removes a large portion of content serving workloads from the service servers. Some sites report that more than 90 percent of the traffic is served from point-of-presence (POP) locations.

Design for high availability using Azure Web Apps in multiple regions

Websites today are visited by people around the world. Even internal business sites need to run from various remote locations to be effective. No one likes waiting for a website, especially if it is an internal one, to load in their browser. Azure supports websites in multiple regions for high availability in a number of ways.

One method that was discussed earlier is to use a CDN that automatically deploys the web application as close as possible geographically to the users requesting the site. The URL for the website is set to the CDN system, and the website is set as the origin domain.

You can deploy websites to multiple regions, such as East US and West US. Then, you can set up Azure to use the Traffic Manager to expose the websites via a single URL. Each endpoint website is added to the Traffic Manager. Keep in mind, though, that to connect a web application to the Traffic Manager, you must be running in the Standard pricing tier. The other limitation is that you can include only one web application from any given Azure Region, meaning, for example, that you cannot add two web applications from East US. Figure 1-12 shows the configuration settings for the Traffic Manager.

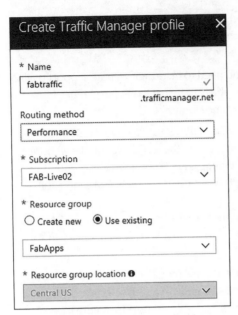

FIGURE 1-12 Screenshot creating Traffic Manager profile

The Load Balancing Method has four possible options: Performance, Weighted, Priority, and Geographic. The default setting is Performance, which is used when you have endpoints in different geographic locations and you want end users to use the "closest" endpoint in terms of the lowest network latency. Priority is used to have a primary service endpoint for all traffic and provide backups in case the primary and other backup endpoints are unavailable. Performance distributes traffic evenly between all of the endpoints. Weighted is used to distribute traffic across a set of endpoints, either evenly or according to weights you define. Geographic uses locations geographically closest to the request. The Geographic option will be the best for improving the performance around the world.

> **NOTE LOAD-BALANCING ROUTING METHODS**
>
> Performance is one of the supported load-balancing routing policies. You also can set up weighted, priority and geographic load balancing. See *https://docs.microsoft.com/en-us/azure/traffic-manager/traffic-manager-routing-methods* for more details.

Determine which App Service Plan to use

The App Service Plan is a way to logically group of Web Apps and other app services together so that they can be scaled and managed together. If an App Service Plan is changed to a different pricing tier, all of the websites and other app services that are under that plan are moved to the new pricing tier as well. In addition, the scaling and auto-scaling for all of the services can be set together. The plan you choose is dependent on location, capabilities, number of apps, max instances, SLA, technology, and capabilities.

MORE INFO APP SERVICE PLAN

You can learn more about App Service Plan: *http://azure.microsoft.com/en-us/documentation/articles/azure-web-sites-web-hosting-plans-in-depth-overview/.* For a side-by-side comparison see *https://azure.microsoft.com/en-us/pricing/details/app-service/plans/.*

EXAM TIP

Keep in mind that App Hosting Plan is now named App Service Plan.

Design Web Apps for business continuity

Websites that are used for business needs must be available and have the security of backups in case of problems, which can range from the catastrophic (the datacenter being consumed by fire) to the more mundane (loss of power in the server room). Today, companies need their data and websites to be up and available as close to 100 percent of the time as possible. This might be to perform work-related activities, but also might be an industry requirement that data is available for the last seven years of manufacturing. No matter the reason for designing and setting up the websites for business continuity, Azure can help perform these functions to help with your business needs. Business continuity is concerned with having your application available to the business as dictated by the business requirements. Often these requirements will dictate high availability, backup and restore, replication of data, and contingencies for when things inevitably go wrong.

Scaling your application, and making sure it is highly available, is the first step to designing a web app for business continuity. Scaling and backing up all tiers of the application are just as important. The backup and restore features for Web Apps are available in the Standard tier. If you are using the Free or Basic tiers, you can still back up the website manually using FTP/FTPS or the GIT Clone URL that is available in the Properties section of the settings for the web application. The Premium tier for Web Apps provides up to 50 backups each day, whereas the Standard tier provides a single backup per day. When planning your backup strategy, you need to determine how often backups are needed. For a site that does not update frequently, you might find that a single daily backup is sufficient. It is not sufficient to just back up and hope all went well. You must also test the restore.

Resiliency, monitoring, diagnostics and patching are also important part of designing for business continuity. Microsoft has guidance on designing resilient applications for Azure at *https://docs.microsoft.com/en-us/azure/architecture/resiliency/.*

EXAM TIP

Recovery Time Objective (RTO) and Recovery Point Objective (RPO) are "business objective" time intervals, typically expressed in number of minutes or hours.

- RTO is the maximum time a workload can be unavailable in a disaster. It is the maximum allowed time to restore services after a disaster. It answers the question, "How much time do we have to get services running after an incident?"

- RPO is the maximum acceptable data loss during a disaster. This is the amount of data (in terms of time) that is already collected that can be lost. RPO defines the amount of time between backup, replication, or synchronization. It answers the question, "What is an acceptable amount of data loss?" It is usually much smaller than RTO.

- Mean Time To Recover (MTTR) is the average time it takes to restore a workload after a failure. If MTTR exceeds RTO, then a failure in the system will cause an unacceptable business disruption, because it won't be possible to restore the system within the defined RTO. If this is the case, the system architecture or configuration should be changed so the MTTR does not exceed RTO.

MORE INFO   BACKING UP A WEBSITE

You can learn more about website backups at *http://azure.microsoft.com/en-us/documentation/articles/web-sites-backup/*.

Determine when to use Azure App Service Environment (ASE)

Azure App Service Environment is an Azure App Service feature that provides a fully isolated and dedicated environment for securely running App Service apps at high scale. They are needed when the application needs very high scale, isolation and secure network access or high memory demand. An ASE always exists within a subnet of a virtual network. You can use the security features of virtual networks (Network Security Groups, NSGs) to control inbound and outbound network communications for your apps. These networks can be bridged to other infrastructure in Azure or on-premises through standard hybrid networking technologies like a VPN or ExpressRoute. An ASE can be either internet-facing with a public IP address or internal-facing with only an Azure internal load balancer (ILB) address. To learn more see *https://docs.microsoft.com/en-us/azure/app-service/environment/intro*.

Design for API apps

To design for API Apps, determine how to break apart aspects of an application. Break them apart in logical places where the individual parts can be built as a standalone application. Then that application, which has one job to do, can do it, return a result, and abstract the complexity of that job away from the developer of other applications that use the API. Re-use of these API calls or apps can be fully automated and secured through background authentication with application keys. Just like any other app, API apps can scale and perform integrations with any other app or service. DevOps is a primary driver for API apps, as these apps are generally built fast and deployed in a very short cycle.

Determine when to use Web Apps on Linux

Web Apps on Linux is a fully managed compute platform that is optimized for hosting websites and web applications on Linux. Customers can use App Service on Linux to host Web Apps natively on Linux for supported application stacks. The supported stacks are: Node.js, PHP, .NET Core, and Ruby. See *https://docs.microsoft.com/en-us/azure/app-service/containers/app-service-linux-intro* for a complete list of versions and updates to stacks. Additional deployments stacks can be used by creating a custom Linux Docker image and deploy to Web App for Containers. If you have Linux apps that need full capabilities offered by the Azure platform (e.g., Scaling), then Web Apps on Linux should be used. DevOps is a primary driver for Web Apps for Linux.

Determine when to use a CDN

A Content Distribution Network (CDN) can be used to speed up access to your site or content around the world by allowing users that are geographically located far from the source to access a copy of the data close to their geography. This content could be web pages, entire sites, images, documents, configuration files, or any file that might delay a page load. If your site users are geographically spread out or you have many images or other large files that take time to load, CDNs can make a huge difference in performance.

Determine when to use a cache, including Azure Redis Cache

Azure Redis Cache is for high throughput and consistent low-latency data access. It provides a highly secure and ultra-high performance access to data. Use Redis Cache for an ultra-fast, advanced key-value store, where keys can contain data structures such as strings, hashes, lists, sets, and sorted sets. This data can be pulled instantly from your application. Redis Cache is often used as a session cache. Managing scores or leaderboards, counts, stats or status are also key scenarios. Items in your app or on your website that are queried constantly are great use cases. As an example, if you are tracking latest items, page history or even navigation, Redis Cache is the right tool.

Skill 1.5: Create compute-intensive applications

As the name suggests, the purpose of *Big Compute* is to perform a lot of computational tasks in a distributed yet coordinated fashion. Typical Big Compute workloads include simulation (such as fluid-dynamics simulation), analysis (such as genome search), and modeling (such as risk modeling), and so on. These often require a large number of compute hours.

Microsoft Azure provides both hardware and software resources with which you can run large-scale batch jobs in parallel in the cloud. Instead of managing expensive infrastructure yourself at your own datacenters, you can dynamically request compute resources at any time, perform compute tasks on them, and then release them to avoid extra costs.

> **This section covers the following topics:**
> - Design high-performance computing (HPC) and other compute-intensive applications using Azure Services
> - Determine when to use Azure Batch
> - Design stateless components to accommodate scale
> - Design lifecycle strategy for Azure Batch

Design high-performance computing (HPC) and other compute-intensive applications using Azure Services

Azure brings raw computing power to your high-performance computing (HPC) applications with high-performance servers, storage solutions, and networks. On the other hand, if you already have computing clusters on-premises, with Azure you can dynamically extend these clusters to the cloud when you need additional resources to handle more complex computing tasks.

Compute-intensive instances

Azure's H-series, A8, A9, A10, and A11 virtual machine (VM) sizes are tailored specifically for HPC workloads. They combine high-speed, multicore CPUs and large amounts of memory, and they are connected by extremely fast networks. The H-series virtual machines are based on the Intel Xeon E5-2667 V3 @ 3.2 GHz (with turbo up to 3.5 GHz) processor technology, utilizing DDR4 memory and SSD-based local storage. The A8-11 VMs come with Intel Xeon E5-2670 @ 2.6 GHz, and for detailed specifications and machine specifications table see: *https://docs. microsoft.com/en-us/azure/virtual-machines/windows/sizes-hpc*.

The H16r, H16mr, A8, and A9 feature a network interface for remote direct memory access (RDMA) connectivity. This interface is in addition to the standard Azure network interface available to other VM sizes. This interface allows the RDMA-capable instances to communicate over an InfiniBand network, operating at FDR rates for H16r and H16mr virtual machines, and

QDR rates for A8 and A9 virtual machines. These RDMA capabilities can boost the scalability and performance of Message Passing Interface (MPI) applications.

Constructing an HPC cluster

Another way that Azure handles HPC environments is through its support for the Intel MPI Library. The Intel MPI Library is designed to boost the performance of applications running on clusters that are based on Intel architecture. It is widely used by many HPC applications and takes advantages of Azure's low-latency network and RDMA capabilities.

An HPC cluster comprises a head node and a number of compute nodes. The head node is responsible for managing the cluster, and the compute nodes run compute jobs. The nodes in a cluster are often connected to one another on a private, low-latency network because they need frequent network communications to coordinate the workloads on the cluster. Figure 1-13 shows a simple HPC cluster deployment on Azure.

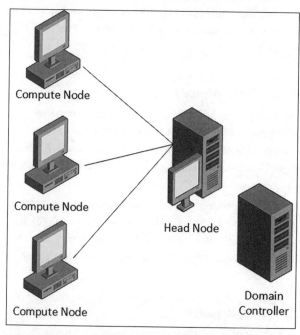

FIGURE 1-13 A simple HPC cluster deployment on Azure

The following is a list of high-level steps for configuring an HPC cluster head node in Azure:

1. Create a virtual network.
2. Create a domain controller on the virtual network.
3. Create a domain user account that you'll use to configure the cluster.
4. Create a VM as the head node.
5. Add the domain user account to the local Administrators group.

6. Install and configure HPC Pack on the head node.

7. Complete the Deployment To-Do List in the HPC Cluster Manager.

You can use Microsoft HPC Pack to create, manage, and run HPC applications on an HPC cluster. The cluster can be made up of dedicated on-premises servers, part-time servers, VMs in the cloud, and even workstations. As of this writing, the latest version of HPC Pack is HPC Pack 2016 R2, which you can download from the Microsoft Download Center. See *https://docs.micro-soft.com/en-us/azure/virtual-machines/windows/hpcpack-cluster-options*.

EXAM TIP

You can deploy an HPC cluster by manually preparing and configuring the nodes. However, because deploying such clusters involves provisioning and configuring a large number of resources, it is recommended that you instead use automated scripts. There's an HPC Pack IaaS Deployment Script, which you can download from the Microsoft Download Center at *http://www.microsoft.com/en-us/download/details.aspx?id=44949*. You can also deploy a cluster with an Azure Resource Template from the gallery: **New** > **Marketplace** > **Every-thing** > search for *cluster or batch*.

Azure Premium storage and large VM instances

There are many existing compute-intensive applications that enterprises would like to use to migrate to the cloud. However, these enterprises don't want to take on the extra cost and risk to redesign and re-implement these applications. For such lift-and-shift scenarios, Azure provides faster storage options and bigger VM sizes so that you can deploy and scale-up these applications on Azure without any code changes.

Premium storage is designed to provide sustained high I/O performance using solid-state drives (SSDs). Premium storage drives provide up to 80,000 I/O operations per second (IOPS) with 2000 megabits per second (Mbps) throughput. Read more about high-performance pre-mium storage at *https://docs.microsoft.com/en-us/azure/virtual-machines/windows/premium-storage*.

> **NOTE** **DIFFERENCES BETWEEN D-SERIES AND DS-SERIES**
>
> D-series is designed for applications with high demand in compute power and temporary drive performance. D-series uses SSDs as temporary drives. DS-series is designed for I/O in-tensive workloads, and uses SSDs for both hosting VM drives and local caches. For compari-son of other series see: *https://docs.microsoft.com/en-us/azure/virtual-machines/windows/premium-storage#scalability-and-performance-targets*.

Determine when to use Azure Batch

Use Azure Batch when you need high-performance compute batch processing but don't want the overhead or expense managing a compute cluster yourself. Using Batch, you can schedule and manage large-scale parallel workloads on Azure-managed compute resources without the need to manage any infrastructure yourself. Azure Batch works well with compute intensive tasks such as:

- Financial risk modeling
- 3D image rendering and other large-scale rendering workloads (*https://docs.microsoft.com/en-us/azure/batch/batch-rendering-service*)
- Image analysis and processing
- Media transcoding
- Optical character recognition (OCR)
- Genetic sequence analysis
- Data analysis and transformation; ETL processing
- Message parsing
- Multi-node AI training
- Fluid dynamics
- Execution of R algorithms on Batch pools

Learn more at *https://docs.microsoft.com/en-us/azure/batch/batch-technical-overview.*

Design stateless components to accommodate scale

Scalability is the ability of a system to handle increased loads without human interaction. There are many design considerations to accommodate for scale. One of these design considerations is stateless components. In a highly scalable system any given task could be run on one or more physical compute nodes. In order to accommodate this architectural challenge all metadata must be stored in a place that can be seen by these multiple compute nodes. This metadata is referred to as state. Stateless is storing this metadata in a location that can be used by all compute nodes.

Some example of this metadata might include:

- Counters, variables and sequence markers
- Session information such as users IP address, name, authentication token
- Navigation history

Often in the past, the application state data was stored on the local hard drive of the compute node. If this data were stored on a single node and the application for the current user sends a secondary request to the server that is automatically redirected to another node because the original node was down or busy, any data that the application needs would be lost. The solution to this challenge is programming the application to be stateless.

Stateless does not mean there is no state; it just means that the information is available regardless of which node the user or application attaches to on subsequent calls. This data can be passed into the subsequent calls as parameters; it can be stored in a highly optimized database, or a location such as an online cache like Redis Cache. Where the state information is stored is not important. What is important is that it is fast, reliable and resilient and available regardless of compute node. In most cases, programmers will eliminate state as much as possible, reduce the amount of data needed, and use a standard technology for obtaining or passing the data that must be available at time of execution. To learn more about designing stateless for scalability see *https://docs.microsoft.com/en-us/azure/architecture/checklist/scalability*.

Design lifecycle strategy for Azure Batch

Azure Batch allows many capabilities and advantages over other HPC environments. The largest of which is the lack of overhead required to manage and sustain a high-performance compute cluster. A close second biggest advantage is obtained by minimizing cost while maximizing capability through an effective lifecycle strategy for Azure Batch.

Managing your Azure Batch lifecycle includes sequencing and developing strategies for how the various components will be leveraged. A strategy will include all or most of the following:

1. Set up and manage accounts (*https://docs.microsoft.com/en-us/azure/batch/batch-account-create-portal*)

2. Authenticate with Azure Active Directory (*https://docs.microsoft.com/en-us/azure/batch/batch-aad-auth or https://docs.microsoft.com/en-us/azure/batch/batch-aad-auth-management*)

3. Create and store application packages in a central repository (*https://docs.microsoft.com/en-us/azure/batch/batch-application-packages*)

    A. Azure Batch will store the versioned binaries

    B. Store code and other components in central code repository (VSTS, Git, other)

    C. Pool application packages

    D. Task application packages

    E. Leverage Batch Management .NET library or the Azure portal

4. Create and manage pools *https://docs.microsoft.com/en-us/azure/batch/batch-automatic-scaling*

5. Manage jobs and tasks (*https://docs.microsoft.com/en-us/azure/batch/batch-job-prep-release*)

6. Persist job and task output

    A. Batch API (*https://docs.microsoft.com/en-us/azure/batch/batch-task-output-files*)

    B. File Conventions library (*https://docs.microsoft.com/en-us/azure/batch/batch-task-output-file-conventions*)

7. Run workloads (*https://docs.microsoft.com/en-us/azure/batch/batch-rendering-service*)

8. Monitor resources (*https://docs.microsoft.com/en-us/azure/batch/batch-diagnostics*)

Thought experiment

In this thought experiment, apply what you've learned about this skill. You can find answers to these questions in the "Thought experiment answers" section at the end of this chapter.

You are the administrator for Contoso. You have more than 100 hosts in your on-premises datacenter. You are replicating and using Site Recovery as part of your BC/DR plan. Contoso just acquired another company, Fabrikam, Inc. The development teams at both Contoso and Fabrikam use Visual Studio and Visual Studio Team Services.

Letter from the CTO:

"As you know, we have finalized the acquisition of Fabrikam. I would like for you to come up with a plan of execution for migrating the workloads running in the Fabrikam datacenter. The lease of the space will be expiring in 9 months at which time we must have everything out. I would prefer that we get everything moved quickly, in the next 4 to 6 months. Then we can do some cleanup later if needed. We MUST make sure we maintain a high degree of confidence in securing all data as we go through this transition. All applications will continue to be used for the foreseeable future, so it is important to minimize system downtime of Fabrikam services. The physical machines at Fabrikam are beyond or nearing their expected usable life. However, we have a directive from leadership to minimize capital expenditures where possible. I would also like you to be conscious of the costs of ongoing maintenance of these services until such a time that they can be evaluated for longer term upkeep projections. Where possible, in the short period of time we have for the migration, leverage our DevOps practices and switch applications to native cloud apps and leverage serverless compute. Some of the Fabrikam apps are already running in containers. Plan on adding these to our existing container infrastructure running on Azure Service Fabric."

Fabrikam has 5 VMware hosts, 10 Hyper-V hosts and more than 60 VMs. They are running a mix of operating systems, some running Linux, but most running Windows Server. The following is a quick list of apps and their architecture:

- 46 web applications running on Windows Server and IIS; 4 are only providing API services to applications. Those that use data, use SQL server. All but three are running stateless.

- 3 websites running on Linux, Apache, PHP, and WordPress.

- 3 containerized applications running .NET core on Linux.

- 8 containerized applications running Node.js.

- 1 Oracle database server.

- 3 SQL servers running more than 20 databases.

- 2 Domain Controllers.

- 2 External DNS servers.
- 2 Monitoring and reporting servers.
- 1 file server.
- 1 3 node cluster for batch processing and analysis running R scripts; usually on a monthly cadence to do analysis of customer purchasing patterns.

With this in mind, answer the following questions:

1. What site should be used to receive Fabrikam VM services and why?
2. What tool could you use to securely migrate the VM workloads? How will this limit downtime?
3. How can you minimize downtime of Fabrikam web services?
4. Can the Linux websites be migrated to PaaS on Azure? If so, how?
5. What are the best destination services for migration of the IIS websites?
6. What is the best way to move the containers to Azure Container Instances?
7. What are the next steps after an application has been moved to Azure?
8. Is the batch cluster a good candidate for migration to serverless compute? Why or why not?
9. What tool might be able to help you understand what is running at Fabrikam and what would be needed for the migration?
10. If you stood up a copy of the various workloads on Azure or on-premises, what tool or service could you use to switch that copy to be the new production location with little or no downtime?
11. What challenges do you think you need to prepare for?

Thought experiment answers

This section contains the solutions to the thought experiments and answers to the skill review questions in this chapter.

1. Azure is the best location to receive the virtual machines and services because the physical machines at Fabrikam are beyond or nearing their expected usable life. Additionally, security is important as well as limiting capital expenditures.
2. All of the VM workloads could be migrating using Azure Site Recovery. This would security synchronize data to Azure and allow for a quick failover to limit downtime.
3. You can minimize downtime of Fabrikam web services by using a Traffic Manager in front of the applications that are running at Fabrikam. Deploy the apps to Azure then switch over to the Azure deployed apps when ready.
4. Yes, the Linux websites are migrated to PaaS on Azure using Azure Web Apps for Linux.

5. The best destination services for migration of the IIS websites would be Azure Web Apps.

6. The best way to move the containers to Azure Container Instances would be to create an Azure Registry, upload the containers to the Azure Registry, then deploy the containers to Azure Container instance.

7. Set up monitoring, backup, and development slots. Development slots will allow for continuous innovation and DevOps practices.

8. A batch cluster is a great workload to move to Azure Serverless compute because it requires much hardware that is rarely used. In addition to being significantly cheaper than deploying the cluster in virtual machines, the cluster is only used periodically which means there would be no cost except when the jobs are running.

9. Azure Migrate.

10. Traffic Manager.

11. The largest challenge will be integrating the directories of the two companies. It may also be a challenge to determining which applications will use which compute service in Azure.

Chapter summary

- Azure supports various VM sizes and a gallery of both Linux images and Windows images.

- Azure provides raw compute power for your HPC needs with instance sizes optimized for compute-intensive workloads.

- With Azure, you can transfer on-premises applications to the cloud and scale them up by using larger VM sizes and Premium storage.

- Azure is a great platform for adding redundancy to your on-premises systems.

- Replicating to Azure can offer an additional layer of protection for single-datacenter environments.

- Replicating to Azure as the replica datacenter can give customers almost instant offsite recovery capabilities without expensive hardware purchases.

- Azure Migrate makes it easy to assess on-premises workloads for migration to Azure.

- Azure Active Directory can protect backend Web Apps using OAuth 2.0 protocol.

- Azure Batch is a hosted Azure service that supports running parallel tasks at large scale. Batch provides flexible programming models as well as comprehensive management and monitoring capabilities to manage your tasks.

- You can use Azure Site Recovery to migrate to Azure using failover.

- Azure datacenters take over some of the responsibilities of infrastructure management by providing trust-worthy and sustainable infrastructures.

- Your application needs to be designed to cope with service interruptions and throttling. In addition, your application needs to adopt appropriate security policies to ensure that your service is only accessed by authenticated and authorized users.

- You can automate VM state management with Azure Automation and third-party solutions such as Chef and Puppet.

- When you build serverless apps you don't need to provision and manage servers, so you can take your mind off infrastructure concerns. There are many serverless option on Azure including: Azure Functions, Logic Apps, Containers, Batch, Event Grid, API Management, Cognitive Services, Azure Bot Service, Azure Storage and more.

- Azure Container Instances allow you to develop apps fast without managing virtual machines or having to learn new tools—it's just your application, in a container, running in the cloud.

- DevOps requires infrastructure to be captured as code. With DevOps, an application consists of both application code and infrastructure code so that the application can be deployed consistently and rapidly across different environments.

- Containers and serverless compute are key enablers to DevOps.

- Azure Resource Template captures the entire topology of your application as code, which you can manage just as you do application source code. Resource Templates are JSON files that you can edit using any text editors.

- Containerization facilitates agility, high compute density, and decoupling of workloads and VMs. It transforms the datacenter from VMs with roles to resource pools with mobilized workloads.

- You can use autoscale to adjust your compute capacity to achieve balance between cost and customer satisfaction. Autoscale can also provide almost limitless performance and reliability.

- Premium storage is designed to provide sustained high I/O performance using solid-state drives (SSDs). Premium storage drives provide up to 5,000 I/O operations per second (IOPS) with 200 megabits per second (Mbps) throughput. With the 16-core DS series VMs, you can attach up to 32 TB of data disks and achieve more than 50,000 IOPS.

- Data Migration Assistant (DMA) enables you to upgrade to a modern data platform by detecting compatibility issues that can impact database functionality in your new version of SQL Server and Azure SQL Database.

- Traffic Manager can distribute user traffic based on availability and performance.

- Traffic Manager uses performance, weighted, priority or geographic load balancing methods to decide to which endpoint to route traffic.

- CDNs serve cached content directly from CDN nodes that are closest to end users.

- CDNs can reduce traffic to original service nodes by serving static content directly.

- The cloud provides QoS opportunities for your cloud applications. However, you need to design your application for the cloud to take advantage of these offerings.

- Availability is commonly realized by redundancy, but redundancy has its associated costs. So, you should pick a realistic availability goal.

- To ensure system-level availability, you need to ensure that all components are available. SPoF has significant negative impacts on system availability.

- You can increase system-level availability by using multisite deployments. You can also increase system-level availability by introducing alternative service paths.

- Azure uses Update Domains and Fault Domains to help you to keep at least a number of service instances running during system failures and software updates.

- Scaling up is when you increase processing power of a single instance. Scaling out is when you increase system capacity by using more service instances.

- Autoscale helps you to reduce operational cost by adjusting the system capacity as workloads change.

- You can create web applications by using .NET, Java, Node.JS, PHP, or Python.

- You can tie Web Apps to Application Insights to save information and telemetry for the website.

- You can use a CDN to distribute web applications to datacenters around the world.

- Using deployment slots, you can deploy websites to a staging location where you can perform testing in the production environment.

- Using App Service Plan, you can scale multiple web applications while still using the same pricing tier.

- You can use deployment slots to minimize downtime when web applications are updated.

- You can use a CDN to copy websites or data storage to other regions around the world, putting them in closer geographic proximity to end users.

CHAPTER 2

Design data implementation

From simple web apps to complex machine learning apps, almost every app needs to store data in some fashion, and apps hosted in Azure are no exception. But not all apps have the same needs for storing and managing information. For instance, backups, virtual machines, regular files, and databases are types of services or solutions that have different storage requirements.

Azure provides you with solutions for your storage needs that can go from unstructured data, such as files or documents, to databases or Big Data storage. This chapter provides coverage on Azure storage solutions, and the different ways to access them.

Skills covered in this chapter:

- Skill 2.1: Design for Azure Storage solutions
- Skill 2.2: Design for Azure Data Services
- Skill 2.3: Design for relational database storage
- Skill 2.4: Design for NoSQL storage
- Skill 2.5: Design for Cosmos DB storage

Skill 2.1: Design for Azure Storage solutions

Every workflow uses and processes some kind of data. Most of that data needs to be stored in a place where you can access it later. Azure Storage solutions are part of the storage options that Microsoft offers. These cloud-based Microsoft-managed storage solutions are highly available, secure, durable, scalable, and redundant. You can access this storage from anywhere using HTTP or HTTPS. Azure Storage also provides you with different levels of access and security for making your data public or private, depending on the configuration that you need.

Azure Storage solutions provide Azure Blob storage or Azure File storage for different data requirements. In this section we will examine those solutions and when to use them.

In order to use Azure Storage you must create an Azure Storage account. Azure offers you three different types of storage accounts:

- General-purpose v1 storage accounts (GPv1)
- General-purpose v2 storage accounts (GPv2)
- Blob storage accounts

General-purpose storage accounts are designed to give you access to blobs, files, queues, tables, and Azure virtual machine disks. GPv1 are the original storage accounts used on the classic deployment model. While the pricing for this type of storage account is lower, it doesn't offer the most recent features like access tiers.

GPv2 shares all of the features offered by GPv1, but it also includes the latest features, like access tiers, that can be used with this type of account. We will review access tiers in detail in the next section.

General-purposes storage accounts, v1 and v2, also offer two different performance tiers: standard and premium storage performance. The premium storage performance tier is available only for Azure virtual machine disks.

Blob storage accounts are a specialized type of storage account. You will use blob storage accounts to store block or append blobs, but not page blobs. We will cover blob storage accounts in depth in the next section.

This section covers how to use:

- Azure Blob Storage
- Blob tiers (hot, cool, archive)
- Azure Files
- Azure Disks
- Azure Data Box
- Azure Storage Service Encryption
- Azure StorSimple

Azure Blob Storage

A blob is a collection of binary data stored as a file that can be of any type and size. You can use blobs for storing files, documents, media files, logs, Azure virtual machine drives, and others. Azure Storage provides three different types of blobs:

- **Block blobs**   Designed for storing and managing large files over networks. The information is stored in blocks inside the blob. Each block can be up to 100MB, and each blob can have up to 50,000 blocks. This means that a single block blob can store a little more than 4.75 TB (100 MB x 50,000 blocks). Text and binary files are the ideal type of data that you should store in this type of blob.

- **Append blobs**   They are like block blobs, but optimized for appending operations. You can only perform append operations to this type of blob. Update or delete operations are not supported here. This way, you will use append blobs for storing log files or similar workloads where you usually add information, but rarely need to delete or update information. Each block in an append blob can be up to 4MB in size, and you can have up to 50,000 blocks in a single append blob. This means that the total size of this type of blob can be more than 196GB (4MB X 50,000 blocks).

- **Page blobs**   They use pages as the unit for storing information. Each page has a size of 512 bytes and is grouped into collections. Pages are optimized for read and write operations and are especially suited for disks used in Azure Virtual Machines. A single page blob can be up to 8TB in size.

Blob storage accounts can store only blocks and append blobs. If you need to store disks for Azure Virtual Machines, you should select general-purpose storage accounts.

NOTE WHICH TYPE OF AZURE STORAGE SHOULD I CHOOSE?

You should not use blob storage accounts if you want to store a virtual disk for Azure Virtual Machines. This type of account does not support page blobs.

The information inside a storage account is organized in three different levels. Those levels are organized in a parent-child relationship and are used for organizing and providing different levels of granularity of settings and security. In the first level we have the storage account itself. Inside a storage account you can create an unlimited number of containers that are the structures where you can create the different types of blobs. A blob must be always created inside a container (see Figure 2-1).

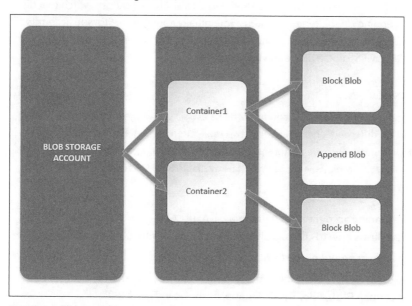

FIGURE 2-1 Blob storage account structure

Microsoft provides high availability and durability to all storage accounts by replicating the information stored in a storage account across different locations. This replication is transparent to the user and is always performed. This replication copies the information to different places in Azure's infrastructure, ensuring that your data is protected against hardware or even datacenter failures.

Depending on where this replica is stored, you can choose between four different replica strategies:

- **Locally redundant storage (LRS)**   Designed to provide 99.999999999% (11 nines) of durability over a given year of your data. Using this strategy, data will be copied inside the same datacenter in different fault domains.

- **Zone-redundant storage (ZRS)**   Designed to provide 99.9999999999% (12 nines) over a given year. The information is copied between different availability zones inside the region where you created the storage account.

- **Geo-redundant storage (GRS)**   The data is copied to a secondary region, and is designed to provide 99.99999999999999% (16 nines). Secondary regions are pre-assigned and cannot be configured or changed. You cannot read data from the secondary region using this replication strategy, unless Microsoft automatically performs a failover to the secondary region.

- **Read-access geo-redundant storage (RA-GRS)**   This works similar to GRS, but it allows read-access to data stored in the secondary region.

You can select the replica strategy during the creation process of a storage account. Once the storage account has been created and you set the replica strategy, you can switch to a different strategy, depending on the type of strategy you initially configured. Storage accounts configured with a ZRS strategy cannot be converted to or from any other replica strategy. You can switch from LRS to GRS, or RA-GRS, and vice versa.

> **NOTE ZRS CLASSIC VS. ZRS**
>
> You should not confuse ZRS storage accounts with ZRS Classic. Although the name is similar, there are important differences between these two replication strategies. ZRS Classic is available only for general-purpose v1 storage accounts, and data is replicated asynchronously within one or two regions. A replica won't be available until Microsoft starts an automatic failover to the secondary site.

You can create a storage account from Azure portal, Azure Cloud Shell, or Azure CLI. The following procedure shows how to create a blob storage account with RA-GRS replication.

1. Sign into the management portal (*http://portal.azure.com*).

2. Click on the Create A Resource Link at the upper-left corner, and then select **Storage** > **Storage Account – Blob, File, Table, Queue**, as shown in Figure 2-2.

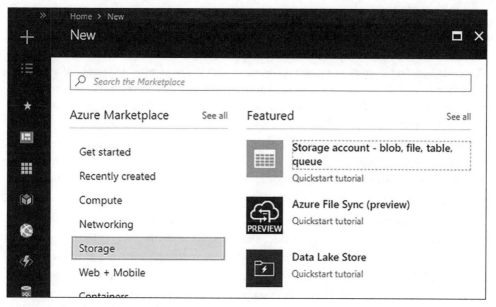

FIGURE 2-2 Creating a new storage account

3. On the Create storage account blade, type the name for the storage account. Notice that the name must be between 3 and 24 characters long and can contain only lowercase letters and numbers. The name must be also unique across all storage accounts in Azure.

4. In the Account Kind dropdown, select Blob Storage. Notice that when you make this selection, the Premium Performance option is disabled.

5. Ensure that Read-Access Geo-Redundant Storage (RA-GRS) is selected in the Replication dropdown. This is the default option.

6. Ensure that Access Tier (default) has selected the Hot option.

7. Keep Secure Transfer Required Disabled

> **NOTE ABOUT SECURE TRANSFER REQUIRED**
>
> This option enforces all connections to the storage account using secure channels. If this option is enabled, Azure rejects any request made to the REST service using HTTP. This option cannot be used with classic storage accounts.

8. Select your subscription, resource group name, and location. You can also select the virtual network that will have exclusive access to the storage account

9. Click on the Create button to create the storage account.

Blob tiers (hot, cool, archive)

One of the features introduced with blob storage and general-purpose v2 accounts are storage tiers. One interesting quality about data is that any kind of information that you may think about has age. And its age has a direct relationship with the requirement of speed of access to the information. This way, the younger the information is (the more recently it has been created, updated, or accessed), the greater the probability you need it. So, why store data that is rarely accessed on high-speed/high-performance and more expensive storage?

Blob tiers have been designed to provide you with different levels of access times to store your data most effectively, depending on your access requirements. This distribution of tiers can also have a positive impact on your storage costs depending on how you use them.

Blob storage provides you with three storage tiers:

- **Hot access tier**   Optimized for storing data that you or your applications usually access. This tier has the highest costs for storing data but the lowest cost for access and transactions. Data read and written frequently by your application is a good example of usage of this tier.

- **Cool access tier**   Optimized for storing data that will be store for at least 30 days. You usually put data here that is infrequently accessed. Access and transaction costs are higher, while storing costs are lower than those from the hot storage tier. You can find short-term backups or large-term storage for telemetry data using this type of storage tier.

- **Archive access tier**   This tier is available only at the blob level. You will typically store data here for at least 180 days. You cannot read, update, or copy a blob that is in the archive tier, since the blob is offline. You can access its metadata and perform some operations like delete, list, get blob's metadata and properties, or change the blob tier. This tier is suitable for storing data required for law compliance or archiving. The archive tier has the highest costs for access and transactions, while the lowest costs for storage.

Once you store information in an archived blob you cannot read it until you un-archive that blob, meaning you convert back to a cool or hot access tier. This process is called blob rehydration. You should plan this operation since it can take up to 15 hours to complete.

Storage tiers can be applied at storage account level or at blob level. If you do not specify any tier configuration for a blob, it will inherit the configuration from the storage account. Remember that you can only configure archive store tier at blobs level, not for storage accounts.

> *NOTE* **EARLY DELETING DATA FROM COOL AND ARCHIVE ACCESS TIERS**
>
> On March 1, 2018 or later, if you move any data to a blob stored in a cool or archive tier, you can perform an early deletion. So, you can delete the data before a 30-day period for cool tiers and a 180-day period for archive tiers. In these cases, costs are proportional to the days that the data is in the storage tier. This early deletion feature for cool access tier is available only for general-purpose v2 storage accounts.

You can switch the storage tier for a storage account or blob from Azure portal, Azure Cloud Shell, or Azure CLI. The following procedure shows you how to change the access tier for a blob using Azure Cloud Shell.

1. Sign into the management portal (*http://portal.azure.com*).

2. Click on the Cloud Shell icon in the upper-right corner, as shown in the Figure 2-3.

FIGURE 2-3 Launching Cloud Shell

> **NOTE SELECT CLOUD SHELL ENVIRONMENT**
>
> The first time that you start Cloud Shell you need to select which environment to use: PowerShell or Bash. You can always change the Cloud Shell environment by selecting the correct one in the upper-left corner of the Cloud Shell.

---

3. On the Cloud Shell, ensure that you have selected PowerShell on the dropdown in the upper-left corner.

4. On the Cloud Shell, get a reference to the storage account and store it in a variable.

```
$storageAccount = Get-AzureRmStorageAccount -ResourceGroupName
<storage resource group> -StorageAccountName <storage account name>
```

5. Get a reference to the container that stores the blob.

```
$storageContainer = $storageAccount | Get-AzureStorageContainer
-name <container name>
```

6. Get a reference to the blob object that we want to change the access tier.

```
$blobObject = $ storageContainer | Get-AzureStorageBlob -Blob
<blob name>
```

7. Change the access tier to archive. Remember that if you want to move from the archive access tier, to any other tier you need to wait for the rehydration time.

```
$blobObject.ICloudBlob.SetStandardBlobTier('Archive')
```

When you change between access tiers, you should consider the costs implications for each access tier. Figure 2-4 shows how prices evolve when you change between access tiers.

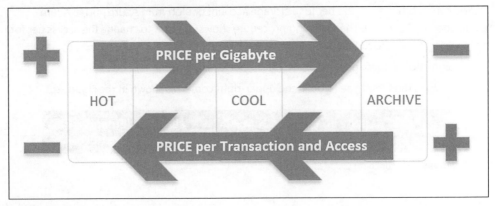

FIGURE 2-4 Price evolution between tiers

Azure Files

The objective of storing files is making the information available to users or applications for accessing when needed. If you think about how users access their daily information, one way is using shared folders hosted by on-premises file servers in their organizations.

Azure Files offers a way to access storage accounts using Server Message Block (SMB), the same protocol used for accessing shared folders on file servers. You can also access to Azure Files services by using the REST interface or the client libraries provided by the storage account. This means that Azure Files is a convenient way of sharing information between applications and users. While applications access information by using REST interfaces or client libraries, shared folders provide a more user-friendly way to get to the information.

In the same way that Azure Blob storage accounts are constructed based on a three-level structure, Azure Files uses a similar structure based on four levels:

- **Storage Account** We need this level since it's the one that provides access to the data.
- **Shares** Like in a file server, a share provides SMB access to files and folders. The storage account can contain an unlimited number of shares with a maximum of capacity of 5 TiB per share. The number of files that you can create inside a share is also unlimited. A share is like a container where you create files and directories.
- **Directory** It's just an optional hierarchical level for your convenience. Each directory must be created on a share or inside a directory that is already inside a share.
- **Files** The actual files. Each file can be up to 1 TB in size.

Figure 2-5 represents the structure of an Azure Files account.

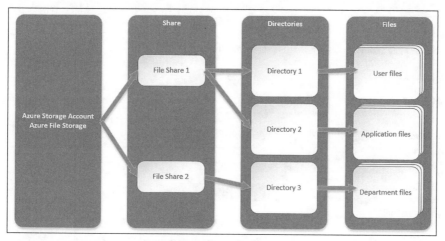

FIGURE 2-5 Azure Files structure

Azure Files is also ideal for migrating applications that depend on file shares to the cloud. You can just create an Azure file share and move the data from the on-premises shared folder to the cloud. Depending on the amount of information that you want to upload to the Azure file share you have different options:

- **Azure File Sync**   This allows you to deploy an on-premises server on your infrastructure that is connected to your Azure Files account and makes a local copy of only the most recent accessed files. You can use this as a long-term solution for improving the performance of accessing your data, or just for the time needed for perform the migration. At the time of this writing, this feature is in preview.

- **Azure Import/Export**   You can copy all of the data that you want to migrate to Azure Files on disks that you send to Azure's datacenter. Then, Microsoft's staff copies the information to your Azure Files storage account.

- **Robocopy**   Just mount an Azure Files Share as a network drive and use the well-known tool robocopy to transfer your data to the cloud.

- **AzCopy**   This is a specialized tool for copying data to and from Azure Storage accounts, including blobs and files.

In the following procedure create an Azure File share.

1. Sign into the management portal (*http://portal.azure.com*), and create a General Purpose v2 storage account.

2. Once the storage account has been created, go to Storage accounts and select the new created storage account to open its blade.

3. On the File Service section, click on Files. This will open the Files blade.

4. On the Files blade, in the upper-left corner of the blade, click on the File share button to create a new file share. This will open the New file share dialog, as shown in Figure 2-6.

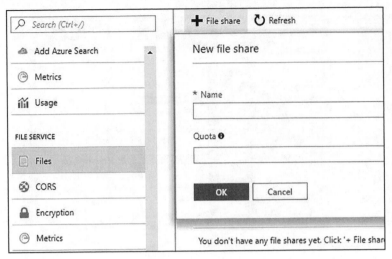

FIGURE 2-6 Creating a new file share

5. Once you have created the share, you need to get the storage account key for accessing to the new share. You will find the key in the settings section of the navigation pane in the storage account blade.

6. Now it's time to mount the file share on your windows server. You can do it by using the net use command.

```
net use <desired-drive-letter>: \\<storage-account
-name>.file.core.windows.net\<share-name> <storage-account-key>
 /user:Azure\<storage-account-name>
```

> **NOTE STORAGE ACCOUNT KEYS**
>
> Microsoft provides you with two different storage account keys for accessing the storage account. The reason for this is that you can use one key with your Azure resources and applications while you regenerate the second one.

Azure Disks

Like any regular computer, Azure Virtual Machines need disks for storing data and operating systems. Whenever you create a new virtual machine, Azure also creates its associated virtual disks. Those disks are stored in Azure Storage accounts as page blobs using the Virtual Hard Disk (VHD) format. By default, Azure always creates two virtual disks attached to the virtual machine: the operating system virtual disks and a temporary disk.

The operating system disk is presented to the virtual machine as a SAS disk and has a maximum capacity of 2048 GB. On the other hand, temporary disks are intended for storing temporary data like a swap area or page files. Although the information of this temporary disk is not deleted across virtual machine reboots, Azure cannot guarantee that the disk remains in case of redeployments of the virtual machine or maintenance events.

You can also create a data disk for storing your application's data inside the virtual machine. Those data disks are presented to the virtual machine as SCSI disks. The number of data disks that you can attach to a virtual machine depends on the size of that virtual machine. Data stored inside a data disk is persistent across maintenance events or virtual machine redeployments.

Azure allows you to use four different types of disks:

- **Standard storage** This type of disk is backed by HDD disks, which provides a good balance between cost-effective disk and performance. Standard storage disk can be configured for replicating locally (LRS), at zone level (ZRS), or geo-redundantly (GRS, RA-GRS).

- **Premium storage** Backed by SSD disks, this type is suitable for intense I/O workloads. This type of disks delivers high-performance, low-latency access to data. You can use only LRS replication for premium storage.

- **Unmanaged disks** This is the traditional way of using disks in VMs. In this model, you oversee the creation of the storage account that hosts the disks and make sure that you do not put too many disks that may go beyond the scalability limits of the storage account.

- **Managed disks** When you use this type of disk, Azure automatically takes care of storage account creation and management along with other details related with scalability limits. You only need to worry about selecting Standard or Premium storage. You can only use LRS replica strategy with this type of disks.

As with any other type of blob, disks must be created inside a container in a storage account. Remember that disks are stored as page blobs and can be only created on General Purpose v1 (GPv1) or GPv2 storage accounts. When you create a disk inside a container and attach it to a virtual machine, that disk is leased on the VHD. This way, the disk cannot be deleted until you detach if from the virtual machine. Azure also puts a lease on the disk if you use it for creating your own images.

If you need to delete a single disk instead of deleting an entire virtual machine, you need to perform some additional steps. The following procedure shows you how to perform the deletion of a single data managed disk using Azure Portal:

1. Sign into the management portal (*http://portal.azure.com*), and locate the virtual machine that has attached the disk you want to delete.

2. In the navigation pane, in the Settings section, select Disks. This will show you all disks attached to the virtual machine. Temporary disks are not shown on this view.

3. At the upper-left corner of the disks blade, click on the Edit button. This will enable you the option for detaching the disk from the virtual machine. You can detach a disk from a virtual machine while is online, but bear in mind that any data stored in the data disk won't be available for the virtual machine.

4. Look for the disk that you want to remove and click on the detach icon, as show in Figure 2-7.

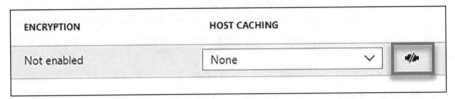

ENCRYPTION	HOST CACHING	
Not enabled	None ∨	⏏

FIGURE 2-7 Detach a data disk

5. On the upper-left corner of the disks blade for the virtual machine, click on the Save button to commit the changes. If you forget this step, you won't be able to delete the disk.

6. Now you can delete the data disk. Since it is a managed data disk, you need to look for it on the Disks' Service blade. Select the All Services button on the navigation bar and type **disk** on the filter text box. Now select the Disks service icon.

7. Look for the managed disk that you want to delete and select the name of the disk. The data disks blade should be open now.

8. On the menu bar at the top of the disk blade, click on the Delete button for removing the disk. If the button is disabled, please ensure that the DISK STATE is Unattached. You cannot remove a disk that is attached to a virtual machine or image.

> *NOTE* **CHANGE DISK PROPERTIES**
> You can change the properties of a disk, like Account Type or Size. You need to detach the disk before being able to make any modification to the disk.

Azure Data Box

Moving an important amount of data to the cloud is not a simple task. It highly depends on the available bandwidth, time, availability, and costs, and should be carefully planned for not impacting on other running workloads or business areas. In some cases, this means that performing the data copy over the network is just not an option. For those situations, Microsoft provides the Azure Import/Export service where you copy all of the information to physical disks that you send to Azure datacenters and then copy the information to your Azure Blob Storage or Azure Files accounts. But you still need to provide an HDD or SSD disk.

Azure Data Box is a storage appliance that you can connect to your on-premises infrastructure for copying all of the data that you want to migrate to Azure Blob Storage or Files accounts without impacting your other running workloads. This appliance is a 45-pound device. It is ruggedized, tamper-resistant, and human-manageable, and also integrates well with other storage solutions that you may have deployed on your infrastructure. Some of the partners that Microsoft has been working with to ease the integration with Azure Data Box are: Commvault, Veritas, Wandisco, Peer, Veeam, CloudLanes, NetApp, Avid, and Rubrik.

This appliance has a capacity up to 100TB of storage and can be accessed using SMB/CIFS protocols. Data in the Azure Data Box can be encrypted using 256-bit AES. You can also track the whole process from the Azure Portal. At the time of this writing, this service is in public preview.

Azure Storage Service Encryption

Data security is one of the main concerns of anyone who works with data in most types of environments, and especially with data on the cloud. You can protect your data during transmission using secured communications like SSL/TLS or tunneling. You can also protect your data by encrypting the information at the filesystem level, by using BitLocker for Windows virtual machines, or by using DM-Crypt features for Linux with Azure Disk Encryption service.

Azure Storage Service Encryption (SSE) provides an additional level of security by automatically encrypting any data that is written to a storage account. The data is also decrypted automatically when the data is read from the protected storage account. SSE service oversees the key management for encrypting the information. It uses 256-bit AES encryption for securing the data.

You enable Storage Service Encryption at the storage account level. You can use this service with blobs, files, and table and queue storage for both deployment models: classic and ARM. Once you enable encryption at the storage account level, all data written to the storage account will be encrypted. Any data that existed previously on the storage account won't be encrypted unless you rewrite it. If you decide to disable the encryption, the data will be decrypted when the user reads it. Any encrypted data remains encrypted until you rewrite it. All encryption keys are managed automatically by Microsoft. If you prefer to manage your own encryption keys, you can integrate Storage Service Encryption with Azure Key Vault. This way, you will have more flexibility since you will be able to create, rotate, disable and define access controls on your own encryption keys.

Since Storage Service Encryption works transparently to the user, you can use any of the already known ways to upload information to an Azure Storage account. This includes REST, AzCopy, Storage Explorer, Storage Client libraries, or SMB.

Azure StorSimple

Storing every single type of data of your company on the cloud sometimes may not be the best option. There is data that your users use more frequently than others, and that data needs to be ready as soon as possible. Moving all of your data to the cloud means that you have a stronger dependency on available bandwidth connections to the Internet.

Here is where Azure StorSimple helps. This is a hybrid storage area network solution for storing more frequently accessed data in an on-premises device while moving less frequently accessed or archived data to Azure.

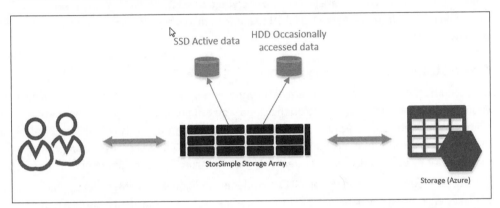

FIGURE 2-8 StorSimple data flow

You can deploy Azure StorSimple on your infrastructure in two different ways:

- **Azure StorSimple Virtual Array**   This is a virtual appliance that can be deployed on a single node virtualization infrastructure (Hyper-V or VMware). It can store up to 6.4 TB in local store and 64 TB in the cloud per virtual array. You can access this storage using iSCSI or SMB protocols.

- **StorSimple 8000 Series**   This is a physical device with SSD and HDD disks that you can install on your on-premises infrastructure. This appliance uses tiering techniques for storing more frequently accessed data in SSD drives while moving less frequently data to HDD drives. When data is valid to be archived, it is moved to Azure, reducing the need for local storage.

You will typically use the StorSimple Virtual Array on file sharing or archival file sharing scenarios, where data is infrequently accessed. You need to consider that each virtual array can write and read from an Azure Storage at a 100Mbps. If you share this between too many concurrent users, the virtual array will be a bottleneck, impacting negatively on the performance.

If you want to use StorSimple for frequently accessed file shares, you need to deploy StorSimple 8000 series devices. These devices come with compression, deduplication, automatic tiering, backup and snapshot capabilities that make it more appropriate for this type of workload. They also have redundant and hot-pluggable components, truly an enterprise-level highly available device. Apart from file sharing, StorSimple 8000 series devices are suitable for other workloads like distributed file sharing, SharePoint, simple file archiving, virtual machines, SQL, Video surveillance, primary, and secondary target backup.

Both StorSimple Virtual Array and 8000 series devices use a heat map to move data between different tiers. Azure Storage is treated as another tier inside the StorSimple virtual array or device. This way, the movement between tiers is transparent to the user, since the most accessed data will be always present on the fastest tier.

For those situations where you prefer not to move data to Azure Storage, you can configure StorSimple with locally pinned volumes. Any data stored on a locally pinned volume won't be copied to Azure Storage.

This skill showed the different services that Azure offers you for storing your data. But storing data is just the beginning of the story. In the next section we will cover how Azure can help you on managing and exploiting the information stored in Azure.

Skill 2.2: Design for Azure Data Services

Information can be originated from several and distinct origins. Storing data is an important part of any workflow but not the end of the road. But once you have stored the data, you need to process, transform, present, and share it. The real value of any data is the information that it provides after you process it and share it with your clients, partners, or colleagues. Depending on the amount of information that you need to process, it can be a challenging task.

Azure Data Services provides you with the tools for managing, transform, present, and share your information efficiently while minimizing the effort and costs. Azure helps you to solve some common problems like:

- Having a central repository of data sources
- Orchestrating all of the operations on information transformation and presentation
- Providing calculation resources for transforming data without impacting on your production environment
- Storing historical information for latter analysis
- Presenting and sharing the information once that it has been processed

> **This section covers how to use:**
> - Azure Data Catalog
> - Azure Data Factory
> - Azure SQL Data Warehouse
> - Azure Data Lake Analytics
> - Azure Analysis Services
> - Azure HDInsight

Azure Data Catalog

Sharing information is a key point in any successful team. But sharing information is not limited only to members of a team, because sharing between teams can be even more important. When some of those teams work with data, it's likely that they'll work with data sources to access those information assets.

Azure Data Catalog is a service that unifies and centralizes the storage and management of data sources used in your company for accessing information assets. This service tries to address some of the most common challenging scenarios for data consumers and data producers:

- A data consumer user may not have any idea about an existing data source unless it is needed as a part of another process. There is no central repository where a user can attend and review existing data sources.

- A data consumer may not necessarily know the location of the data source documentation. In those cases, understanding the intended use for the data may be difficult. The documentation and the data source itself are usually stored in a variety of locations.

- From the point of view of a data consumer there is no direct relationship between the information asset and those that have the expertise on the data usage.

- Even if the data consumer has the data source and the documentation, she may not know the procedure for asking access to the information asset.

- For a data producer, creating and maintaining the documentation for the data sources is usually a time-consuming and complex task. If the documentation is not correctly maintained, the data consumer user may start losing trust in the documentation since it can be perceived as being out of date.

- Data producers may try to document data sources by using metadata associated to it, but those metadata are usually ignored by client applications.

- Trying to restrict the access to data sources based on security groups can be also challenging.

Azure Data Catalog tries to address all of these challenges by providing a central store for data consumers and data creators that make data sources discoverable and understandable for those users that need to work with them. These cloud services allow you to register a data source by copying to the Data Catalog data source's metadata and also to a reference to its location.

Once you have registered a data source into the Data Catalog, any allowed user in your company can update and enrich this registry by adding or updating tags, description or more metadata to the registered data source. You can also attach documentation and requesting procedures. When you register a new data source you need to consider two different types of metadata.

- **Structural metadata** This is basically the information related with column names and data types extracted from the data source when you connect it to the server for the first time.

- **Descriptive metadata** This is the metadata that you provide to the registry, like descriptions, tags, or any other metadata that helps to understand better how this data source can be used.

When provisioning a new Data Catalog, you need to bear in mind that your user needs to be a member of the Azure Active Directory associated with your subscription. You cannot use guest users for creating a new Data Catalog. Once you create your first Data Catalog, you can register for your first data source. The following procedure shows how to register your first data source using the Azure Data Catalog application:

1. Sign into Azure Data Catalog web site (*https://www.azuredatacatalog.com*).

2. On the Home page, select Publish Data. You can also select Publish button on the upper-right corner of the page, as shown in Figure 2-9.

FIGURE 2-9 Data Catalog control buttons

3. In the Publish Your Data Now! page, click on the Launch Application button. This will download the Azure Data Catalog application that you will use for registering your first data source.

4. Once you install the application, you need to sign in using your Azure Active Directory account.

5. Next, you need to select the data source type that you want to register and click on Next. The information that you need to provide on the next page depends on the type of data source that you select. For this example, we will use Azure Blob.

6. For an Azure Blob data source, you need to provide the account name and the access key and click on Connect. Remember that you can get that information from the Azure portal. For the account name you don't need to provide the suffix .core.windows.net.

7. On the last page, you need to select which blob or blobs you want to register on the portal.

8. Once you have registered all of the blobs you decided on, you can go to the Azure Data Catalog portal for reviewing your newly registered data sources.

Azure Data Factory

Working with Big Data usually involves dealing with storage, processing or transforming data, and moving data between datasources, and presenting information. The enormous amount of raw data that usually represents Big Data doesn't have any real value until it's processed. For this kind of workload, you need a way of automatically performing the movements between different systems that Big Data requires.

Azure Data Factory is a cloud-based service provided by Microsoft that allows you to orchestrate all of these movements between services involved on big data management and processing. Using Azure Data Factory, you can get raw data from relational data sources, like databases, line of business applications, CRMs, or ERPs, and non-relational data sources, like social media, IoT devices, web sites, or raw media. Once you get the information from the different data sources, you can move it to those services in charge of processing and transforming the information, such as Azure HDInsight, Hadoop, Spark, Azure Data Lake Analytics, and Azure Machine Learning. Figure 2-10 shows the data flow in a typical Big Data process.

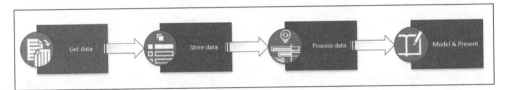

FIGURE 2-10 Big Data process, getting data

Once you have processed and transformed the information, you can instruct Data Factory to move the information to some other service for storing and presenting the processed data. You can use, for example, Azure SQL Data Warehouse, Azure SQL Database, Azure Cosmos DB, or any other analytics engine that your users may consume for feeding their business intelligence tools.

Azure Data Factory provides the tools for automating the process of moving the information between different systems. It also provides enterprise-level monitoring tools for reviewing success and failure of the scheduled activities in Data Factory. The tools that provide monitoring features to Azure Data Factory are Azure Monitor, API, PowerShell, Microsoft Operations Manager Suite, and health panels on the Azure Portal.

Inside Azure Data Factory you use a pipeline for performing the movement of information between the different steps. A pipeline is a data-driven workflow, which is basically a group of activities that work together to perform a task. Each activity in your pipeline defines those actions you need to perform on your dataset. Based on this you can find three types of activities:

- **Data movement activities**   You use these kinds of activities for copying data between on-premises and/or cloud data stores. After you process and transform the data, you typically use these type of activities to publish your results.

- **Data transformation activities**   After copying the data to the data transformation system, you use these activities to execute the transformation in a computing environment. You can trigger activities in on-premises or cloud systems.

- **Control activities**   You use these activities for controlling the flow execution of the pipeline. As with any other type of workflow, you can also set activities dependencies to control workflow execution. Depending on the execution result of an activity, you can indicate which activity should be executed on an specific time

Another important part of any pipeline is the group of data that will be processed by the activities. That group of data is known as the dataset. You can think on the dataset as a pointer or reference to the real data on the data source that is used for each activity in the pipeline. Before any activity can use any dataset, you also need to provide the connection to the source of the data. We know that connection as a linked service. In the same way a connection string defines the properties needed by an application to connect to a database, linked services define the properties needed by Azure Data Factory for connecting to different data sources.

Azure SQL Data Warehouse

When you work on Big Data workflows, you need to perform several steps for getting the results you want to achieve. Azure Data Factory helps on automating and orchestrating the data flow between different parts. Once the data has been processed by other transformation engines, it can be moved to an Azure SQL Data Warehouse, where you will store your data into relational tables with columnar storage.

As you see in Figure 2-11, Azure SQL Data Warehouse is at the end of the chain, where the data needs to be modeled before you can present it to business intelligence applications or reporting services.

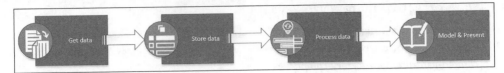

FIGURE 2-11 Big Data process, modeling

Thanks to the columnar storage format used in SQL Data Warehouse, queries executed in this service are several times faster than in traditional databases. This means that you can run data analysis at the massive scale that Big Data usually needs without impacting your production environments and databases.

Azure SQL Data Warehouse offers two different performance tiers. These two performance tiers allow you to choose the option that better fits your compute needs:

- **Optimized for Elasticity**   On this performance tier, storage and compute are in separate architectural layers. This tier is ideal for workloads of heavy peaks of activity, allowing you to scale the compute and storage tiers separately depending on your needs.

- **Optimized for Compute**   Microsoft provides you with the latest hardware for this performance tier, using NVMe Solid State Disk cache. This way, most recently accessed data keeps as close as possible to the CPU. This tier provides the highest level of scalability, by providing you up to 30,000 compute Data Warehouse Units (cDWU).

In order to measure the resources allocated to SQL Data Warehouse, Microsoft defines a compute scale called Data Warehouse Unit (DWUs). This unit is a bundle of CPU, memory and IOs, that provides an abstract and normalized measure of compute resources and performance. This way, if you need to assign more performance to your system, you increase the number of DWU. Although the concept is similar for both performance tiers, we use DWU for measuring resources assigned to the Optimized for Elasticity performance tier while we use cDWU for Optimized for Compute performance tier.

> **NOTE DATA WAREHOUSE UNITS**
>
> For a complete list of DWU and cDWU you can refer to *https://docs.microsoft.com/en-us/azure/sql-data-warehouse/performance-tiers* for a comprehensive list of CPU, IO and memory resources assigned to each DWU/cDWU level.

Thanks to compute and storage tiers separation, you can increase or decrease assignment of resources to the compute tier without affecting the pricing in the storage tier. The architecture used for providing the scale-out capabilities to Azure SQL Data Warehouse is composed by four main layers:

- **Azure storage**   This service is used for storing user data. Since multiple compute nodes need access to the data, the information is shared into distinct storage units called distributions to optimize the performance of the overall system. You can choose between three different sharing patterns, Hash, Round Robin, and Replicate, for distributing the information in the storage account. You are charged separately for Azure storage account consumption.

- **Control node** This is the entry point to the system and the header that orchestrates and manages the whole system. The Massive Parallel Processing, or MPP, engine runs on this node, and provides the needed interfaces for interacting with different applications.

- **Compute nodes** This layer provides the calculation power of the system. Compute nodes get the data needed for doing their job from the Distributions defined in the Azure storage layer. Each distribution maps to a compute node for its processing.

- **Data Movement Service** This service ensures that each node in the service receives needed information when doing parallel queries for returning an accurate result.

Azure Data Lake Analytics

Following with Big Data workflows, once you gather and store your data, you need to process it. You use a processing data activity for data analysis or applying machine learning techniques that will produce new refined data that can be later modeled by other tools.

Microsoft provides Azure Data Lake Analytics for performing on-demand analytics jobs on your data sets. This service is focused on performance for managing huge amounts of information, so it's ideal for big data workflows. Figure 2-12 shows where Azure Data Lake Analytics play its role in the workflow.

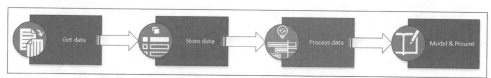

FIGURE 2-12 Big Data process, processing

Azure Data Lake Analytics provides you with an evolution of SQL, called U-SQL. This language extends the declarative nature of SQL with C# capabilities. This way, your developers do not need to learn a new language, just using their already acquired skills to analyze data. Thanks to integration with other Azure data services, you can take advantage of the highest performance and throughput when using Azure Storage Blobs, Azure SQL Database, or Azure SQL Data Warehouse.

Another interesting capability of Azure Data Lake Analytics is that is able to integrate with your existing IT infrastructure. This means that you can manage users and security by using your Active Directory. In the same way, Data Lake Analytics can be also integrated with Visual Studio for developing your data transform programs. The following procedure shows how to create and run a small U-SQL script.

1. Sign into the management portal (*http://portal.azure.com*).

2. *Create* a new Data Lake Analytics account. Click **Create A Resource** > **Data + Analytics** > **Data Lake Analytics**.

3. Provide needed information for creating the Data Lake Analytics account. As you can see in the Figure 2-13, you can choose between two pricing packages, Monthly commitment and Pay-as-You-Go. You need to create or select an existing Data Lake Storage account, which is covered in the Skill 2.4 section.

FIGURE 2-13 New Data Lake Analytics account

4. Once you provide all needed information, click on the **Create** button and wait while the account is provisioned.

5. Go to your newly created Data Lake Analytics account by clicking **All services** and typing **data lake** on the filter textbox. Then select Data Lake Analytics and click your new account.

6. We need to create a new job for running a U-SQL script. On the Overview blade of your Data Lake Analytics account, select New job located in the upper-left corner.

7. You need to provide a name for the new job. You will also use this blade for writing your U-SQL script. The script shown in Figure 2-14 is a very simple script for an imaginary industrial temperature measuring system that works well for our example. When running

this job, you can decide to assign from 1 to 30 Analytics Units for executing the job in parallel. The more units you use, the more performance you get, and the more cost you have to pay.

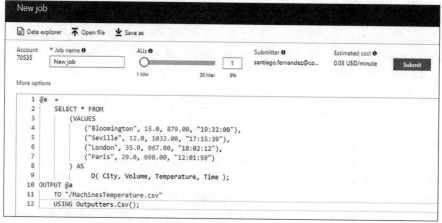

FIGURE 2-14 Creating a new job for running a U-SQL script

8. Once you are happy with your script, click on Submit for creating the job and submitting the script for being processed.

9. As soon as you submit your job, you will get the job details blade, where you can review the progress of the execution, the graph that represents the tasks performed by the script, and the output of your script. If you select the Data tab, on the Outputs tab you will see the output file created by the execution of your script.

Azure Analysis Services

Once you have all your data processed and modeled, you need to present it to different applications. Based on SQL Server Analysis Services, Azure Analysis Services allows you to connect distinct data sources from different origins for combining and relating the information of each source into tabular models that you can use later with Business Intelligence analysis tools, like Power BI, Excel, SQL Server Reporting Services, Tableau, or custom applications. Thanks to this, Azure Analysis Services is compatible with SQL Server Analysis Services Enterprise Edition tabular models at 1200 and 1400 compatibility models.

Azure Analysis Services integrates with Azure Active Directory, Azure Data Factory, Azure Automation and Azure Functions. These integrations provide features like role-based access control that secures the access to your data, the orchestration for feeding your models using Azure Data Fabric, or the lightweight orchestration, writing custom code using Azure Automation and Azure Functions.

You can choose between three different tiers: Developer, Basic and Standard. The processor power, Query Processing Units (QPUs), and memory size, as well as the costs, depend on the pricing tier you select. Developer and Standard tiers have the same list of features available.

The difference between both tiers is the amount of resources you can assign to each tier. The Developer tier only has one instance type, while you can choose between six different instance types. For the most recent feature and instance types definition, visit the Analysis Services pricing page (*https://azure.microsoft.com/en-us/pricing/details/analysis-services/*).

When selecting a tier, you need to create a server for Azure Analysis Services, then select a plan or instance type within a tier. Once you select your tier, you can move your instance type up and down within the same tier. You can also move up your tier, but you cannot move down. If you select Standard tier and instance type S2, you can move to an S1 or an S4, but you cannot move to any plan on Developer or Basic tiers.

For those cases where you need to provide more power to your server, but you don't want to increase the instance type, Azure Analysis Services provides you scale-out capabilities. When you use a single server, it is in charge of acting as the processing server and query server. If the server starts exceeding the number of assigned QPUs, because of the number of clients making queries is too high , clients will start experiencing bad performance issues. By using Azure Analysis Service's scale-out feature, you can deploy up to seven additional instances of your server. You can create a query pool for serving client's queries. You can have up to eight servers in your pool, which is your current server plus seven additional severs.

When you create a query pool, the processing workload is not distributed between servers in the pool. Just one server acts as the processing server. Once the processing operation is completed there is a synchronization of the processed model between all replicas in the query pool. Any single replica in the query pool only serves queries against the synced model. You can configure scale-out only for servers in the Standard tier. Each additional server in the query pool is billed at the same rate of the main server. You can configure scale-out replicas and synchronization, as well as start a manual synchronization by using Azure Portal, PowerShell, or REST API.

Between the different types of data sources that you can connect to using Azure Analysis Services, you can choose to connect to data sources located on your on-premises infrastructure. In those cases, you need to deploy and configure an on-premises data gateway. This gateway is like a bridge that provides secure transfer of your data between your on-premises data source and your Azure Analysis Services servers deployed in the cloud.

Azure HDInsight

Azure Data Lake Analytics is a good tool for processing data, but in some cases it isn't the best option for doing the job. Different scenarios may require more specific tools for having the best results.

Azure HDInsight is a cloud native solution for deploying an optimized cluster of several Big Data open source solutions. HDInsight includes frameworks like Hadoop, Spark, Interactive Query, Kafka, Storm, HBase and R Server. The main advantage of using HDInsight is that you can select the best option to fit your specific scenario. Any of the options existing in HDInsight share some important enterprise-level features:

- **Cloud native** When you choose any of the frameworks available in HDInsight, Azure automatically creates for you an optimized cluster for your selection. This also means that Microsoft can provide you with an SLA that ensures the level of service that you will receive.

- **Low-cost and scalable**   As with most services in cloud, you can add or remove nodes or resources to your cluster, enabling you to pay only for what you use. Using orchestration techniques with HDInsight, you can also dynamically grow or shrink your cluster based on the needs of your operation. Compute and storage resources are managed separately, which also helps to achieve performance and flexibility levels.

- **Secure and compliant**   You can also integrate HDInsight with Azure Virtual Network, encryption, and Azure Active Directory. This way you can protect your communications with the cluster and manage users' access to the cluster using role-based access control.

- **Monitoring**   The integration of HDInsight with Azure Log Analytics enables you to have a central location for managing all of your Azure resources, including HDInsight clusters.

- **Extensibility**   HDInsight provides a full-featured cluster, but you may still need some specific features that don't exist with any available option in HDInsight. You can easily extend HDInsight capabilities by installing additional components or integrating with third party Big Data applications.

Skill 2.3: Design for relational database storage

Traditionally, relational databases have been the way applications store information in an ordered and effective way. If you are moving to the cloud or developing a new application in the cloud from the beginning, there is a possibility that you want to use a relational database for storing your application's data.

As with many other services, Microsoft offers you the option of moving your databases to the cloud using a managed service. This allows you to focus on the development of your product and abstracting from tasks that need to provide enterprise-level services, like High Availability, backup and restore, or Disaster Recovery. You can also take advantage of the scale-up and scale-out capabilities that Azure offers through Azure SQL Databases.

This section covers how to use:

- Azure SQL Database
- SQL Server Stretch Database
- Design for scalability and features
- Azure Database for MySQL
- Azure Database for PostgreSQL
- Design for HA/DR and geo-replication
- Backup and recovery strategies
- Optimization strategies for Azure SQL Data Warehouse columnar storage

Azure SQL Database

Based on the well-known SQL Server database engine, Azure SQL Database allows you to deploy and consume databases in Azure without worrying about the details of deploying a SQL Server and its associated infrastructure needs.

You can create three different types of databases in Azure SQL Database:

- **Single databases** You create a single database inside a resource group. You assign to that resource group a set of compute and storage resources for running the needed workloads.

- **Elastic pools** You typically use this type of database when you are not sure or cannot predict the demand for the database. You create a database inside a pool of databases on a resource group. All databases in the elastic pool share the resources assigned to the pool.

- **Managed instance** This type of database is most similar to the on-premises SQL servers that you typically use. This is the ideal option when you want to migrate existing applications to Azure, minimizing the impact of the migration process.

When you decide to create a single instance database or an elastic pool you need to use a logical server prior to creating your first database. A logical server is the entry point for the databases and controls logins, firewall rules, auditing rules, thread detection policies and failover groups. You should not confuse an Azure SQL Database logical server with an on-premises SQL Server. The logical server is a logical structure that doesn't provide any way for connecting to instance or feature level. The following procedure shows how to create an Azure SQL Database:

1. Sign into the management portal (*http://portal.azure.com*).

2. In the upper-left corner of the portal, click on Create A Resource icon.

3. On the New blade, select Databases and then SQL Database.

4. On the SQL Database blade, provide the name for the database.

5. Select the subscription where the database will be created.

6. Create a new resource group or use an existing one.

7. You can choose to create a new blank database, use the sample database (AdventureworksLT) or restore a database from a backup. We will cover how to create and manage backups later in this skill.

8. You need to provide a logical server that you will use for connecting to the database. If you do not already have one, you need to create one. Figure 2-15 shows needed information for creating a new logical server.

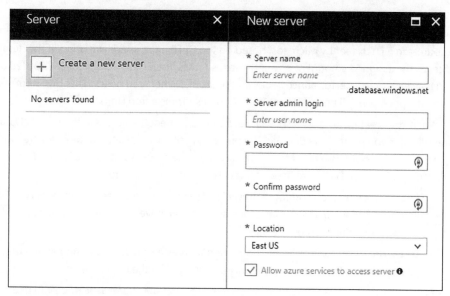

FIGURE 2-15 Creating new logical server

9. Next, select if you what to include the database in an elastic pool. For this procedure, keep the default selection Not Now.

10. Select the pricing tier.

11. Configure the collation for the database. Keep the default collation for this procedure.

Because of how Azure provides high availability to the databases, there is no need for the logical server to be on the same region as the databases it manages. Azure SQL Database does not guarantee that the logical server and its related databases will be on the same region. When you create the logical server, the first user you create is granted with administrator privileges on the master database and any following database that you create. This first account is a SQL login account. You can only use SQL login and Azure Active Directory login accounts. Windows authentication is not supported with SQL logical server. Once you have created the logical server, you can also add an Azure Active Directory administrator. You can use either a single user or a security group. If you plan to manage control access to SQL Database using Azure Active Directory you need to configure an Azure Active Directory administrator.

When you provision resources for the database, depending on the usage pattern of your database you may find that those resource are not used most of the time. If you need to deploy several databases you may find that you are not optimizing resource usage. Elastic pools are designed for solving this issue. An elastic pool allows you to share assigned resources to the pool between all databases in the pool. This way, when one database is not using those assigned resources to the pool, another database in the pool can take advantage of it. This way you minimize the waste of resources. The elastic pool is the best option when you need to deal with unpredictable databases workloads. The elastic pool ensures that all databases in the pool will always have a minimum amount of resources.

Resources assigned to a database are measured in DTU or Database Transaction Units. This unit is a combination of CPU, memory, and data and transaction log I/Os. The ratio of assigned resources in a DTU is set by Microsoft based on the OLTP benchmark workload. If the database exceeds the assigned amount of any of those resources, then the throughput is throttled and you may experience performance issues and timeouts. When you need to assign resources to an elastic pool, you will use eDTU or elastic Database Transaction Units.

When you create your database, you need to also protect the access to it. The SQL Database firewall helps you protect the database by preventing the access to the database. After you create your logical server, you need to specifically allow the access to the server from outside your subscription. The SQL Database firewall offers two levels of protection:

- **Logical server** You configure firewall rules for allowing access to logical server. Each IP that you allow to access to the logical server will have access to all databases and elastic pools managed by the server.

- **Database** You can configure more granular firewall rules, by granting access only to specific databases or elastic pools inside managed by the logical server.

If you want your Azure applications to connect to a database or elastic pool, you need to ensure that the Azure Connections option in the firewall is enabled. This way, you will be able to connect your virtual machines inside a virtual network to a database, elastic pool, dataware-house, or storage account using the virtual network service endpoints.

Microsoft offers three different service tiers (Basic, Standard and Premium) for single data-bases and elastic pools and offers a single General-Purpose service tier for Managed Instances. A service or pricing tier is a group of differentiated range of performances, storage, and pricing levels. This means that each service tier is a compound set of resources. When you want to set a limit for the resources that are available to your database or elastic pool, you choose between those limits existing on a service tier. You assign two different types of resources: DTUs or eD-TUs, and storage. The following procedure shows how to switch between service tiers and how to assign more resources to a database:

1. Sign into the management portal (*http://portal.azure.com*).

2. On the navigation pane on the left side of the portal, select SQL Databases. This open the SQL Databases Management blade.

3. Look for your database on the databases list and select your database.

4. On the database blade, select Pricing Tier (scale DTUs). You can also access this panel from the Overview blade, clicking on the current pricing tier.

5. On the Configure Performance blade, select the new pricing tier. You can also change the assignment of resources by changing the DTU and Storage slicers (Figure 2-16).

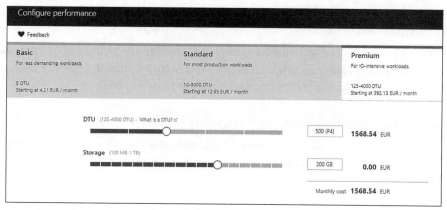

FIGURE 2-16 Changing resources for a database

6. Once you are happy with your selection. Click on the Apply button at the left corner of the blade.

Since a Logical server is not equivalent to an on-premises traditional SQL Server, there are situations where migrating an application from your infrastructure to Azure can be a challenging task. For those scenarios, Microsoft has released Managed Instances. This is a new capability added to Azure SQL Database that makes this service almost 100% compatible with a traditional SQL Server. Managed Instances depend on virtual networks for addressing security concerns and achieving instance security isolation. As with Azure SQL Database logical servers, with Managed Instances you can use SQL or Azure Active Directory authentication. Although this feature is near 100% compatible with on-premises SQL Server, it's still a PaaS (Platform as a Services) service. This means that it's a fully managed service, and you don't need to worry about services patches, provisioning, configurations and other IaaS (Infrastructure as a Service) related tasks. At the time of this writing, Azure SQL Database Managed Instance is in public preview.

SQL Server Stretch Database

The older your data gets, the less it is usually accessed. This is also true for databases, because records in a table that get older are less accessed. But you still need to store them just in case you need to access them. This means that there are occasions where you may be using expensive storage for storing cool data. You can apply archiving techniques for moving that cool data to cheaper storage, but in those cases where you need to access to that data, you need to put the data online again or tune your queries for accessing that data.

Microsoft provides you with a cool data management that integrates transparently with your on-premises SQL Server 2016 or newer databases. SQL Server Stretch Database migrates your cool data securely and transparently to Azure. The main advantage of this solution is that your data is always online, and you not need to change any query or any configuration or code line in your application to work with SQL Server Stretch Database. Since you are moving your cool data to the cloud, you reduce your need for high performance storage for the on-premises database servers.

You can migrate full tables or just parts of online tables by using a filtering function. Although not all tables are appropriate for migrating to Stretch Database, Microsoft provides a separate tool for analysis to identify the suitable tables to be migrated.

> *NOTE* **MICROSOFT DATA MIGRATION ASSISTANT**
>
> **You need to download this tool separately from *https://www.microsoft.com/en-us/download/details.aspx?id=53595*. This tool is no longer part of the installation media of SQL Server 2016.**

You need to bear in mind that not all tables are suitable for being migrated to Azure using SQL Stretch. You will find a full list of table limitations that avoid you from using SQL Stretch at the Limitations for Stretch Database page (*https://docs.microsoft.com/en-us/sql/sql-server/stretch-database/limitations-for-stretch-database*). The following procedure shows you how to enable SQL Stretch for a database:

1. Open SQL Server Management Studio and connect to your database server. Remember that your SQL Server needs to be at version 2016 or later.

2. Expand the list of databases and right click on the database where you want to enable SQL Stretch. From the contextual menu, select Tasks > Stretch > Enable. This will launch the Enable Database for Stretch wizard.

3. Click Next on the Introduction page.

4. Select the table or tables you want to migrate to Azure and select Next. Selecting the Tables page will review all tables on the database and show you which tables are candidates for migrating. When you select a table, you can migrate all rows or migrate just a group of rows. On the migrate column Entire Table appears by default. This means that you will migrate all rows in the table. If you want to migrate only a group of rows, you need to create a filter that includes the rows you want to migrate. Once you define the filter for the table, the name of the filter appears in the migrate column. Figure 2-17 shows an example of a filter.

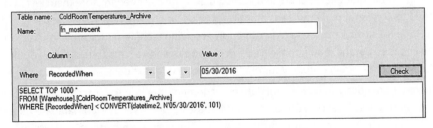

FIGURE 2-17 Creating a filter

5. You need to sign in your Azure Subscription. Select the Sign In button and provide an account with administrative privileges.

6. You need to select which subscription you will use for storing the Azure SQL Database. You also need to provide the region for the database. As with any other database, you need to provide a SQL logical server. If you don't already have a logical server for Azure SQL Database, you can create one using this wizard.

7. Provide a database master key (DMK) for protecting the credentials that you provided in the previous step. If you already have a DMK for this database, then you need to provide it here.

8. You need to provide the IPs that will be able to connect to the logical server. By default, logical servers do not allow access from outside Azure.

9. On the summary page, review the information about the configuration and then click on Finish.

10. Once the operation finish, the Results page will show you the status and result for all actions performed during the setup.

Design for scalability and features

When you need more computing resources, you have two options: assigning more resources, also known as *scale up,* or creating more identical elements and distributing the load across all elements, also known as *scale out*. You can use both strategies with Azure SQL Databases for achieving the best results for your needs. When you add more DTUs to a database, you are growing vertically or scaling-up your resources assigned to the database. If you want to grow horizontally or scale-out, you need to add additional databases to your application. There are different techniques for distributing the load and data when you scale-out, but Azure SQL Database uses a *Sharding* technique. Using this technique, the data is divided and distributed among databases structured identically. You use the Elastic Database client library for managing scale-out.

Sharding is especially useful when you need to store data for different customers. These final customers are also known as tenants. When you need to distribute the data for each tenant you can do it using two different patterns:

- **Single-tenant sharding pattern**   You assign a single database to each tenant. All data associated to each tenant will be always stored in the same database. Your application is responsible for routing each request to correct database. This pattern offers isolation, backup/restore ability and resource scaling at the tenant level. When you use this pattern, you don't need to provide an ID or customer key value to each tenant.

- **Multi-tenant sharding pattern**   You use each database for storing one or more tenants inside the database. This pattern is useful when your application needs to manage large numbers of small tenants. Each tenant needs to be identified by an ID or customer key value and is the application layer that is responsible for routing the request to the appropriate database. The elastic database client library helps with this kind of scenarios. You can also apply row-level security to filter which rows can be accessed for each tenant.

These patterns are not mutually exclusive. You can use the multi-tenant sharding pattern for small tenants, and when the tenant requires more resources or additional level of isolation/

protection or whatever other criteria you decide. And you can use the split-merge tool for migrating tenant's data from one database in one pattern to another database using a different pattern. Microsoft provides the Elastic database client library for helping administrators and developers manage and implement the multi-tenant sharding pattern. When you use the Elastic client library, you deal with shards, which is conceptually equivalent to a database. This client library helps you with:

- **Shard map management**   When you store tenant data in databases you need to keep a tracing system for knowing in which database each tenant's data is stored. This feature creates a shard map database for storing metadata about the mapping of each tenant with its database, allowing you to register each database as a shard. This feature makes the management and evolution of the tenant's data inside the system easier for you, since you don't need to worry about implementing your own mapping system.

- **Data dependent routing**   This feature allows you to select the correct database based on the information that you provide on the query for accessing the tenant's data. You can also use the context in your application for providing the needed information that will route your request to the correct shard.

- **Multi-shard queries (MSQ)**   This feature is used when you make a request that involves more than one shard. This type of query executes the same T-SQL on all shards that participate with the query and returns the resultant data as the result of a UNION ALL.

Azure Database for MySQL/PostgreSQL

Like Azure SQL Databases, Azure also offers support for other SQL engines like MySQL or PostgreSQL. Based on the community edition of these popular SQL database management systems, Microsoft offers a full managed service for those users who want to store their data using MySQL or PostgreSQL database engines, without worrying about management tasks. At the time of this writing, Azure Database for MySQL and Azure Database for PostgreSQL is in public preview, but it stills offers a good level of capabilities and features like:

- **High availability**   Already included in the price.

- **Predictable performance**   You can choose between different performance layers using pay-as-you-go model.

- **Scale on the fly**   You can always assign more resources to your database server.

- **Secured**   All data at-rest or in-motion is encrypted.

- **Automatic backups**   You can have automatic backups from a 7 to 35-day retention period. Azure Database for MySQL also offers point-in-time-restore.

- **Enterprise-grade security and compliance**   Azure Database for MySQL or PostgreSQL offers three different performance tiers: Basic, General Purpose and Memory Optimized. Each performance tiers offers different limits of resources that you can assign to the database server. You can modify the resources assigned to the database server, but you cannot modify the pricing tier, the Compute Generation, or the type of Backup.

When you want to use Azure Database for MySQL or PostgreSQL, you need to create a server first. This MySQL or PostgreSQL server is pretty the same as an on-premises MySQL or PostgreSQL server and is the entry point for the databases that you will create. The server is also the parent resource for those databases. This means that the resources that you assign to the server are shared among all databases managed by the server. You can decide to create a server per database on a server with more resources assigned that hosts more databases. The following procedure shows how to create a new Azure Database for MySQL server using Azure Cloud Shell. You can use the same procedure for creating a PostgreSQL server:

1. Sign into the management portal (*http://portal.azure.com*).

2. Click on the Cloud Shell icon in the upper-right corner, as shown in the Figure 2-18.

FIGURE 2-18 Launching Cloud Shell

3. Create a resource group for the MySQL server.

   ```
   az group create --name <resource group name> --location <location>
   ```

4. Add the latest Azure Database for MySQL management extension.

   ```
   az extension add --name rdbms
   ```

5. Create a database server. In this example, this command creates a server in General Purpose Gen 4 performance tier with 2 vCores assigned. The MySQL engine version is 5.7. You can choose between versions 5.6 and 5.7.

   ```
   az mysql server create --resource-group <resource group name> --name <mysql
   server name> --location <location> --admin-user <username for admin>
   --admin-password <password for admin> --sku-name GP_Gen4_2 --version 5.7
   ```

6. You need to create a firewall rule on this server if you want that external applications to be able to connect to the database.

   ```
   az mysql server firewall-rule create --resource-group <resource group name>
   --server <mysql server name> --name <rule name> --start-ip-address <start ip
   address> --end-ip-address <end ip address>
   ```

7. Once you are done creating the server, you can review connection the connection information. You will use this information for connecting with your MySQL IDE or for connecting your application to the database. You need to create a database before start using it in your application.

   ```
   az mysql server show --resource-group <resource group name> --name <mysql
   server name>
   ```

When you want to assign resources to your server, MySQL or PostgreSQL, there are a couple of concepts that you need to know:

- **Compute generation**   This represents the physical CPUs that are used for the logical CPUs. Gen4 logical CPUs are based on Intel E5-2673 v3 2.4GHz processors while Gen5 logical CPUs are based on Intel E5-2673 v4 2.3GHz processors.

- **vCore**   This is the number of logical CPUs that you assign to your server. The amount of memory assigned to a vCore depends on the pricing tier that you choose. The amount of memory assigned to each vCore is also doubled as you increase the pricing tier. That is, the memory assigned to a vCore in the Memory Optimized tier is double than the memory assigned in the General Purpose tier, and this double than the memory assigned in the Basic tier.

- **Storage**   This is the amount of storage you provide for storing database files, temporary files, transaction logs and server logs. The performance tier and IOPS of the storage also depends on the pricing tier. This way, Basic tier IOPS is not guaranteed and the Standard performance tier is used for storage. For General Purpose and Memory Optimized tiers, Premium performance tier is used for storage. The IOPS reservation scales in a ratio of 3:1 with the storage size. The range of storage size that you can select on all pricing tiers is from 5GB to 1TB.

> *NOTE* **SERVICE LIMITATIONS**
>
> The pricing tier also affects other aspects like the number of max connections. The service itself also has some other limitations that you can review by visiting: *https://docs.microsoft. com/en-us/azure/mysql/concepts-limits*.

Although you don't need to restart the server for scaling up or down your server, you should bear in mind that the connection to the database is interrupted. This means that any current connection will be disconnected and any uncommitted transactions will be canceled. This happens because when you scale up or down, Azure creates another server with the new requested resources. Once the server is ready, it disconnects the current server from the storage and attaches it to the new server.

Design for HA/DR and geo-replication

High availability (HA) and disaster recovery (DR) design depends on the service you are using and your needs. We will review these features separately for SQL databases and MySQL or PostgreSQL.

Azure SQL Databases

Fails happen. This is a fact, and High availability techniques are here for minimizing the impact that a fail may have on your infrastructure. Although there is a myriad of situations that may lead to a failure, to clearly scope and address the solution for these situations, Microsoft defines three main types of failures that HA should deal with:

- Hardware and software failures
- Human error failures made by operational staff
- Planned servicing outages

Azure SQL Database uses direct attached disks for providing fault tolerance to the databases. Depending on the service tier that you configure for your database, this direct storage is a Local Storage (LS) for Premium database service tier or Remote Storage (RS) on Azure Premium page blobs, for both Basic and Standard service tiers.

Premium service tier will use LS replication, while Basic and Standard service tiers will use RS replication. Regardless of the service tier that you decide to use, the internal mechanism that uses Azure SQL Database is based on Always ON SQL server feature.

When you use a Local Store (LS) configuration, Azure configures three copies of the database, all located inside the same datacenter, but in distinct physical systems. These three copies make up the control ring managed by the management service (MS). The copies are always distributed with one primary replica and two secondary replicas or quorum-set. When you request any read or write operation, the gateway (GW) sends the request to the primary replica. Write operations are then asynchronously replicated between primary and secondary replicas. The transaction is not considered as committed until the data is written to the primary replica and at least one of the secondary replicas. In case of a failure, the Service Fabric failover system automatically rebuilds the failing node and replaces it. Figure 2-19 shows a diagram of how LS configuration works.

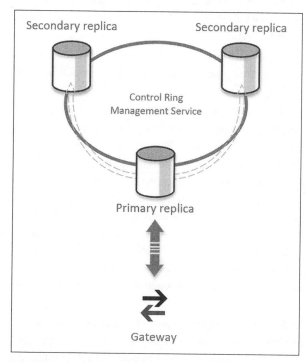

FIGURE 2-19 Local store replication

Failure detection depends on Azure Service Fabric. If a failure arises in the primary replica, the error is quite evident since you made the gateway forward all reads and writes to the primary replica. In this case, a secondary replica is immediately promoted to the primary replica. The recovery time objective (RTO) for this operation is 30 seconds, while the recovery point objective (RPO) is 0. As a best practice for mitigating the RTO, you should encourage your application to reconnect several times with a smaller wait time.

If the failure happens on a secondary replica, the service fabric initiates a reconfiguration process. There is a waiting time for determining if the failure is permanent. After this time, the service fabric creates another replica, but only if the failure is not due to operating system failure or upgrades. This happened due to allowing the failed node to restart instead of immediately creating a new replica.

Although high availability is a great feature, it does not protect against a catastrophic failure of the entire Azure region. For those cases, you need to put in place a disaster recovery plan. Azure SQL Database provides you with two features that makes it easier to implement these type of plans: active geo-replication and auto-failover groups. At the time of this writing, auto-failover groups were in public preview.

With active geo-replication you can configure up to four readable secondary databases in the same or different regions. In case of a region outage, your application needs to manually failover the database. If you require that the failover happens automatically performance, then you need to use auto-failover groups. When a secondary replica of a geo-replication is activated on the secondary region or promoted to primary, all of the other secondary replicas are automatically pointed to the new primary. Once the failover to the new primary is complete, all DNS endpoints will be redirected to the new region.

If you need active geo-replication to failover automatically in the event of a failure, you need to use auto-failover groups. In that case, all databases in the group can be replicated only to one secondary server in a different region.

When you use active geo-replication, data is replicated to the secondary region automatically and asynchronously. This means that the transactions in the primary database are committed before they are copied to the secondary databases. You can increase the level of protection by creating up to four secondary replicas. You can also use those secondary databases for read-only operations, and to enable geo-replication on any database in any elastic pool. The secondary database can also be a regular database or a database in an elastic pool. Primary and secondary databases need to be on the same service tier, although it's not required to be on the same performance level. This means you can have a primary database in a P6 and the secondary at a lower level, like a P2. Although this flexibility is possible, it is not recommended, since it can impose lag on the replication process. In case of a failover, the performance of the application will be greatly impacted by the lower resources assigned to the secondary database.

To minimize the complexity of configuration and potential downtimes due to configuration issues, Microsoft recommends using database firewall rules for replicated databases. This way, firewall rules are replicated with the database and there is no need to maintain server rules on the replicas. The same recommendation applies to user access. You should use Azure Active Directory or a user-contained database for granting access to the database.

Built on top of active geo-replication, the auto-failover group manages the replication of a group of databases configured in a primary server that will automatically failover to the secondary server in case of failure. The secondary server cannot be deployed on the same region as the primary server. You should bear in mind that replication between regions happens asynchronously due to high latency on the communication between datacenters. Because of this, there is a potential of some data loss in case of a failure.

You can configure active geo-replication and auto-failover groups using the Azure Portal, PowerShell, T-SQL, or the REST API. The following procedure shows how to configure active geo-replication on an existing database:

1. Sign into the management portal (*http://portal.azure.com*).

2. Select the SQL database in the navigation bar.

3. In the SQL databases blade, look for the database you want to configure and select your database.

4. On the navigation bar, in the selected database blade, select Geo-Replication on the Settings section.

5. On the Geo-Replication blade, you should see a map of the world that displays the different regions location. Select the secondary region that you want to add to the replication. Figure 2-20 shows a partial view of the regions.

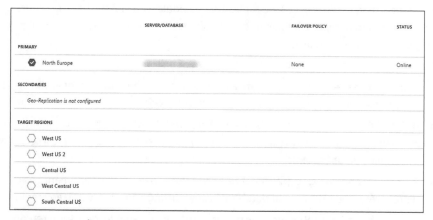

FIGURE 2-20 Configuring geo-replication

6. Choose the configurable region for the secondary replica, and the Create Secondary blade will appear. Select the target server. If you don't have a server available you can create a new one here. You can't select the current primary server as your secondary server without raising an error. Select the Pricing tier. Remember that the primary and secondary replicas need to be on the same service tier.

7. Click on OK.

Azure SQL Databases for MySQL or PostgreSQL

Azure Database for MySQL or PostgreSQL provides high availability by default. This high availability is provided by the already built-in fail-over mechanism at the node-level. When a node-level interruption happens, the database server automatically creates a new node and attaches the storage to a new level. Like with the scale-up and down, any active connection with the database will be dropped, and any in-flight transaction won't be committed. The application using the MySQL or PostgreSQL server database is responsible for providing the mechanism of reconnection and transaction retries.

Design a backup and recovery strategy

When you deploy an Azure SQL Database, Microsoft provides you with an automatic backup for your databases at no additional charge. This backup is also geo-redundant because it transparently uses read-access geo-redundant storage (RA-GRS). Depending on the service tier, the retention period of this backup is 7 days, for Basic tier or 35 days for Standard and Premium tiers.

Automatic backup in SQL Databases is based on the SQL Server technology. This means that it creates full, differential and transactions back up automatically. The schedule of each backup depends also on the type of backup. A full backup is scheduled to happen weekly, differential backups happen every few hours, while transactional log backups happen every 5 to 10 minutes. The exact time when each backup happens is automatically managed by the Azure SQL Database services to automatically accommodate the current system load. Geo-replicated backup depends on the Azure Storage replication schedule. The first full backup occurs when you create your database, which takes about 30 minutes. It can take longer, however, if you are copying or restoring a database.

With this feature you can perform different types of restores:

- **Point-in-time restore**   You create a new database in the same server as the original. The restore can take place within the retention period.
- **Deleted database**   You can restore a full deleted database to the point in time that it was deleted. You can only restore the deleted database to the same logical server where the original database existed.
- **Restore to another geographical region**   This allows you to implement basic disaster recovery. You restore your database in any existing logical server in any region.
- **Restore from Azure Recovery Services vault**   If you enable long-term retention, you can restore a specific version of your database from your Azure Recovery Services vault.

As mentioned earlier, retention policy depends on the service tier configured for the database. If you decide to switch to another service tier, then the access to the backup changes depending on the movement. For example, if your database is configured with a Standard or Premium service tier, and you switch to Basic, only backups with seven days or less are available. If you change the service tier from Basic to Standard or Premium, then the existing backups are extended until they are 35 days old.

If you want to extend the default retention period beyond the 35 days, you need to configure long-term retention. This feature depends on Azure Recovery Services, and you can extend the retention time up to 10 years. To enable SQL Database long-term retention, you need to create an Azure Recovery Services vault in the same subscription, geographical region and the resource group as the SQL logical server. Once you configure the retention policy, the weekly full database backups are copied to the vault automatically. When you enable long-term retention, you can recover any of these backups to a new database in any server in the subscription. The following procedure shows how to enable long-term retention using the Azure Portal:

1. Sign into the management portal (*http://portal.azure.com*).

2. Select **Create A Resource** in the upper-left corner of the portal. On the Azure Marketplace, select **Storage** and select **Backup And Site Recovery (OMS)**.

3. Create a Backup Service vault. You need to create this vault in the same resource group as the SQL logical server where you want to enable the long-term retention.

4. Select the resource groups on the navigation bar. Look for the resource group that hosts your database server and select the name of the resource group.

5. On the Overview blade, select the name of the server.

6. **Select Long-term Backup Retention** under the Settings section.

7. Select the database you want to configure and select **Configure** on the top menu.

8. Select the Recovery service vault. Select the vault that you just configured in step 3. If you see that your vault is listed, but it's disabled, ensure that you created the vault in the same subscription, region, and resource group as the SQL logical server.

9. Create a new retention policy. Provide a name for the retention policy and a retention period. Click on **OK** to accept the configuration.

10. Click on Save in the upper-left corner of the long-term backup retention blade. Confirm that you want to apply the configuration.

11. Once the long-term retention has been correctly configured, your database should show the assigned retention policy and the retention period (Figure 2-21).

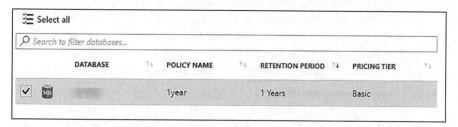

FIGURE 2-21 Database with long-term retention enabled

When you need to recover a database from an automatic backup you can restore it to:

- A new database in the same logical server from a point-in-time within the retention period.
- A database in the same logical server from a deleted database.
- A new database from the most recent daily backup to any logical server in any region.

When you restore a database, you can incur additional costs if the size of the database that you want to restore is greater than the amount of storage included on the performance level. This usually happens when you want to restore from a larger performance level, like P11 to P15, to a smaller performance level, like P1 to P6, or S4 to S12.

You also need to remember the recovery time when you want to perform a database restore. That time depends on several factors, like the size of the database, the performance level, the number of transaction logs involved, the amount of activity that need to be replayed when performing a recover to a point-in-time, and the network bandwidth when you perform a restore to a different region.

When you want to make a restore, you can use two different approaches:

- **Replacement** Here you want to restore the full database and replace the old one. You cannot make a database restore into an existing database. If you need to make a database replacement, you need to restore your backup to a new database. Then rename the old database using the ALTER DATABASE command in T-SQL. After you have successfully renamed the old database, change the name of the new restored database to the name of the database that you want to replace.
- **Data recovery** This is for those situations where there was some data loss due to application or user error. With data recovery you don't need or want to perform a full database replacement, but just restore the missing or corrupted data. You need to write your own data recovery scripts for performing the data recovery.

Design optimization strategies for Azure SQL Data Warehouse columnar storage

When you use Azure SQL Data Warehouse it's important to apply some techniques and best practices for maintaining a good level of performance in your operations:

- **Maintain statistics** SQL Data Warehouse requires that you create and update columns statistics manually. These statistics directly impact the quality of the execution plan created by the optimizer. A good strategy for this manual maintenance is to update the statistics every time your data is significantly updated, on a daily basis or after each load. If you notice that the statistics update is impacting the performance, then review which columns have statistics and which columns need to be update frequently.
- **Avoid using singleton INSERTS** Using one-time inserts performs well on small tables. But if you need to insert a big amount of data, like thousands or millions of rows, this approach may greatly impact the performance. In those cases, writing data to a file and periodically loading this file into the table has a better performance.

- **Use Polybase** Polybase is designed to work better with the MPP architecture of SQL Data Warehouse, so this is the ideal tool for loading and exporting data. While Polybase is the right tool for loading and exporting, you should avoid using Polybase for querying SQL Data Warehouse since it needs to load the data to tempdb before being able to process the query.

- **Avoid Round Robin distribution** In MPP, a distribution is the basic unit for storage and processing parallel queries. Every time you run a query, this is divided into 60 different queries that run on one data distribution. When you use a round-robin algorithm for distribution, rows are evenly distributed across all distributions. This assignment is random, which cannot guarantee that rows with equal value are assigned to the same distribution. The hash algorithm computes a hash for assigning data to each distribution. This ensures that rows with the same values calculate the same hash and are assigned to the same distribution.

- **Watch partitions** Having too many partitions can affect performance loss since it reduces the effectiveness of clustered indexes for partitions with fewer than one million rows. By default, SQL Data Warehouse distributes your data across 60 different distributions or databases. If you create a table with 100 partitions, you will end with 6000 partitions.

- **Minimize transaction size** When you use INSERT, UPDATE and DELETE statements, you run it in a transaction. If any of those statements fail during the execution of the transaction, they must be rolled back. The bigger the transaction is, the longer it takes to roll back. You should consider splitting big transactions into smaller chunks for minimizing the risk of a rollback.

- **Use adequate column size** You should use the minimum column size that supports your data. This will improve performance, especially with CHAR and VARCHAR columns. If you need to store strings that will contain only ASCII chars use VARCHAR instead of NVARCHAR. NVARCHAR is more flexible since it can store Unicode strings, but requires more space for storing the data.

- **Use temporary tables** When you are importing data to SQL Data Warehouse, using temporary heap tables before applying more transformation will speed up the process.

- **Optimize clustered columnstore tables** When you work with columnstore tables, the quality of the segment directly impacts on the performance of the table. You can measure the quality of segments in the columnstore by the number of rows in a compressed Row Group. The quality of the columnstore segment can suffer under conditions of memory pressure when data is written to the table.

- **Use appropriate resource classes** Depending on you want to improve performance or concurrency, you need to adjust the size of the resource class that SQL Data Warehouse assigns to each database for running queries in memory. By default, SQL DW grants 100 MB of memory per distribution. This means that the total system-wide memory allocation is 6000MB, since SQL DW uses 60 distributions out of the box. If you have queries with large joins or loads to clustered columnstore tables, you will benefit from larger memory allocations, thus improving the performance. On the other side, if you notice that queries start to have a long delay, you should consider reducing the size of the resource classes, since those queries maybe consume a lot of concurrency slots, causing other queries to be delayed.

In this section we covered the different solutions that Azure offers for working with relational databases, as well as high availability, disaster recovery, and business continuity options related with the Azure SQL Database service. Next, we detail what Azure can offer when working with NoSQL systems.

Skill 2.4: Design for NoSQL storage

Relational databases have been very popular for a long time due to their capacity for managing data in different scenarios. Sometimes, using relational databases may not be the best option for some scenarios. Relational databases can be challenging when you need to scale out through different servers. There are also other challenges like storing JSON documents, or using key-values, or graphs structures, that do not fit well on relational databases. For example, if your application needs to store an object that does not have a defined schema, using a relational database for storing it will perform poorly with this type of data.

To address these current challenges, NoSQL storage is a new way of storing this type of data. Although models that are used on NoSQL storage vary from system to system, all of them share some common features:

- Simpler horizontal scale
- Flexibility on the data structure
- Most of them are BASE (Basic Availability, Soft-state, Eventual consistency) instead of ACID (Atomic, Consistent, Isolated, Durable)
- Schema-free
- Simple API

Despite its name, NoSQL storage doesn't always mean that it doesn't provide you with SQL capabilities, like using indexes, having a structured query language, or being able to create relationships between elements. But they are not stored and organized as SQL databases and they provide more than just SQL features.

> **This section covers how to use:**
> - Azure Redis Cache
> - Azure Table Storage
> - Azure Data Lake
> - Azure Search
> - Azure Time Series Insights
> - Design pipelines for managing recurring jobs

Azure Redis Cache

Redis Cache is an open source in-memory NoSQL data structure storage that you can use as a database, cache and message broker. This system is based on a key-value model, where keys can be of different types of data structures such as strings, hashes, list, sets and sorted sets.

Based on this open source solution, Azure Redis Cache is a managed service that can be accessed from any application from inside or outside Azure. This service is aimed to speed up your application by processing data in memory datasets.

Depending on your needs, Azure Redis Cache offers three different pricing tiers:

- **Basic** Ideal for development and testing. Redis is deployed in a single node, available in multiples sizes. There is no SLA associated to this tier.
- **Standard** This is the first tier that has high availability and has an SLA associated. Redis is deployed in a two-node cluster in a master/slave configuration managed by Microsoft. This tier is also available on multiple sizes.
- **Premium** This tier extends Standard tier capabilities providing better performance, bigger workloads, disaster recovery, and enhanced security.

While you are deciding which pricing tier is more appropriate for your needs, you should bear in mind that you can always scale up in the pricing tier, because moving down from an upper tier to a lower tier is not allowed.

Since all data managed by Redis Cache is stored in a memory dataset, there are some risks of data loss in case of failure of the system. You can configure Redis Cache for persisting data in an Azure Storage account. Data from Redis Cache is persisted using RDB, which is a point-in-time representation of your data stored in a compact single file. This feature works well as a backup for your in-memory data. Data persistency is available only on the Premium tier.

> **NOTE PERSISTING DATA**
>
> Redis Cache uses two different mechanism for persisting data: RDB and AOF. AOF persists every single write operation received by the server, recovering the data in case the server is restarted. At the time of this writing, using AOF is in public preview.

You can access Azure Redis Cache from the Internet. This access from the public network is protected by using access keys, which is included in the Premium tier. You can also apply network filters based on a network address by deploying Redis Cache in an Azure Virtual Network. If you want to import or export data from your Azure Redis Cache, you can use RDB files stored in page blobs in an Azure Storage account. This enables you to migrate from other Redis Cache systems, even if they are in another cloud service, as long as they use compatible RDB files.

For those cases where you want to deploy a disaster recovery configuration, you can configure geo-replication by linking two instances of Azure Redis Cache in the Premium tier. Using this configuration, one cache is designated as the primary cache, while the other is designated as the secondary linked cache. All write operations are performed against the primary cache and replicated to the secondary cache, which becomes a read-only cache. You need to ensure that data persistence is disabled on both caches. You also need to ensure that the secondary cache is at the same service tier as the primary cache.

The size of the cache that you can create with Azure Redis Cache is limited to 53 GB for Basic and Standard tiers. If you need more capacity for the cache, you can configure a cluster with up to 10 nodes. This extends the maximum capacity of your cache up to 530GB. Creating a cluster is available only in the premium tier. The following procedure shows how to configure an Azure Redis Cache cluster using the Azure Portal:

1. Sign into the management portal (*http://portal.azure.com*).

2. Click on **Create A Resource** on the upper-left corner of the portal. On the **Azure Marketplace**, select Databases and then select Redis Cache.

3. On the New Redis Cache blade, you need to provide the information needed for creating the new cache.

4. In the DNS name provide a name for the cache. This name must be unique across Azure.

5. In the Subscription field, select the subscription where you will create the cache.

6. In the Resource Group field, select if you want to create a new resource group or use an existing one.

7. Select the Location for the cache.

8. Select the Pricing tier. Since we want to configure a cache cluster, you need to select a Premium pricing tier (see Figure 2-22). When you select a Premium pricing tier, Redis Cluster, Redis data persistence and Virtual Network options will be enabled.

FIGURE 2-22 Selecting pricing tier

9. Select Redis Cluster. If this option is disabled, ensure that you selected a Premium pricing tier.

10. On the Redis Cluster blade, in the Clustering section, select Enabled. Once you enable this option, it can't be changed after you create the cache.

11. On the Redis Cluster blade, in the Shard count section, select the number of nodes or shards that you want to assign to your cluster. You can modify the number of shards later if you need.

12. Click on **Create**.

Azure Table Storage

Based on Azure Storage Accounts, Azure Table Storage is a NoSQL service that allows you to store key-value data in the cloud. Since this service allows you to use a schemaless design, you can easily adapt your entities as the application evolves. The number of tables and entities stored in the table depends only on the available space and the limits on the Azure Storage account that you use.

You can access a table from inside or outside Azure applications. All access to the data is protected through authenticated calls. Since it's a NoSQL service, it is ideal to store structured and non-relational data. This type of data is typically used by web scale applications, address books applications, device information applications, or any other type of application that requires you to store metadata. You can access data using the OData protocol or LINQ queries when using WCF Data Service .NET libraries.

Azure Table Storage uses a structure like the one used in an Azure Storage Account (see Figure 2-23).

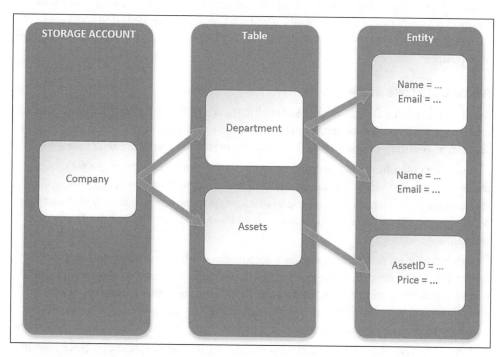

FIGURE 2-23 Azure Table Storage structure

When you need to work with an Azure Table, you need to understand some concepts:

- **URL**   This will be the entry point for your Azure Table. The URL has the form http://<storage account name>.table.core.windows.net/<table name>.

- **Account**   This is the Azure Storage account that hosts your Azure Table.

- **Table**   This is where you store your entities. Since entities don't have a defined schema, you can store different types of entities in the same table.

- **Entity**   An entity is a group of properties. Each entity can be up to 1 MB in size.

- **Properties**   An entity can have up to 255 properties. A property is each of the key-value pairs that store information. Azure Tables need three properties: PartitionKey, RowKey, and Timestamp, for correctly managing the entities for you. These three properties are included in the limit of 255 properties per entity, which means that you can have up to 252 custom properties. PartitionKey and RowKey conform to a clustered index for all entities in the table. You cannot create any additional index.

You can create an Azure Table in any General-Purpose Azure Storage account. Once you create the storage account, you can create a new table in the Table Service section, you only need to provide the name for your table. Once you have created your table, you can access it using the OData protocol. If you need to manually explore the data stored your table, you can also use Azure Storage Explorer (*https://azure.microsoft.com/en-us/features/storage-explorer/*).

Since Azure Tables is based on an Azure Storage account, it also shares all enterprise-level capabilities for replication and availability. If you still find that Azure Table doesn't fit your needs, you can also opt for Cosmos DB Tables. We will review Cosmos DB in the last skill section of this chapter.

Azure Data Lake Store

Based on the Hadoop Distributed File System (HDFS), Azure Data Lake Store is the storage solution for Big Data applications. It can be integrated natively with any Hadoop solution that supports a WebHDFS-compatible REST API, like Azure HDInsight or Azure Data Lake Analysis.

Azure Data Lake Store provides storage with no limit on the account size, the file size, or the amount of data that can be stored. While Azure Data Lake Store doesn't impose any limit for storage it still performs multiples copies of your data for ensuring durability of stored data. Azure Data Lake Store doesn't impose any limit on the duration of time that the data can be stored in the account.

Data stored in an Azure Data Lake Store account doesn't have to comply with any specific format. There is no need, from the point of view of the storage system, to make any kind of transformation for storing data in the data lake. It is the responsibility of the application that consumes the data lake to apply any transformation that may be needed for its correct function. You can create a hierarchy of folders and files inside the data lake for managing your data.

Azure Data Lake Store is the data storage solution for Big Data applications. This means that the access to the data needs to be very fast. When you store a file in a data lake, Azure divides the file into several parts and spreads each part across several storage servers, improving the read throughput of the file.

You can access data stored in a data lake using a WebHDFS compatible REST API, or by using AzureDataLakeFilesystem (adl://). This new filesystem offers further performance optimizations compared with traditional WebHDFS API. Applications and services in Hadoop environments can take advantage of this filesystem.

Some of the Azure services that you can integrate with Azure Data Lake Store are:

- Azure Data Lake Analysis
- Azure HDInsight
- Azure Active Directory, for controlling the access to the data lakes
- Azure Event Hub
- Azure Data Factory
- Third-party applications using Azure Data Lake Store .NET SDK
- Azure SQL Data Warehouse

Azure provides several mechanisms for managing security, depending on the scope of the security. Azure Active Directory provides needed authentication mechanisms for accessing a data lake. Thanks to this integration, you have a centralized point for managing identity and authentication. Azure Active Directory provides some mechanism that directly benefits Azure Data Lake Store, like multi-factor authentication, authentication through OAuth or OpenID standard protocols, or federation with enterprise directories and cloud identity providers.

Once the user has been authenticated, you need to provide access to the resource. The authorization process is managed by two different mechanisms, depending on the scope of authorization:

- **Role-based access control**   Provides authorization control at the account level. At this level you can grant privileges on the operations that a user can make at the account level. Depending on the role, this might also grant access to the data level.
- **POSIX ACLs**   This is like Unix/Linux privileges and controls the access of user at the data level. There are three different privileges: read (r), write (w), and execute (x). You can grant privileges for users or security groups. As a best practice, you should always create security groups, add users to the security group, and grant privileges to the security group.

You can also control network access security and data protection. You can control which IP or range of IPs can access your data lake. Azure Data Lake Store provides data protection for in-transit data, by using TLS encryption, for stored data, and by optionally encrypting your data. If you opt for encrypting your data, Azure Data Lake Store automatically encrypts for you the data prior to being stored, and automatically decrypts the data when you want to read it. Data is encrypted using Master Encrypt Keys (MKEs). You can allow Data Lake Store to manage MKEs for you, or you can integrate Data Lake Store with Azure Key Vault for managing MKEs on your own. You can only select the type of encryption while you are creating the Data Lake

Store account. Encryption is enabled by default. The following procedure shows how to create a Data Lake Store connected to an existing Azure Key Vault:

1. Sign into the management portal (*http://portal.azure.com*).

2. Click on **Create A Resource** on the upper-left corner of the portal. On the Azure Marketplace, select **Storage** and then select **Data Lake Store**.

3. On the **New Data Lake Store** blade, provide information for Data Lake's name, subscription, resource group, and location. The name for the data lake needs to be lowercase and unique across Azure.

4. On the pricing package, select the option that better fits your need. Not all options are available for all locations.

5. Select **Encryption Settings** for opening the blade.

6. On the Encryption Type dropdown select **Use Keys From Your Own Key Vault**. Remember that you cannot change the encryption type once you create the Data Lake Store.

7. When you select Use keys From Your Own Key Vault option, two additional options will appear (see Figure 2-24) for configuring the key vault and the key you will use for encrypting the data in your Data Lake.

FIGURE 2-24 Encryption settings

8. Select **Key Vault** for selecting an existing key vault. If you did not create a key vault previously, you can create a new one here. Select the key vault that has the keys encryption for the Data Lake.

9. Select the Encryption key to select the key that will be used for encrypting data on your Data Lake. If you did not previously create an encryption key, you can do it here by selecting Create A New Key.

10. Once you have configured encryption settings, click OK on the **Encryption Settings** blade and click on **Create On The New Data Lake Store Blade**.

Azure Search

You can easily add search capabilities to your application by using the features provided by Azure Search service. This is a cloud solution that provides developers an API for consuming advanced search capabilities on their web, mobile, or enterprise applications. Azure Search services provides following features:

- **Full text search and text analysis**   Your application sends queries to the engine using a supported syntax. In the simplest query syntax, Azure Search supports logical operators, phrase search operators, suffix operators, and precedence operators. The Lucene query syntax extends the simple query syntax with fuzzy search, term boosting, and regular expressions.

- **Data integration**   As long as you provide the information using a JSON data structure, you can feed Azure Search with data from any kind of data source. You can also take advantages from indexers that Azure provides to you for pulling information from Azure Cosmos DB, Azure SQL Database, or Azure Blob Storage.

- **Linguistics analysis**   Azure Search provides you with language and lexical analyzers that enable you to perform searches based on phonetics matching, regular expressions, verb tenses, genders, irregular plural nouns, and more.

- **Geo-search**   Based on the proximity to the user, you can provide the user with the search results nearest to a physical location.

- **User experience features**   This is like search suggestions, faceted navigations, filters, hit highlighting, sorting, or paging.

- **Relevance**   By using scoring profiles you can model the relevance of certain items based on different criteria. This way, you can provide newer or discounted products higher scores that makes them to appear earlier in the results.

- **Monitoring and reporting**   This feature provides insights about what users type when they do their searches. There are other interesting metrics that are also collected, like queries per second, latency, or throttling that helps you to monitor and decide if you need to scale the service.

- **Tools for prototyping and inspection**   Azure Portal provides you with two important tools: Import Data Wizard and search explorer. The Import Data Wizard helps you design and configure indexes. The search explorer tool allows you to test your queries and refine scoring profiles before you make the final change in your code.

- **Infrastructure**   Depending on the pricing tier, Azure Search provides high availability and scalability.

Azure Search is offered in three different pricing tiers, Free, Basic and Standard. Standard tiers offer four additional configuration sets. Free tier doesn't have any SLA associated. For Basic and Standard tiers, the SLA depends on the resource configuration you make. Once you have configured the service, you cannot change to a higher pricing tier. If you need to upgrade, you need to create a new search service at the new desired tier and reload your indexes.

When you configure the resources in a pricing tier, you need to know about two different concepts:

- **Partitions**   This is where the Search service stores those indexes that you create. It provides storage and I/Os for read/write operations. If your application needs more performance on the searching service, you may need to configure more partitions.

- **Replicas**   These are copies of the indexes used for load balancing. Each replica stores a single copy of an index. If you need high availability, you need to create at least two replicas for read operations HA and three replicas for read/write operations HA.

Capacity for the Search services is billed in search units (SU), where a search unit is a partition or replica. This way, you can use following formula for calculating your billing: Replica x Partitions = SU. Cost per SU depends on the pricing tier.

Time Series Insights

This service helps you with analyzing data that is based on time series like the one that comes from IoT devices or any other time-based records. You can easily recognize this type of data because it usually represents values that are bound to time. For example, you can have an IoT device that measures the temperature of a room. It may send the temperature measurement every five minutes. It is quite rare that you need to modify a time-based record, because the information comes from the evolution of the measure, the temperature in our example, during a period of time.

Time Series Insights is fully integrated with Azure IoT Hub and Azure Event Hub. Once you connect the service with one of the hub services, Time Series Insights parses the JSON data that comes from the hub and joins metadata with telemetry in a columnar store. Time Series Insight also creates needed indexes for you.

You don't need to worry about providing a storage configuration for Time Series, since it's automatically managed by the services. Data is stored in memory and SSD for best performance, so depending on your configuration, you can maintain data in the SSD storage for up to 400 days.

One of the big benefits of using Time Series Insight is that you don't need to create complex graphs or integrate with other services for visualizing and analyzing the data. Time Series Insight (TSI) provides you with a graphical interface, called TSI Explorer, that allows you to visualize your data as it's loaded in TSI, near in real-time. You can also perform queries on your data, using the query service provided by TSI. You can use this query service in TSI Explorer or use the provided REST Query API.

The key point with TSI is to work with values that change over time. Its internal database has been designed with time series data in mind. The value of this type of data comes from the evolution of the metric during the time. You can analyze this evolution using patterns and perspective views to perform root-cause analysis. These tools are present in TSI Explorer. You can also connect TSI with Azure Stream Analytics to monitor and set alerts based on these patterns that detects anomalies.

Relating information from different data sources is also another key value for this type of analysis. You can join and correlate information that comes from different data sources and locations while viewing all of this data together.

When you configure your Time Series Insight environment, you need to understand how works storage and which is the data retention time. You configure data retention time in days. You need to configure what should be the priority for TSI when the system reaches the data retention time or storage limits. There are two modes of operation:

- **Purge old data**   The objective for this mode is to keep the services running, discarding any old data.
- **Purge ingress**   In this mode, the priority is data history and data retention. Data ingress is paused if the storage capacity of the environment is hit.

Time Series Insight offers two different SKUs: S1 and S2. Storage and ingress capacity depends on the SKU you select. You should select carefully the SKU since you cannot switch between tiers once you deploy your environment. You can configure for both SKUs up to 10 units in a single environment. When you are planning your capacity needs, you should calculate total ingress that you may need on a per-month basis. Then, calculate your ingress needs per-minute. You use a per-month calculation for selecting the correct event size allocation. You use per-minute calculations for selecting the correct events count per-minute allocation. If you have a spike in your data ingress that lasts less than 24 hours, Time Series Insight provides you with a double capacity in the ingress ration without you experiencing any latency. The following procedure shows how to adjust capacity and data time retention in an existing Time Series Environment:

1. Sign into the management portal (*http://portal.azure.com*).
2. Select All Services at the upper-left corner of the portal. In the All Services blade, type **Time series** in the filter text box, and select Time Series Insight environments.
3. Select the name of the environment that you want to configure.
4. In the Time Series Insights environment, select Configure in the Settings section.
5. In the Configure blade, move the Capacity slider to the desired new capacity. This action has costs impacts.
6. In the Configure blade, adjust the data retention time (in days).
7. Check I Have Reviewed The Documentation Prior To Making Any Changes To The Environment, And I Am Aware Of The Potential Risk Of Data Loss, and click Save.

Design pipelines for managing recurring jobs

As discussed in skill 2.2, the Azure Data Factory allows you to automate or orchestrate the data movement between different elements in your solution. Those automating operations are defined inside Data Factory as activities, and a group of one or more activities composes a pipeline. One of the objectives of creating pipelines is performing the same task several times, so you should be able to run a pipeline automatically.

You can start the execution of a pipeline using two different methods: manually (also known as on-demand) or scheduled. The scheduled execution of a pipeline is governed by a trigger. Triggers are objects that define how and when a single or group of pipelines should be executed. This means that a single trigger can run multiples pipelines, and multiples triggers can run a single pipeline. There are two different types of triggers:

- **Schedule** The pipeline is invoked based on a clock schedule. There is a many-to-many relationship between scheduled triggers and pipelines.

- **Tumbling window** You define a periodic interval specifying a start time for pipeline execution. The state of the pipeline is retained. A tumbling window trigger can only reference a single pipeline.

Although both types of triggers run at scheduled intervals, there are some important differences between them:

- Tumbling window triggers can be scheduled for windows in the past. This is useful for backfilling scenarios.

- Tumbling window triggers are 100% reliable.

- You can retry failed pipelines using tumbling window triggers.

- You can configure concurrency options with tumbling window triggers. The concurrency controls the number of simultaneous rungs that can be fired for windows that are ready to be executed. This is meaningful on back fill scenarios. Imagine that you configure today a trigger and set the startTime for yesterday, the frequency for hours, and an interval to one. This will create 24 execution windows for your pipeline. If you configure a concurrency of four, then the first four windows will be executed in parallel, then the next four, and so on, until the trigger runs out of ready windows.

- Tumbling window triggers can use WindowStart and WindowEnd system variables. You can use these variables as parameters in your pipeline definition.

The following procedure shows how to create a tumbling window trigger:

1. Sign into the management portal (*http://portal.azure.com*).

2. Select All Services at the upper-left corner in the window. In the All Services blade, type **data factory** in the filter text box and select Data Factories.

3. Select the name of the data factory that you want to configure.

4. In the Quick links section, select Author & Monitor (see Figure 2-25).

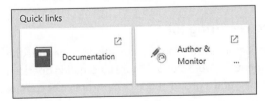

FIGURE 2-25 Quick links

5. In the Azure Data Factory authoring tool, select the Author button on the left margin (see Figure 2-26) to open the Authoring blade.

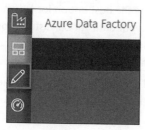

FIGURE 2-26 Azure Data Factory authoring tool menu

6. In the Factory Resources pane, look for the pipeline that you want to configure and select its name. This will open the pipeline editor.

7. In the pipeline editor select Trigger and then on New/Edit. This will open the Add Triggers blade.

8. In the Choose Trigger dropdown, select New.

9. In the New Trigger blade, fill the properties for the new trigger. In the Type selector, select Tumbling Window.

10. Select the start date. Since this is a tumbling window trigger, you can set this value in the past.

11. In the Recurrence section, select Hourly and keep every value set to one. This will execute the pipeline every hour starting at the start date you defined in step 10.

12. Keep No End selected for the End field. You can optionally set an end time for this trigger.

13. You can set a delay for starting the execution of the pipeline. This delay applies to every pipeline run.

14. Set the max concurrency for back filling pipelines.

15. Configure the Retry Policy. Count parameter controls the number of times that the trigger tries to run a pipeline before it's marked as Failed. The Interval In Seconds option sets the time that the trigger waits between each retry.

16. Click on Next.

17. If your pipeline has any parameters, you need to configure them in this blade. Configure your pipeline parameters and click on Finish. You need to publish the pipeline for the trigger being able to run the pipeline.

In this section we reviewed some of the services that Azure offers for NoSQL storage. Although all of the options that we have reviewed are prepared for production environments and have enterprise-level capabilities, some of them may lack some features that you may need. In the next skill section we will review more advance features available through Cosmos DB, which is a NoSQL storage.

Skill 2.5: Design for Cosmos DB storage

Azure Table Storage is a good NoSQL service, but it may not be the best option for your needs. If you need more advance features like secondary indexes for your data, global distribution, or latency guarantee, you should use Cosmos DB. This also allows you to move from your on-premises NoSQL storage, like MongoDB or Casandra, to a SaaS model..

This is a NoSQL storage service that offers more advanced capabilities than Azure Table Store, but it is still compatible with it. This way, you can move from your current Azure Table Store solution to Cosmos DB without changing your code.

> **This section covers how to use:**
>
> - Azure Cosmos DB
> - MongoDB API
> - SQL API
> - Graph API
> - Azure Tables API
> - Design for cost, performance, data consistency, availability, and business continuity

Azure Cosmos DB

There are situations where you need to provide a solution for data storage that can be distributed across several regions in the world, while ensuring a good level of throughput and elasticity. If you need to globally distribute your solution, it makes sense to think that latency is also a requirement for your application.

Azure Cosmos DB provides you with a service that is a multi-model database, globally distributed, with guaranteed throughput, latency, availability and consistency; it also enables you to scale independently each part of the distribution.

One of the main advantages of the global distribution that Cosmos DB offers is that you don't need to make changes to your application when you want to change or add additional regions to the replication. When you use the Cosmos DB multi-homing API, you can configure your application for using logical endpoints, which are region-agnostic endpoints, for accessing your Cosmos DB account. These logical endpoints allow your application to access the storage transparently in the case of a failover of the region. If you need more granular control from the application to redirect read and writes to specific regions, you can use physical endpoints.

Cosmos DB allows you to configure an unlimited number of replicas, outside of geo-fencing restrictions like Germany or China. You can add or remove new replicas from your configuration dynamically. You can also configure each region for read, write, or read/write operations. You can only have a single write region, but you can have as many read regions as you want. Read queries are always routed to the nearest region to the request. This way Cosmos DB can ensure that the latency for read requests is always minimal. When you add a new region to the database account, Azure ensures that the region will be available within 30 minutes anywhere in the world, as long as your database size is up to 100 TB.

While working with Highly Available (HA) services, automatic failover is a key feature of the any HA system. Cosmos DB provides two different levels of automatic failover for the region that is configured for write operations:

- **Regional** If a regional outage happens, Cosmos DB automatically moves the requests to another region. During this transition there is a potential data loss during the regional outage.

- **Internal** There are internal failover mechanism for protecting you from failures at the database, collection, or partition level. These automatic failovers are transparent for you, and you don't have any control over them.

If you need to test the availability features of Cosmos DB with your application, you can manually start a failover operation. When you make a manual failover operation, Azure guarantees that there will be zero data loss. When dealing with failover, Cosmos DB allows you to configure failover priorities. You can use these priorities for instructing Cosmos DB in which order an automatic failover should happen. The following procedure shows how to add additional regions to your database replication and configure failover priorities:

1. Sign into the management portal (*http://portal.azure.com*).
2. Select Azure Cosmos DB on the navigation panel on the left side of the window.
3. Select the name of your database, which opens the Overview blade for your database.
4. Under the Settings section, select Replicate Data Globally (see Figure 2-27).

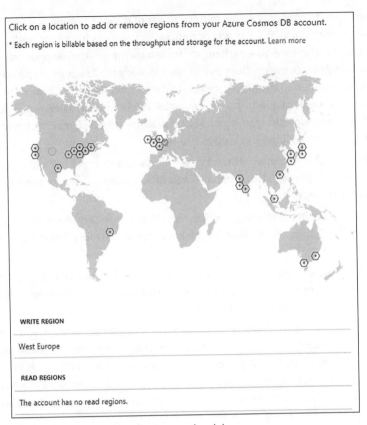

Click on a location to add or remove regions from your Azure Cosmos DB account.

* Each region is billable based on the throughput and storage for the account. Learn more

WRITE REGION

West Europe

READ REGIONS

The account has no read regions.

FIGURE 2-27 Configured replicas across the globe

5. In the Replicate Data Globally blade click on Add New Region. The button switches into a dropdown control. You can also add new regions by clicking on the hexagon icon in the world map.

6. Select a region in the dropdown and click OK. You need to repeat this operation with every region you want to add to the database replication.

7. Once you are done adding regions, click the Save button in the upper-left corner of the Replicate Data Globally blade.

8. For enabling and configuring the failover priority, click on the Automatic Failover icon. This is the fourth icon in the upper menu.

9. Select Enable Automatic Failover to On. You can change the order by dragging each region to the new position in the list.

Cosmos DB also ensures, by SLA, that Latency is P99 for reads and synchronously indexed writes. This means that 99% of the operations will have a latency, measured in milliseconds (ms), below 10ms. Azure can achieve this by ensuring that database operations are performed locally in the nearest region to the user. To achieve this level of low latency, Cosmos DB needs to perform asynchronous replication. This also means that Cosmos DB cannot employ strong consistency, because this consistency model imposes big restrictions that lead to greater latency values. Cosmos DB uses well-defined, relaxed consistency models.

> **NOTE COSMOS DB CONSISTENCY MODELS**
>
> Cosmos DB allows you to configure the default consistency model for your database. You can choose between five different consistency models: strong, bounded staleness, session, consistent prefix, and eventual. You can find a detailed description of each model at: *https://docs.microsoft.com/en-us/azure/cosmos-db/consistency-levels*.

Cosmos DB uses different data models like document, graph, key-value, table or column-family. You can work with these data models through different APIs, which expose different features, depending on your needs. We will review these APIs in the next sections.

MongoDB API

You can connect to your Azure Cosmos DB using the MongoDB API. MongoDB is a NoSQL storage system that uses a document data model. Similar to JSON objects, a MongoDB document is composed of pairs of fields-value, where a value can be other documents, arrays, or arrays of documents.

When using the MongoDB API, you can reuse your already existing libraries, code, and tools for accessing your Cosmos DB databases. MongoDB API is compatible with MongoDB 3.4 (version 5) wire protocol as well as MongoDB aggregation pipeline. By using MongoDB API you can take advantage of the features of Cosmos DB:

- **Scalability**   You can scale up and down storage and throughput elastically. You can configure the resources assigned for each collection on each database.
- **Multi-region replication**   As with any other Cosmos DB database, the MongoDB database is replicated across all regions that you configure. Cosmos DB provides transparent failover capabilities through the use of multi-homing APIs.
- **No server management**   As with any other managed service, you don't need to worry about MongoDB servers' configuration and management details.
- **Tunable consistency levels**   You can change the consistency level at the account level. Since MongoDB 3.4 has such a session consistency level, if you configure this level and access Cosmos DB using the MongoDB API, this will be treated as eventual consistency.
- **Automatic indexing**   When you create a MongoDB database, Cosmos DB will automatically create an index for all properties of each document in the database. There is no special need for a schema or secondary index for this automatic action.
- **Enterprise grade**   Out of the box, Cosmos DB provides you with several local replicas of your database. These replicas are part of the way that Azure uses for ensuring the 99.99% level of availability. You don't need to make any special configuration for this.

The following procedure shows how to create your first Cosmos DB database. The procedure is equivalent to all APIs, so you just need to select the API that you want to use for accessing the database. Once you select the API for accessing the database, you cannot change it:

1. Sign into the management portal (*http://portal.azure.com*).

2. Click on Create A Resource on the upper-left corner of the window. On the Azure Marketplace, select Databases and then select Azure Cosmos DB.

3. On the Azure Cosmos DB New Account blade, enter an account ID. This will be the name of your account. You can create several databases inside your account.

4. On the API property, choose MongoDB in the dropdown (see Figure 2-28). Remember that you cannot change this value later.

FIGURE 2-28 Selecting Cosmos DB API

5. Depending on your needs, select an existing resource group or create a new one.

6. Select the location more appropriate for you. This will be the write region for your account.

7. If you want to enable geo-redundancy, click on the checkbox below the location dropdown. If you don't enable geo-redundancy during account creation, you can enable that later. If you decide to enable the geo-redundancy at this point, you need to add additional replicas later.

8. Click on Create.

SQL API

Another way to access to your Cosmos DB databases is using SQL API. This way, you can access your NoSQL storage by using your SQL skills. Added to the features that we already mentioned in previous sections, you can program your own stored procedures, triggers and user defined functions (UDFs) using standard JavaScript.

When you work with SQL API, you use a document model. This means that the information is organized in databases, collections, and documents. There are other types of items like triggers, stored procedures, or user defined functions that are also stored as JSON documents inside a database. We have two different types of resources inside a Cosmos DB account:

- **System-defined resources**   These resources have a well-known schema since they are part of the system itself. System-defined resources are databases, users, permissions, and collections.

- **User-defined resources**   These are the resources defined by the user with an arbitrary schema. These resources are documents, stored procedures, triggers, UDFs and attachments.

Figure 2-29 shows the relationship between different resources types.

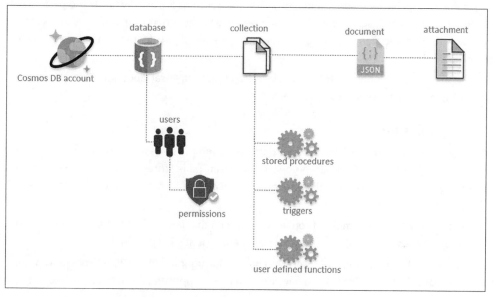

FIGURE 2-29 Resources relationship in Cosmos DB

You can access your databases, collections, and documents by using the existing REST API making requests using HTTP/HTTPS. Microsoft also provides SDKs for languages .NET, Node.js, Java, JavaScript, and Python.

> **NOTE PROGRAMMING FOR COSMOS DB**
>
> When you need to develop applications that integrate with Cosmos DB, there is no need to provision a Cosmos DB account for development purposes. Microsoft provides you with an Azure Cosmos DB Emulator for development and testing purposes on your local environment when you want to work with SQL API. You can download the Cosmos DB Emulator from *https://docs.microsoft.com/en-us/azure/cosmos-db/local-emulator*.

Graph API

When you deploy your Cosmos DB for use with the Graph API, you are telling Azure that you want to use a Graph data model. Graph API appears as a Gremlin (graph) option in the API dropdown during the deployment of a new Cosmos DB account.

A graph data model is useful when your entities and the relationship between them are equally important and you need to define properties for both types of elements. Azure Cosmos DB implements the property graph model. In this model each entity is known as a vertex and represents discrete objects like a car, a person, or a place. Vertices have relationships between them called edges. Both vertices and edges have properties. Using NoSQL engines is usually a good option for implementing graphs, thanks to the schema-free structure.

You typically use a graph for solving problems related with social networking, content management, geospatial, or recommendations. Graph algorithms are usually faster and perform better than traditional SQL and NoSQL databases, usually by orders of magnitude, thanks to the algorithms associated with the graph mathematics, like depth-first search or breadth-first search.

Graph API is compatible with Apache TinkerPop graph traversal language, Gremlin, or any other TinkerPop-compatible graph system.

Azure Tables API

Cosmos DB allows you to connect to your database using the same API calls that you use for your Azure Table Storage. This allows you to move from Table Storage to Cosmos DB without changing a line of code. Making this change, you will benefit from the improvements made for Cosmos DB:

- **Latency** With Cosmos DB you are guaranteed that latency is less than 10ms for reads operations and less than 15ms for write operations at 99th percentile.

- **Throughput** Using Table Store you have a throughput limit of 20,000 operations per second. With Cosmos DB you have no such limit, supporting more than 10 million of operations per second.

- **Global distribution** You can configure only a single region for read/write operations with an optional read-only second region for high availability when you use Table Storage.

- **Indexing** Azure Table Store provides a single primary index based on PartitionKey and RowKey properties. You cannot configure additional indexes.

- **Query** Table Store use indexes for queries only when you include the primary key on your query. For any other query without primary key, it uses scans, which have great impact on performance.

- **Consistency** You cannot choose the consistency model with Table Store. Within the primary site a strong consistency model is used along with a consistency model inside the secondary site.

- **Pricing** It's optimized for storage when using Table Storage. Cosmos DB pricing is optimized for throughput.

Design for cost, performance, data consistency, availability, and business continuity

When planning for deploying Azure Cosmos DB, one of the aspects that you need to consider is the amount of resources that you need for your solution and the associated costs for those resources. When dealing with resources and costs, you need to consider an important concept, Request Unit (RU). This unit is the measure for assigning resources per partition and for billing. You can consider a partition or physical partition as a server. When you need to assign resources to your Cosmos DB account, you make it by adding RU per seconds. Remember, billing is performed hourly. Each RU has assigned a fixed amount of resources (Memory, Core and IOPS). This unit or currency simplifies the model for provisioning throughput to the application, since you don't need to differentiate between read and write capacity units. As a rule of thumb, you should consider that a write operation needs five times the number of RUs needed for a read operation of the same size. This means that if you need one RU for reading a document of 1KB size, you will need five RUs for writing a document of 1KB size.

Cosmos DB offers a low latency guarantee for read and write operations. Azure can provide this feature thanks to consistency models used on data replication. Depending on your needs, you can configure five well-defined different consistency models for your Cosmos DB account:

- **Strong** Guarantees that the read operation returns the most recent version of an item. Any write operation will be available for reading only when has been committed by the majority quorum of replicas. The client never sees partially committed data. If you configure your account with this consistency model, you cannot associate more than one region with your account. The cost associated with read operations is higher than sessions or eventual consistency models.

- **Bounded-staleness** You configure a staleness value based on the number of versions K or the time interval t. This level of consistency guarantees that reads may lag writes by a maximum K number of versions or t time-interval. This consistency level is ideal when you want to keep low latency guarantee, but have a strong consistency. You can associate any number of regions with your account when you use this consistency model. Costs associated with read operations are equivalent to a strong consistency model.

- **Session** The consistency model is scoped to a client session. This consistency model is ideal for scenarios where a user or device typically reads its own writes. You can associate any number of regions with your account when using this consistency level. Costs associated with read operations are lower than strong or bounded-staleness, but higher than eventual consistency.

- **Consistent Prefix** The replication within the group will eventually converge only if there are no further write operations. This model of consistency guarantees that reads are always ordered. This means that if you wrote A, B, C data, when you read it, you can receive A or A, B or A, B, C, but never A, C or B, A, C. You can associate any number of regions with your account when you use this consistency model.

- **Eventual**   The replication within the group will eventually converge only if there is no further write operations. There is no guarantee of the order when you perform read operations. You can associate any number of regions with your account when you use this consistency model. This consistency level has the lower cost when performing read operations.

Cosmos DB also provides business continuity features, like high availability (HA) and backup.

High availability is provided at several levels. You can configure high availability at a regional level by enabling and adding regions to geo-replications. Azure replicates your write operations across all regions that you configure in your account. But Azure also provides HA locally to each region. When you create an Azure Cosmos DB account, Azure creates a Cosmos DB container. This container automatically is divided in three different partitions. Each partition is made highly available by creating a replica set. When you configure geo-replication and add additional regions, a new layer of partition is added to the Cosmos DB container.

Azure performs backups of your Cosmos DB account automatically every four hours and keeps the last two backups. To ensure that the backup process does not impact on the latency of your account, Cosmos DB uses a separate Azure Blob Storage account. Taking a backup doesn't consume any provisioned RU from your account. These automatic backups are also resilient against regional disaster by replicating the backup data to another region using geo-redundant storage (GRS). Although only two last backups are available for recovery, if you accidentally delete a database or collection, your backup is maintained up to 30 days. If you need to have a longer retention time, you can use Azure Cosmos DB Data Migration Tool and schedule additional backups. You can only perform a restore by opening a support ticket.

> *NOTE* **PROTECTION AGAINST DATA CORRUPTION**
>
> Automatic Cosmos DB backups protect your data against accidental deletes, but cannot detect if your data have been corrupted in any way. To ensure that you can recover correct data from your backups in case of data corruption, Microsoft recommends deleting the affected database or collection before eight hours. This way you can be sure that data corruption is not propagated to the automatic backups. Then you can request a database or collection recovery.

We have reviewed the advanced features that Microsoft offers you when using Cosmos DB and how this unique NoSQL service can help you with your storage needs. This service is especially useful for applications that need to replicate worldwide. You can also take advantage of the multi API provided by Cosmos DB to transparently migrate your application from other services like MongoDB, Casandra, or Azure Table Storage.

Thought experiment

In this thought experiment, you can demonstrate your skills and knowledge about the topics covered in this chapter. You can find the answers to this thought experiment in the next section.

Your company is developing an application for IoT devices that measures the volume of liquid and temperature that flows through a pipe section. Your company will use data gathered from IoT devices for detecting problems on the monitored liquid flows. You also need to provide a mechanism for rising alerts when you detect weird values on the temperature and volume measurements.

With this information in mind, answer the following questions:

1. What technology should you use for performing the data analysis and data presentation?

2. What should you do for rising alerts in case the system detects a deviation from defined patterns?

Thought experiment answers

This section contains the solutions to the thought experiment.

1. You should use Azure Time Series Insight. You can connect your IoT devices to Azure IoT Hub. Time Series Insight can be connected to Azure IoT Hub for loading data and analyzing it. Time Series Insight provides you with tools for detecting patterns on your data as well as a graphical interface for visualizing your data.

2. You can connect Time Series Insight with Azure Stream analysis for monitoring any rising alerts based on the patterns that you detected and configured on Time Series Insight.

Chapter summary

- Azure provides storage solutions for your needs, from single location storage to geo-replicated highly available storage. It also provides different levels of performance. You can also encrypt your information stored in Azure Storage.

- You can extend your on-premises storage to the cloud using the StoreSimple service.

- If you want to move your storage to the cloud and have a big volume of data, you can use Azure Import/Export or Azure Data Box.

- Azure provides solutions for big data and regular data storage, transformation, orchestration, and presentation.

- Azure HDInsight provides Big Data analysis compatible with open source solutions.

- You can run your relational database workloads in Azure, using Azure SQL Database, Azure SQL Database for MySQL, or Azure SQL Database for PostgreSQL.

- You can optimize the costs for your on-premises databases by moving cool and archive data to Azure by using Azure Stretch Database.

- Azure Redis Cache provides with an enterprise-level managed cache services for your application.

- Azure Table Storage provides simple NoSQL storage based on key-value pairs of data.

- Azure Data Lake Store provides optimized storage for HDInsight workloads.

- Azure Search is a search as a service for abstracting from your application the details of the implementation of a search engine.

- If you need to perform an analysis of data that evolves along the time, Time Series Insight provides you with the tools for focusing on detecting patterns and analyzing the evolution of your data.

- Cosmos DB is a multi API NoSQL service that provides geo-replication of your data with guaranteed low latency read and write access.

Design networking implementation

The foundation of the cloud is a large pool of storage, compute, and networking resources, allowing you to acquire any amount of cloud resources at any time, from anywhere, without managing any underlying infrastructure. Once resources are complete, return them to the cloud to avoid any unnecessary costs. Azure resources are managed by Azure Resource Manager (ARM), providing a unified API to management tools and automation scripts for provisioning, monitoring and releasing Azure resources.

Some cloud services give access to the infrastructure, such as Virtual Machines (VMs) and virtual networks, and are called Infrastructure as a Service (IaaS). Platform as a Service (PaaS) provides support for building your own services on the cloud. And, Software as a Service (SaaS), makes it possible to handle workloads on the cloud.

Azure provides networking features similar to on-premises datacenters. This chapter provides coverage on networking, introducing key components, services, and tools used to implement various networking scenarios.

Skills covered in this chapter:

- Skill 3.1: Design Azure Virtual Networks
- Skill 3.2: Design external connectivity for Azure Virtual Networks
- Skill 3.3: Design security strategies
- Skill 3.4: Design connectivity for hybrid applications

Skill 3.1: Design Azure Virtual Networks

Today, just about any computer you see is connected to a network. Computers on Azure are no exception. Provisioning a new VM on Azure prevents physical access to the hosting machine. Instead, you can operate the machine through remote connections, such as remote desktop or Secure Shell (SSH), which is made possible by Azure's networking infrastructure.

Azure Virtual Network, introduced here, creates virtualized private networks on Azure. VMs deployed on a virtual network can communicate like they do on an on-premises local area network (LAN).

Connect virtual networks with on-premises networks, or with other virtual networks, through cross-network connections. Skill 3.2 covers hybrid networks.

> **This section covers how to:**
> - Create and manage virtual networks
> - Implement load balancing
> - Use User Defined Routes (UDRs)

Create and manage virtual networks

It's easy to create a new virtual network on Azure. Here we will set up a new virtual network with two subnets on Azure, covering the differences between a virtual network and an on-premises network required when designing network infrastructures in the cloud.

> *NOTE* **REVIEW OF BASIC NETWORKING CONCEPTS**
>
> A deep networking knowledge isn't required here, since you may not routinely maintain networks. We provide refreshers of basic networking concepts in notes found throughout this chapter. Feel free to skip these notes if you're already familiar with the concepts.

Creating a virtual network by using the Azure management portal

There are ways to create a new virtual network on Azure, including using the Azure management portal, Azure PowerShell, and Azure CLI. Here you will use the management portal to create a new virtual network, and scripting options are discussed later in this chapter.

1. Sign in to the management portal (*http://portal.azure.com*).
2. Click on the New link at the upper-left corner, and then select Networking | Virtual Network, shown in Figure 3-1.

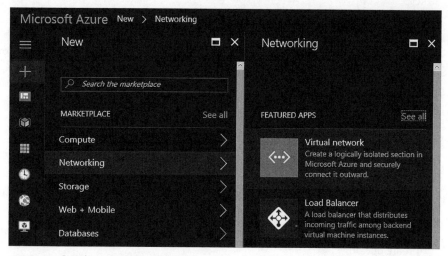

FIGURE 3-1 Creating a new virtual network

3. On the Create Virtual Network blade, type a name for the virtual network. In the Address space box, change the CIDR to 10.0.0.0/16. You can pick any address space you like. In this example, we'll use an address space and create two subnets on the network.

> **NOTE** **ABOUT ADDRESS SPACE CONFLICT WARNINGS**
>
> When entering the CIDR, you might see a warning message that says the address space '10.0.0.0/16' overlaps with another existing address space. This is because you've already created another virtual network whose address space overlaps with the current address space. This is not a problem if you use the two virtual networks in isolation. You'll face problems, however, when you try to connect them through cross-network connections (see Skill 3.2).

4. Change the subnet name to **frontend** and the subnet address range to **10.0.0.0/24**. Later in this exercise, you'll create a backend subnet. When managing a large virtual network, create multiple subnets to improve performance. To describe this briefly, a network is like a web of roads. When you have more computers sending and receiving packets on the same network, packets can collide and must be resent. Using subnets, you can control and limit traffic in different areas. It's similar to using local roads for a short commute and using shared highways to travel longer distances.

In many cases, subnets are created not only for performance but also for manageability. You can create subnets in alignment with business groups, such as creating one subnet for the sales department and another subnet for engineering. You can also create subnets based on server roles. Create a subnet here for a frontend and another subnet for a backend.

1. If you have multiple Azure subscriptions, pick the subscription to use in the Subscription dropdown box.

2. All of your Azure resources are organized in resource groups. You can choose to create a new resource group or put the virtual network into an existing resource group.

3. Pick the Azure region where you want to deploy your network and then click on the Create button.

4. Once the virtual network is created, click on the Subnets menu and then the +Subnet icon, as shown in Figure 3-2.

FIGURE 3-2 Adding a new subnet

5. On the Add subnet blade, type in **backend** as the subnet name, and verify that the CIDR block is 10.0.1.0/24. Then, click on the OK button to add the subnet.

Managing virtual networks with Azure Cloud Shell or Azure CLI

Azure CLI is a cross-platform command-line tool for managing Azure resources. You can download and install Azure CLI for macOS, Linux, and Windows. You can also access Azure CLI directly from Azure management portal through a feature called Cloud Shell. In this exercise, you'll use Cloud Shell to perform a couple of administrative tasks. You'll first inspect an existing virtual network and then create and delete another virtual network.

1. On Azure management portal, click on the Cloud Shell icon in the upper-right corner, as shown in Figure 3-3. This launches a new Cloud Shell instance at the bottom of the portal screen.

FIGURE 3-3 Launching Cloud Shell

2. If you have multiple Azure subscriptions, use the following command to choose the subscription you want to use. Otherwise, skip to step 3.

    ```
    az account set --subscription '<your subscription name>'
    ```

3. To list existing virtual networks in a table format, use the following command.

    ```
    az network vnet list --output table
    ```

4. To add a new virtual network with address space 192.168.0.0/16 to your resource group, use the following command.

    ```
    az network vnet create --name <virtual network name> --address-prefix
     192.168.0.0/16 --resource-group <existing resource group name>
    ```

5. To delete the virtual network, use the following command.

    ```
    az network vnet delete --name <virtual network name> --resource-group
     <resource group name>
    ```

IP Addresses

You've learned how to perform basic virtual network management tasks, so let's dig deeper into how the Azure Virtual Network works, beginning with IP addresses.

You can assign two types of IP addresses to an Azure resource: public IP and private IP. Public IPs are used for communication with the Internet. Private IP addresses are used for communication within a single Azure Virtual Network or connected virtual networks.

> **NOTE   AZURE DEPLOYMENT MODELS**
>
> Azure provides two deployment models for managing resources: resource and classic. It's recommended to use Resource Manager to provision any new Azure resources. The classic deployment model is not discussed further in this book.

Private IP Addresses

Private IPs can be assigned to resources sitting in a virtual network and provide addresses for them to reach one another. For example, you can assign a private IP to the network interface card (NIC) of a VM, making the VM addressable within the scope of the virtual network. If the VM has multiple NICs, you can assign a private IP to each of the NICs.

Figure 3-4 depicts a sample topology of a virtual network (10.0.0.0/16) with two subnets (10.0.0.0/24 and 10.0.1.0/24). A default system route table allows VMs (10.0.0.4, 10.0.1.4 and 10.0.1.5) to communicate with each other. When a VM tries to reach the Internet, its private IP address is Source Network Address Translated (SNAT) into a public IP address by the Azure infrastructure.

A private IP address can be either dynamic or static. A dynamic IP address is automatically allocated from the resource's subnet address space using DHCP. When a resource is stopped and restarted, it may get a different private IP address. A static IP address, on the other hand, remains the same throughout the lifetime of the resource.

Dynamic private IP addresses are allocated by an Azure-provided DHCP server. The DHCP server also assigns a DNS server and a default gateway. The DNS server is by default the host server IP address, and the gateway is an address on your Azure virtual network subnet. Later in this chapter, you'll learn about how to set up a custom DNS server.

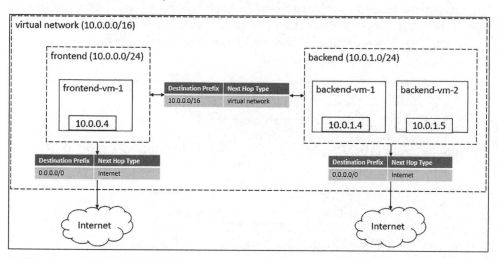

FIGURE 3-4 Sample network topology

Public IP Addresses

A public IP address is an independent Azure resource with its own properties. It can be associated to resources such as VMs, Azure Load Balancers, VPN gateways and Application Gateways to allow direct communications to and from the Internet.

Public IPs come from an IP address pool owned by Microsoft, and they are assigned to Azure resources either dynamically or statically. A dynamic public IP is allocated when you start or create the associated resource and is released when you stop or delete the resource. A static IP is released only when you delete the resource.

Available public IPs on the Internet are limited resources. You can allocate up to 60 dynamic pubic IP addresses and 20 static public IP addresses per Azure subscription. You need to contact Azure support to raise the limit if you need more.

Name resolution

Azure provides a built-in recursive resolver for name resolutions. This virtual DNS server is located at a fixed virtual public IP address of 168.63.129.16. It filters DNS lookup requests so that you can only resolve hostnames of your own deployments. Because VMs residing on the same virtual network share the same DNS postfix (*.internal.cloudapp.net), they can reach one another directly by their hostnames.

You can bring your own DNS server when needed. For example, when you need cross-virtual network name resolutions, you can set up a DNS server on each of the virtual networks and cross-forward DNS queries, as shown in Figure 3-5. In this scenario, a DNS server is configured in each of the virtual networks and forwards DNS queries to the other DNS server. The two virtual networks are connected by an inter-network connection, which will be discussed later in Skill 3.2. The DNS servers also forward DNS queries to Azure-provide name resolution servers for other name resolutions. Please note that when you set up your own DNS servers, you should assign static IP addresses to them.

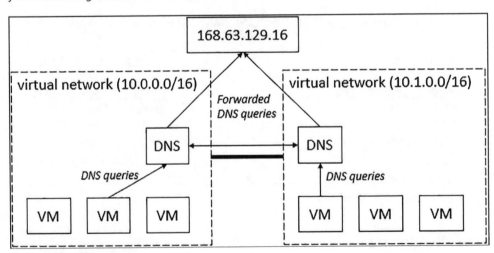

FIGURE 3-5 Custom DNS servers

You can assign DNS name labels to public IPs that you allocate. These DNS name labels are scoped with system-defined postfixes in the format of <region>.cloudapp.azure.com. For example, a DNS name label in the West US region has the name <label>.westus.cloudapp.zure.com. If you prefer your own domain name, you need to set up corresponding DNS records pointing to the public IP in your own domain DNS servers. Or, you can use Azure DNS to host DNS records for your domain.

In the following exercise, you'll use Cloud Shell to create three virtual machines on the virtual network you've provisioned in the virtual network management exercise. One of the VMs is put in the frontend subnet and assigned a public IP. The other two VMs are put in the backend subnet with only private IPs. Then, you'll assign a DNS label to the public IP of the frontend machine. And finally, you'll use Azure DNS to set up a custom domain record for the frontend machine.

1. Open Cloud Shell.

2. Use the following command to create the frontend machine, which creates an Ubuntu LTS server using the *Standard_DS1_v2* machine size. You can choose a different VM size if needed. If you don't specify a --public-ip-address parameter, the az vm create command automatically allocates a public IP (using dynamic allocation method) for you. If you don't want a public IP address to be allocated, you need to pass an empty string to the parameter. Please also note the machine is placed in the frontend subnet by the --subnet parameter.

```
az vm create --resource-group <your resource group name> --name
frontend-vm --admin-password <machine admin password> --vnet-name
<virtual network name> --authentication-type password --admin-username
 <machine admin name> --size Standard_DS1_v2 --image UbuntuLTS --subnet
 frontend --nsg ""
```

3. Once the machine is provisioned, you can observe the assigned public IP in the command's output JSON. To query the public IP at a later time, use the following command:

```
az vm list-ip-addresses --name <virtual machine name> | grep ipAddress
```

4. Create an availability set. You don't need it in this exercise, but you'll need to use it in later exercises. In step 5, you'll create two backend VMs on the availability set.

```
az vm availability-set create --name <availability set name> --resource-group
<resource group name>
```

5. Create two backend VMs on the backend subnet:

```
az vm create --resource-group <your resource group name> --name backend-vm-1
--admin-password <machine admin password> --vnet-name <virtual network name>
--authentication-type password --admin-username <machine admin name> --size
Standard_DS1_v2 --image UbuntuLTS --subnet backend --nsg "" --public-ip-
address "" --availability-set <availability set name>

az vm create --resource-group <your resource group name> --name backend-vm-2
--admin-password <machine admin password> --vnet-name <virtual network name>
--authentication-type password --admin-username <machine admin name> --size
Standard_DS1_v2 --image UbuntuLTS --subnet backend --nsg "" --public-ip-
address "" --availability-set <availability set name>
```

6. Once all of the machines are created, you can SSH into the frontend machine and do some experiments, by using the following command:

```
ssh <machine admin name>@<frontend machine public IP>
```

7. Once connected to the frontend machine shell, try a domain lookup on one of the backend machines:

```
nslookup backend-vm-1
```

You should see an output like the following output:

```
Server:     168.63.129.16
Address: 168.63.129.16#53
Name:    backend-vm -1.mtji5hmdhvgudmao4fdntopbwe.dx.internal.cloudapp.net
Address: 10.0.1.5
```

8. Exit the SSH by typing in **exit** and pressing Enter. Now let's assign a DNS label to the frontend VM's public IP address. To do this, you'll need to get the resource name for the public IP address. Use the vm list-ip-addresses command again and note the name of the public IP address resource:

```
[
  {
    "virtualMachine": {
      "name": "frontend-vm-3",
      "network": {
        ...
        "publicIpAddresses": [
          {
            ...
            "ipAddress": "40.78.109.13",
            "ipAllocationMethod": "Dynamic",
            "name": "frontend-vm-3PublicIP",
            ...
]
```

9. Assign a DNS label to the public IP address:

```
az network public-ip update --name <public IP address name> --resource-group
<resource group name> --dns-name <DNS label>
```

The above command associates a *<DNS label>.<region>.cloudapp.azure.com* FQDN to the public IP address.

10. Now, the frontend VM can be accessed from a client by either its public IP address or its FQDN.

Azure DNS provides high-performance and high-availability DNS hosts in Azure. You can manage and query your DNS records over the Azure global infrastructure. In the following exercise, you'll create a new Azure DNS zone and then set up a custom domain record for the frontend machine.

1. In Cloud Shell, use the following command to create a new Azure DNS zone. The DNS zone name should have at least two parts, separated by ".", for example: haishi.com.

```
az network dns zone create --name <DNS zone name> --resource-group <resource group name>
```

2. Add a new A record that points a <DNS prefix>.<DNS zone name> label to the frontend VM's public IP address:

```
az network dns record-set a add-record --record-set-name <DNS prefix> --zone-name <DNS zone name> --ipv4-address <frontend vm public IP> --resource-group <resource group name>
```

3. Now, you can query your records using the following command:

```
az network dns record-set ns show --name @ --zone-name <DNS zone name> --resource-group <resource group name>
```

For example, the above command generates the following output in a given system:

```
{
    "etag": "c75…",
    "id": "/subscriptions/46…/resourceGroups/70-534/providers/Microsoft.
Network/dnszones/mydnszone.com/NS/@",
    "metadata": null,
    "name": "@",
    "nsRecords": [
        {"nsdname": "ns1-06.azure-dns.com."},
        {"nsdname": "ns2-06.azure-dns.net."},
        {"nsdname": "ns3-06.azure-dns.org."},
        {"nsdname": "ns4-06.azure-dns.info."}
    ],
    "resourceGroup": "70-534",
    "ttl": 172800,
    "type": "Microsoft.Network/dnszones/NS"
}
```

When you purchase your domain name, you should configure the name servers with the domain name registry.

Load balancing

So far, you've got a frontend VM and two backend VMs that can communicate by private IP addresses and hostnames. However, for the two backend VMs to provide a high-available backend, you don't want the frontend VM to address them separately. Instead, you need a load balancer in front of the backend VMs, as shown in Figure 3-6.

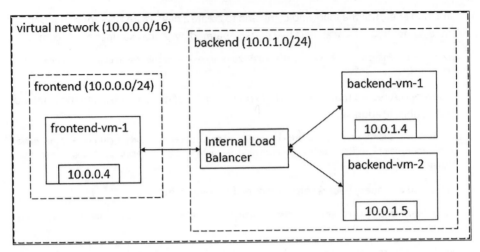

FIGURE 3-6 Internal Load Balancer

The internal load balancer provides the following benefits: First, it provides high-availability. As long as one of the backend VMs is functioning, they can provide continuous backend services to support the frontend. Second, it provides scalability. When you need more capacity in the backend, you can join more VMs behind the load balancer, and the load balancer will evenly distribute workloads to running VMs. This allows you to scale out backend without impacting the frontend.

Availability set

The availability of the system in Figure 3-6 is jeopardized if both backend VMs fail. Azure uses a concept of availability set to minimize the risk. An availability set is a management boundary that defines multiple fault domains (FDs) and update domains (UDs).

A fault domain is roughly a rack in an Azure datacenter. In Azure datacenters, unplanned maintenances are triggered by unexpected physical infrastructure problems such as network failures, rack-level failures, and other hardware failures. When such a failure is detected, Azure automatically moves your VMs to a healthy host. Fault domains don't share a common power source or network switch, so the probability of two fault domains failing at the same time is low. When you add VMs to an availability set, they are evenly distributed into available fault domains.

Azure periodically performs maintenances on the hosting infrastructure. Many of these maintenances occur at the hosting operation system level and the platform software level without any impacts to the hosted VMs. However, some of these updates will require your VMs to be shut down or rebooted. When Azure updates VMs, it guarantees that not all machines in the same availability set will be shut down at the same time. Instead, it walks through update domains, bringing VMs down group by group. This process ensures that at any given time during updates there are at least a few machines running to provide continuous services.

Internal Load Balancer

Azure Internal Load Balancer provides load-balancing capacity within a virtual network. An internal load balancer is defined by the following components:

- **Frontend IP configuration** You can associate multiple IP addresses to a load balancer. The load balancer can be reached via any of the associated IP addresses. This allows a many-to-many mesh between the frontend VMs and the backend VMs.

- **Backend pools** Backend pools hold the candidate VMs to which the traffic is routed. You can add individual VMs and available sets into backend pools.

- **Health probes** A load balancer uses its health probes to detect the health of VMs. Traffic is routed only to VMs that pass health checks. Health probes periodically use either the TCP protocol or the HTTP protocol through the configured port to talk to the VMs. For TCP protocol, a successful TCP handshake is considered a positive response. For the HTTP protocol, a response with 200 return codes is considered a positive response. If a VM fails to provide a positive response within configured iterations, it's considered unhealthy and is taken out of the load-balancing pool. Please note that even if a VM is taken out of the load-balancing pool, health probes keep checking the VM and rejoin the VM back to the pool when the VM comes back.

- **Load balancing rules** Load balancer behaviors are driven by load balancing rules. A load balancing rule binds front IP address, backend pool, and the health probe together. Traffic from the front IP address is evenly distributed to healthy VMs in the backend pool, which is determined by the health probe. You can also specify session persistence behavior of a load balancing rule. If this value is set to "None," successive requests from the same client during a session may be handled by any virtual machines in the backend pool. If the value is set to "Client IP," requests from the same client IP address that are handled by the same virtual machine. "Client IP and protocol," on the other hand, specifies that successive request from the same client IP address and protocol combination are handled by the same virtual machine.

  Session persistence is useful to route traffic to stateful services. For example, when you add multiple items to a server-held shopping cart, you want all the add requests to be routed to the same server that holds the shopping cart instance for your session. If the requests are scattered to different servers, you'll get inconsistent shopping cart state across the servers, unless the state is replicated across the VMs.

- **Inbound NAT rules** You can set up NAT rules to route traffic to <load balancer IP>:<port> to different VMs in the backend pool based on port numbers. For example, to enable SSH connection to each VM instance, you can set up a few NAT rules that maps a series of ports to port 22 on individual VMs, so that a client can use the load balancer IP with a different port to select different VMs.

An internal load balancer resides in a virtual network subnet and is assigned a private IP address from the network address space. To facilitate security configurations, you may want to assign static private IPs to internal load balancers.

Public load balancing

You can setup public-facing load balancers, which are associated with public IP addresses and can be directly accessed over the Internet. A public load balancer is configured in the same way as configuring an internal load balancer. The difference is that a public load balancer can route traffic to VMs across multiple virtual networks.

Figure 3-7 shows an extended topology of the previous samples. In this case, two frontend VMs form the frontend and join the public load balancer. Two backend VMs form the backend and join the internal load balancer. Internet traffic is routed to the frontend VMs via the public load balancer. The frontend VMs talk to the backend via the internal load balancer. And the internal load balancer distributes requests to backend VMs.

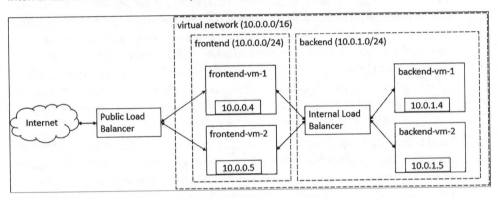

FIGURE 3-7 Public Load Balancer

A public load balancer is an independent ARM resource that sits in the Azure infrastructure and is different from an internal load balancer that resides in your virtual network.

ARM object model

Before moving on to further discussions, it's worthwhile to review the ARM object model behind the diagram in Figure 3-7. ARM treats all Azure artifacts it manages as resources. These resources are organized into resource groups. Resources can have dependencies among them either by reference or by association. Reference is a hard dependency. If resource A depends on resource B, it can't be provisioned until resource B is already in place. Association, on the other hand, is a weak dependency. Association is often established by setting one resource as another resource's property.

Figure 3-8 shows the object model behind Figure 3-7. Rectangles in the figure represent different Azure resource types. Ovals in the figure represent child properties of a resource type. The object model also includes Network Security Groups (NSGs), which will be covered later in this chapter. It's important to understand the ARM object model and how resources are linked together. This will help you to focus on correct resources when working with a complex ARM topology. For example, although public IP addresses are often directly denoted on VMs, they are assigned to network interface resources, which is a different resource type.

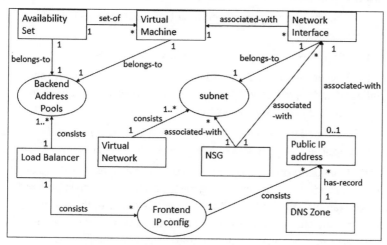

FIGURE 3-8 ARM object model (partial)

Traffic Manager

When you implement a globally-available web application, you need a global routing service. Azure Traffic Manager routes incoming traffic to your application deployments at different geographic locations based on performance and availability.

To use Traffic Manager, you define a Traffic Manager profile that consists of a domain name, a list of endpoints, and a load-balancing policy. When a user tries to access a service, the following activities happen:

1. The user accesses the service by the domain name provided by Traffic Manager (*.trafficmanager.net). If a custom domain is used, another DNS resolution is performed to first resolve the custom domain name to the Traffic Manager domain name.

2. When Traffic Manager receives the DNS resolution request, it evaluates its policy and picks an endpoint address based on availability, performance, weighted priorities or geo locations.

3. Traffic Manager returns a CNAME record that maps the Traffic Manager domain name to the selected endpoint.

4. The user's DNS server resolves the endpoint address to its IP address and sends it to the user.

5. The user calls the endpoint directly by the IP address.

A couple of points are worth discussing here. First, Traffic Manager works during the DNS resolution phase. The actual traffic doesn't go through Traffic Manager. Second, because DNS records are often cached, Traffic Manager isn't involved in every service request. Third, the endpoints don't need to be on Azure. They can be on other cloud platforms, or even in on-premises datacenters.

Traffic Manager picks endpoints based on one of the following four methods:

- **Priority** Traffic is routed to a primary service endpoint and routed to backup end-points when the primary fails.
- **Weighted** Traffic is distributed across a set of endpoints based on weights.
- **Performance** Traffic Manager periodically updates a table that records the response time between various IP ranges to Azure datacenters. When a new request comes in, it picks the datacenter with the best response time in corresponding IP range.
- **Geographic** Traffic is routed to the same region where the DNS query originates from. This feature is important to meet data sovereignty requirements in some regions.

You can also nest Traffic Manager profiles, which means a profile at a higher level uses other Traffic Manager endpoints as candidate endpoints. Using nested profiles, you can implement more complex policies. For example, you can have a top-level profile that uses the priority method to establish a primary site and a secondary site, and a second-level profile that distrib-utes user traffic based on performance. You can have up to 10 levels of nested profiles.

> ✔ **Quick check**
>
> As mentioned above, Traffic Manager can manage endpoints from different environ-ments, as long as the endpoints are reachable over Internet. Can you leverage this feature in your hybrid deployment scenarios?
>
> **Quick check answer**
>
> Traffic Manager can help you to achieve hybrid scenarios such as failover-to-cloud. In this case, you'll set up your primary endpoint to be your pubic on-premises entry point, and a secondary endpoint on Azure. The on-premises services provide fast, private ser-vices to your customers. And when the on-premises system fails, your customers are au-tomatically redirected to Azure hence, the service continuity is ensured. Similarly, you can set up cross-cloud failovers to have your primary system running on your preferred cloud platform while having a backup system running on a secondary cloud.

CDN

Azure operates out of facilities located in over 30 regions around the world, and the number is increasing every year. In addition, Azure also strategically places CDN point of presence (POP) locations to deliver content to end users. You can cache content from Azure Storage, Azure Web Apps, and Azure Cloud Services.

When a user requests content by the CDN URL, the content is directly served from the CDN node if the content exists. Otherwise, the content will be retrieved from the content origin and stored at the CDN node for future requests.

Using CDN has two major benefits. First, because content is served directly from the CDN node that is closest to the user, user experience can be greatly improved. Second, because a large portion of requests will be served from CDN nodes instead of from the original service nodes, the loads on the original service nodes are greatly reduced, making it possible for the service to scale out to support a much greater number of users.

CDN is mostly used to cache static contents. However, you can cache dynamic outputs from your websites and Cloud Services, as well because CDN content is identified by URLs, including the query parameters. For example, http://<identifier>.vo.msecnd.net/chart.aspx?item=1 and http://<identifier>.vo.msecnd.net/chart.aspx?item=2 represent two different cached objects. You need to be careful not to cache volatile data in CDN, because doing so can adversely affect your performance or even cause content problems, all at increased cost.

Routes

Now, let's dig deeper into how network packets are routed on Azure. When you place multiple VMs on an Azure Virtual Network, the VMs can communicate with one another by their private IP addresses or host names. The VMs can also reach the Internet. All of these are made possible by Azure-provided system routes.

System routes

When you provision a VM on a virtual network subnet, a few default routes are defined, as listed in Table 3-1.

TABLE 3-1 Default routes for a VM

ADdress Prefixes	Next Hop Type	Next Hop Type IP Address
Virtual network CIDR, for example: 10.0.0.0/16	Virtual network	-
0.0.0.0/0	Internet	-
10.0.0.0/8	None	-
100.64.0.0/10	None	-
172.16.0.0/12	None	-
192.168.0.0/16	None	-

In Table 3-1, other than how the Virtual Network hop type is always set to the virtual network's address space, all other system routes are static. Routes are processed via the Longest Prefix Match (LPM) method; thus, the most specific routes have the highest priority to be applied. Being the least specific, 0.0.0.0/0 is the "catch-all" route when no other routes apply.

VM-TO-VM ROUTES

Figure 3-9 depicts how traffic between two VMs on different subnets is routed. In this case, the most specific 10.0.0.0/16 route is activated, and the packet is routed through local virtual network to the destination. Please note that although 10.0.0.0/8 and 0.0.0.0/0 could also apply, they are not used because they are less specific.

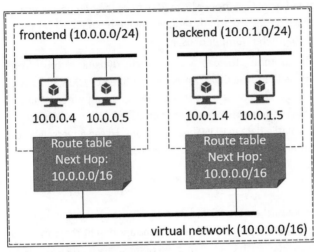

FIGURE 3-9 VM-to-VM Routing

Consider another example: a packet is targeted at address 10.1.1.2. In this case, 10.0.0.0/8 would be the most specific matching route, and the packet is dropped because the next hop type of the route is "None."

VM-TO-INTERNET ROUTES

Private IPs are not routable outside the virtual network (or connected virtual networks). For a VM to communicate with the Internet, it needs to be associated with a routable pubic IP. As introduced earlier in this chapter, if a VM doesn't have a public IP, Azure uses SNAT to associate a public IP so that it can participate in packet routing. If a VM is in a load balancer pool, Azure uses the public IP associated with the load balancer for SNAT. If a VM has a public IP address, there's no SNAT needed. Packets are directly routed in this case.

Figure 3-10 shows the details of how a packet from a VM with private IP 10.0.0.4 is routed to bing.com. From the perspective of bing.com, the request comes from the load balancer public IP. From the perspective of the VM, it never knows about the intermediate hop and thinks it's directly communicating with bing.com.

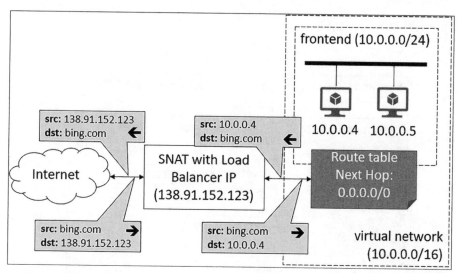

FIGURE 3-10 VM-to-Internet Routing

User Defined Routes

You can define custom routes to implement complex routing scenarios. For example, you may want to inspect all packets flowing through your network. Or you may want to implement a custom firewall and force all traffic to go through the firewall. You may even want to set up a common NAT. For these scenarios, you can create a custom routing table, using User Defined Routes (UDR) to gain fine-grained control over network traffic.

DEFINING USER DEFINED ROUTES

The best way to learn UDR is to see it in action. In the following exercise, you'll extend your virtual network topology and insert a simple virtual network appliance between the frontend subnet and the backend subnet. Then, you'll define a UDR to force all traffic from the frontend to the backend to go through the virtual network appliance you configure. The finished topology is shown in Figure 3-11.

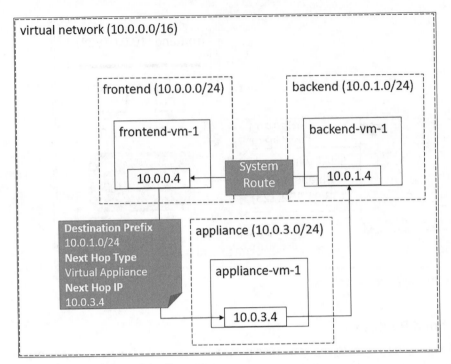

FIGURE 3-11 Virtual Network Appliance

1. First, create a new subnet to host your virtual appliance. Name this subnet "appliance" and set its CIDR to 10.0.3.0/24:

```
az network vnet subnet create --name appliance --vnet-name <virtual network name>
--resource-group <resource group name> --address-prefix 10.0.3.0/24
```

2. Create a NIC. There are a few things worth noticing in the following command. First, the NIC is assigned with a static private IP 10.0.3.4. When we set up UDR, this IP address will be the routing destination. Second, the NIC is created with the ip-forwarding flag, which allows the NIC to forward network packets.

```
az network nic create --vnet-name <virtual network name> --private-ip-address
10.0.3.4 --name appliance-nic --ip-forwarding --subnet appliance --resource-group
<resource group name>
```

3. Now, create the virtual appliance VM with the above NIC.

```
az vm create --resource-group <resource group name> --name appliance-vm
--admin-password <admin password> --authentication-type password --admin-
username <admin user name> --size Standard_DS1_v2 --image UbuntuLTS --nsg ""
--nics appliance-nic
```

4. Create a custom route table named appliance-route:

```
az network route-table create --resource-group <resource group name> --name
appliance-route
```

5. Define a custom route on the route table to route all traffic targeted at 10.0.1.0/24 to the virtual appliance at 10.0.3.4:

```
az network route-table route create --resource-group <resource group name> --name
route-to-backend --route-table-name appliance-route --address-prefix 10.0.1.0/24
--next-hop-type VirtualAppliance --next-hop-ip-address 10.0.3.4
```

6. Apply the custom routing table to the frontend subnet:

```
az network vnet subnet update --resource-group <resource group name> --vnet-name
<virtual network name> --name frontend --route-table appliance-route
```

7. SSH into one of the frontend VMs via its public IP:

```
Ssh <admin user name>:<front VM public IP>
```

8. Use the traceroute command to trace the route from the frontend VM to 10.0.1.4 (if you don't have traceroute installed, use the command sudo apt-get install traceroute to install it):

```
traceroute 10.0.1.4 -m 3
```

The above command will fail with the following outputs:

```
traceroute to 10.0.1.4 (10.0.1.4), 3 hops max, 60 byte packets
1  * * *
2  * * *
3  * * *
```

This is because the virtual appliance doesn't forward any traffic yet. You'll fix this next.

9. From the SSH session, use SSH again to connect to the appliance VM:

```
ssh <admin user name>@10.0.3.4
```

10. Enable IP forwarding:

```
sudo sysctl -w net.ipv4.ip_forward=1
```

11. Type **exit** to exit the SSH session to 10.0.3.4 and return to the SSH session to the frontend VM.

12. Use the traceroute command again to trace the route to 10.0.1.4. This time, you should see how the packet is routed through the virtual appliance (10.0.3.4) and sent to the destination (10.0.1.4):

```
traceroute to 10.0.1.4 (10.0.1.4), 3 hops max, 60 byte packets
1  10.0.3.4 (10.0.3.4)  1.357 ms  1.336 ms  1.324 ms
2  10.0.1.4 (10.0.1.4)  1.808 ms  1.797 ms  1.788 ms
```

13. The traffic going from the backend to the frontend doesn't go through the virtual appliance. To verify this, SSH into the backend VM:

```
ssh <admin user name>@10.0.1.4
```

14. Use the traceroute command to trace the route back to 10.0.0.4:

```
traceroute 10.0.0.4
```

The above command should succeed showing a direct route to 10.0.0.4:

```
traceroute to 10.0.0.4 (10.0.0.4), 30 hops max, 60 byte packets
1  10.0.0.4 (10.0.0.4)  1.883 ms  1.859 ms  1.849 ms
```

> **NOTE EXPERIMENT ON WINDOWS**
>
> If you're using Windows Server instead of Ubuntu, you should use the tracert command instead of *traceroute*. Furthermore, to enable a Windows server to route traffic, install the Routing and Remote Access role, and then configure the role to enable the server as a IPv4 router for Local area network (LAN) routing.

VIRTUAL NETWORK APPLIANCE

You created a simple IP forwarder in the above exercise. In a real-life deployment, you should use existing virtual network appliances from your favorite brands to deliver advanced networking features. Azure Marketplace provides many popular networking products such as Barracuda Web Application Firewall (WAF), Cisco Cloud Services Router (CSR) 1000V, F5 WAF Solution for ASC and FortiGate Next Generation Firewall for HA. Please visit *https://azuremarketplace. microsoft.com/en-us/marketplace/apps/category/networking?page=1&subcategories=applianc es* for a complete list of virtual network appliances.

Skill 3.2: Design external connectivity for Azure Virtual Networks

Microsoft realizes that for many of its existing enterprise customers, a migration to the cloud is a long process that might take years or even decades. In fact, for some of these customers, a complete migration might never be feasible. To ensure smooth cloud transitions, Azure provides a pathway for enterprises to adopt the cloud at their own pace. This means that for the foreseeable future, many enterprises will be operating *hybrid* solutions that have components running both on-premises and in the cloud. Thus, reliable, secure, and efficient connectivity between on-premises datacenters and cloud becomes a necessity. This skill discusses two of the connectivity options: Azure Virtual Network and Azure ExpressRoute. Then, we briefly introduce some other hybrid solution options.

> **This section covers how to:**
> - Design hybrid solutions with Virtual Network and ExpressRoute
> - Leverage other hybrid solution options

Hybrid connectivity

The virtual network offers several types of hybrid connections that bridge resources located at different facilities. You can choose one or several connection options that best suit your requirements. Note that this skill does not focus on detailed steps of setting up the connections. Instead, it describes the steps in general and then focuses on how each connection type suits different scenarios.

Point-to-Site VPN

Point-to-Site VPN is the simplest hybrid connection that enables you to securely connect your local computer to an Azure virtual network. No specific VPN devices are needed in this case. Instead, you install a Windows VPN client through which you can connect to any VMs and Cloud Services within the virtual network. Figure 3-12 shows the topology of a Point-to-Site VPN.

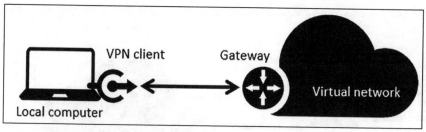

FIGURE 3-12 Point-to-site connectivity

Establishing a point-to-site connection involves several steps:

1. Specify an IP address range. When your VPN clients connect, they will receive IP addresses from this range. You need to ensure that this range doesn't overlap with IP ranges within your on-premises network.

2. Add a gateway subnet.

3. Create a Route Based VPN (previously known as dynamic routing gateway). You can create up to 128 P2S connections through a single gateway.

4. Create a client certification to be used for client authentication. The client machine that makes the VPN connection needs to have the certificate installed.

5. Download the VPN client configuration package from your virtual network's dashboard page. When the client is installed, you'll see a new VPN connection with the same name as your virtual network.

With Point-to-Site connection, you can connect to your VMs on Azure from anywhere. It uses Secured Socket Tunneling Protocol (SSTP), which means that you can establish the connection through firewalls and Network Address Translation (NAT). It works well to support a small mobile workforce. However, because each client PC in this case establishes a separate connection to the gateway, you are limited to the number of P2S connections that the gateway can support.

Point-to-Site enables scenarios such as remote administration of cloud resources, trouble-shooting, monitoring, and testing. It can be applied to use cases such as remote education, mobile office, and occasional command and control. However, for bridging on-premises networks and Azure Virtual Networks, you'll probably want to use Site-to-Site VPN.

Site-to-Site VPN

Site-to-Site VPN is designed for establishing secured connections between site offices and the cloud or bridging on-premises networks with virtual networks on Azure. To establish a Site-to-Site VPN connection, you need a public-facing IPv4 address and a compatible VPN device or Routing and Remote Access Service (RRAS) running on Windows Server 2012. (For a list of known compatible devices, go to *https://docs.microsoft.com/en-us/azure/vpn-gateway/vpn-gateway-about-vpn-devices*.) You can use either policy-based or route-based gateways for Site-to-Site VPN. However, if you want to use both Site-to-Site VPN and Point-to-Site VPN at the same time, you'll need a route-based gateway. Figure 3-13 shows the topology of a Site-to-Site VPN.

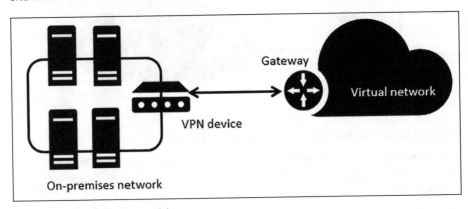

FIGURE 3-13 Site-to-Site connectivity

Site-to-Site VPN extends your local network to the cloud. As you gradually move your workloads to the cloud, you often need the servers in the cloud and the local servers to still work together before the migration is complete. Using Site-to-Site VPN, these servers can communicate with each other as if they are on the same local network. This becomes handy when you move some domain-joined servers to the cloud, but you still want to keep them on your local Active Directory.

Site-to-Site works in the other direction as well: it brings your VMs in the cloud into your local network. You can join these servers into your local domain and apply your security policies on them. In many migration cases, moving the application servers is easier compared to moving a large amount of data. And some enterprises prefer to keep their data local for various reasons. With Site-to-Site VPN, your cloud VMs can reach back to your on-premises data. They also can be joined to Azure Load Balancer to provide high-availability services.

Although Site-to-Site connections provide reasonable reliability and throughput, some larger enterprises require much more bandwidth between their datacenters and the cloud. Moreover, because VPNs go through the public Internet, there's no SLA to guarantee the connectivity. For these enterprises, ExpressRoute is the way to go.

ExpressRoute

ExpressRoute provides private connections between your on-premises datacenters and Azure datacenters. You can achieve up to 10 Gbps of bandwidth with the dedicated, secure, and reliable connections. These connections don't go through the public Internet, and you can get connectivity SLAs from your selected service providers. If you have frequent large-volume data transfers between your on-premises datacenters and Azure, ExpressRoute provides a faster solution that in some cases is even more economical.

There are two ways to use ExpressRoute to connect to Azure. One way is to connect to Azure through an exchange provider location. The other way is to connect Azure through a network service provider. The exchange provider option provides up to 10 Gbps of bandwidth. The network service provider option provides up to 1 Gbs of bandwidth. In either case, Azure configures a pair of cross-connections between Azure and the provider's infrastructure in an active-active configuration to ensure availability and resilience against failures. Figure 3-14 shows the topology of an ExpressRoute connection.

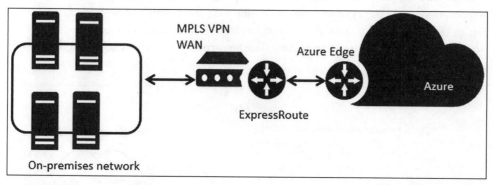

FIGURE 3-14 ExpressRoute connectivity

ExpressRoute's fast and reliable connection is ideal for scenarios such as data storage access, backups, and disaster recovery. For example, you can transfer and store a large amount of data to Azure Storage service while keeping your applications running on your own datacenter. For backup and disaster recovery, ExpressRoute makes data replication faster and more reliable, improving the performance as well as the reliability of your disaster recovery strategies. Moreover, you can access other Azure-hosted services such as Office 365 by using the same private connection for fast, secure access.

When working together, many servers need frequent exchanges of data. When some of the servers are moved to the cloud, the additional latency introduced by Internet connections can have a serious impact on the performance of the overall system and sometimes render the entire system unusable. ExpressRoute provides a fast connection between your on-premises datacenters and Azure so that you can extend your local infrastructure to the cloud without having to make significant architecture or code changes.

vNet-to-vNet VPN

Just as you can establish Site-to-Site connections between your on-premises datacenters and Azure, you also can connect two virtual networks on Azure by using a VPN connection. Figure 3-15 shows the topology of a vNet-to-vNet connection.

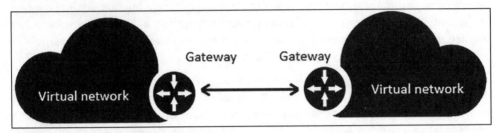

FIGURE 3-15 vNet-to-vNet connectivity

You can use vNet-to-vNet VPN to support geo-redundancy and geo-presence. For example, you can use vNet-to-vNet VPN to set up SQL Always On across multiple Azure regions. Figure 3-16 shows another example, which is a cross-region three-node MongoDB replica set with a primary node and a secondary node in West US, and another secondary in West Europe. The West Europe node is for disaster recovery and is not allowed to be elected as a primary.

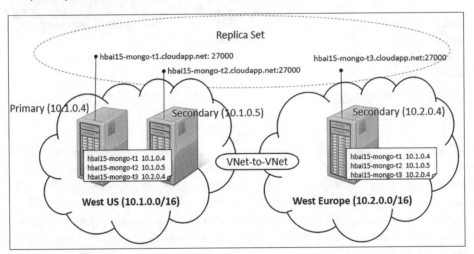

FIGURE 3-16 Cross-region mongodb replica set

You also can use vNet-to-vNet VPN in business integration scenarios. With global corporations, business units sometimes remain independent from one another, but at the same time some workflows need to be integrated. Using vNet-to-vNet, resources owned by different business units can communicate with one another while maintaining isolations between the resources (refer to the later discussions on ACLs and NSGs). Some multitiered applications need such kind of isolations as well. For instance, a new corporate website might need to consume services and data from multiple regional sites, which have their own virtual networks and security policies.

Multi-site VPN

You can use an Azure Virtual Network gateway to establish multiple Site-to-Site connections. This capability makes it possible to join multiple on-premises networks. Figure 3-17 shows the topology of a Multi-site VPN.

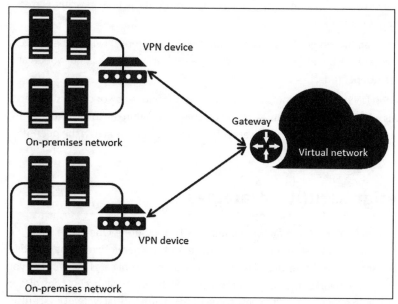

FIGURE 3-17 Multi-site VPN

Using Multi-site VPN, branch offices from different geographic locations can connect with one another to exchange data and share Azure-based resources, such as a common hosted service. This topology is also referred to as a *hub-and-spoke* topology, which is quite common for scenarios in which a head office connects to multiple branch offices.

Network peering

When you connect two virtual networks without overlapping IP ranges in the same region together, you can use virtual network peering to connect the two networks through the Azure backbone network without gateways. Network peering has a few advantages over vNet-to-vNet connections:

- Traffic between virtual machine in peered virtual network is routed directly through the Azure backend infrastructure instead of the gateway. The network latency for a round trip between two virtual machines in peered virtual network is the same as for a round trip within a single virtual network.
- There aren't additional bandwidth constraints other than the bandwidth allowed for the virtual machine.

Network peering has some limitations:

- Peered virtual networks must be in the same Azure region (at the time of writing cross-region peering is in preview).
- Peering is between two networks and is not transitive. For example, if virtual network A is peered with network B and virtual network B is peered with network C, network A and network C are not peered.
- Azure-provided DNS name resolution for virtual machines doesn't work across peered network. VMs with internal DNS names are resolvable only within the local virtual network. You can set up your own DNS server for name resolutions across the peered networks.

Skill 3.3: Design security strategies

Network security is always an important factor in enterprise IT operations. One of the main responsibilities of a network administrator is to ensure the enterprise network remains effective, extensible, auditable, and secure. Azure virtual network environment replicates the features you usually see in on-premises networks, including connectivity, isolation, firewall, access control, and application gateways. In this section, you'll review some of the Azure Virtual Network security features, and study a couple of security scenarios.

> **This section covers how to:**
> - Apply Network Security Groups (NSGs)
> - Deploy Azure Application Gateway

Network Security Groups

A Network Security Group (NSG) defines a list of prioritized security rules that allow or deny traffic to subnets or individual network interfaces attached to VMs (see Figure 3-8).

NSG rules

An NSG rule is defined by the following properties:

- **Name** A region-wide unique name.
- **Protocol** Protocol to match for the rule. You can use TCP, UDP, or * that matches UDP, TCP as well as ICMP.
- **Source port range** Source port range to match for the rule. It can be a single port number from 1 to 65535, a port range such as 8080-8088, or * for all ports.
- **Destination port range** Destination port range to match for the rule.
- **Source address prefix** Source address prefix or tag to match for the rule. It can be a single IP address such as 10.0.2.4, a subnet such as 192.168.1.0/24, a default tag, or * for all addresses.

> **NOTE** **DEFAULT TAGS**
>
> Default tags are system-provided identifiers that indicate IP address categories. There are three default tags: VirtualNetwork, AzureLoadBalancer, and Internet. VirtualNetwork includes virtual network address spaces, connected on-premise address spaces as well as connected virtual networks. AzureLoadBalancer indicates Azure's load balancers. It resolves to an IP where Azure's health probes originate. Internet denotes the IP address space outside the virtual network address space and reachable by the Internet.

- **Destination address prefix** Destination address prefix or tag to match for the rule. It can be a single IP address, a default tag, or * for all addresses.
- **Direction** Direction of traffic. It can be either inbound or outbound.
- **Priority** Priority is a number between 100 to 4096, inclusive. A smaller priority number indicates a higher priority. When Azure applies NSG rules, it goes from highest priority rule to the lowest priority rule. Once it finds a matching rule, the rule is applied, and no further matchings are tested. If no matching rules are found, the packet is dropped.
- **Access** Allow or deny access.

DEFAULT RULES

Each NSG comes with a set of default rules that can't be deleted. These rules are assigned with low-priority numbers so that they can be easily overridden by your own custom rules. Table 3-2 lists the default inbound rules of an NSG. The first rule allows all internal traffic within the same virtual network. The second rule allows health probes from Azure Load Balancer health probes. And the third rule denies all other inbound traffic.

TABLE 3-2 Default inbound rules of an NSG

Priority	Source IP:Port	Destination IP:Port	Protocol	Access
65000	VirtualNetwork:*	VirtualNetwork:*	*	Allow
65001	AzureLoadBalancer:*	*:*	*	Allow
65500	*:*	*:*	*	Deny

Table 3-3 lists the default outbound rules of an NSG. The first rule allows outbound traffic to the virtual network. The second rule allows outbound traffic to Internet. And the third rule denies all other outbound traffic.

TABLE 3-3 Default outbound rules of an NSG

Priority	Source IP:Port	Destination IP:Port	Protocol	Access
65000	VirtualNetwork:*	VirtualNetwork:*	*	Allow
65001	*:*	Internet:*	*	Allow
65500	*:*	*:*	*	Deny

SPECIAL RULES

Besides the default rules, a NSG also contains two special rules that allow essential Azure infrastructural traffic to go through. If you block the following two rules, your VMs won't work properly as expected.

- **Traffic to 168.63.129.16**   As introduced earlier in this chapter, 168.63.129.16 is a special virtual IP address where infrastructural services such DHCP, DNS and health monitoring services reside. This IP maps to the physical IP of the host where the VM is hosted. The host acts as a DHCP relay, DNS recursive resolver, and probe target for load balancer and health probes.

- **Outbound traffic through port 1688**   All Windows images running in VMs need to be licensed. Queries to a hosted Key Management Service are sent through port 1688. To ensure proper licensing, you should not block outbound traffic through port 1688.

RULE FOR REMOTE ACCESS

When you associate a public IP to a NIC, Azure automatically creates an NSG with an inbound rule that allows SSH at port 22 for a Linux VM, or RDP at port 3389 for a Windows VM. If a VM has multiple NICs, you can associate different NSGs to different NICs.

Apply NSGs

NSGs are applied in different orders for inbound traffic and outbound traffic. For inbound traffic, subnet-level NSGs are applied first and then the NIC-level NSGs. For outbound traffic, the order is reversed: NIC-level NSGs are applied first and then the subnet-level NSGs.

Now, let's consider how to add network protections to the topology depicted in Figure 3-7. Logically, the overall deployment is split into two tiers and each corresponds to a separate subnet (frontend and backend). Let's consider each layer separately.

THE FRONTEND TIER

Assume the frontend is comprised of two load balanced Windows web servers that are accessible through both port 80 for HTTP and port 443 for HTTPS. The two web servers are joined to an Azure Load Balancer with HTTP-based probes periodically querying the root path "/". In addition, one of the web servers is double-purposed as a jump box to access VM instances in the virtual network. A Load Balancer NAT rule is configured to map RDP connections at port 3389 to the selected server.

You don't need to define a rule for load balancing because it's already covered by the default rules. For HTTP and HTTP traffic and RDP connection, however, you'll need to define additional inbound rules, as listed in Table 3-4.

TABLE 3-4 Inbound rules for the frontend

Priority	Source IP:Port	Destination IP:Port	Protocol	Access
1000	Internet:80	*:80	TCP	Allow
1001	Internet:443	*:443	TCP	Allow
1002	Internet:3389	*:3389	TCP	Allow

Please note that for the RDP access, the destination IP is set to * instead of a specific IP. This is because in the case of using dynamic private IPs, you can't predict or guarantee a stable IP address for a VM. Alternatively, you can define a separate NSG with the third rule only and apply it directly to the jump box VM. This avoids accidentally granting access to other frontend server's remote access if the NAT rules on the load balancer is configured incorrectly.

Because there are no needs for the web servers to send outbound traffic, all outbound traffic to the Internet should be blocked, as shown in Table 3-5.

TABLE 3-5 Outbound rules for the frontend

Priority	Source IP:Port	Destination IP:Port	Protocol	Access
2000	*:*	Internet:*	*	Deny

THE BACKEND TIER

Assume the backend runs two SQL database servers with data replication enabled. You need to open port 1433 for database accesses. Moreover, you may want to open port 3389 to allow RDP traffic from the jump box. The inbound rules are listed in Table 3-6.

TABLE 3-6 Inbound rules for the frontend

Priority	Source IP:Port	Destination IP:Port	Protocol	Access
1000	10.0.0.0/24:3389	*:3389	TCP	Allow
1001	10.0.0.0/24:1433	*:1433	TCP	Allow

Please note that in both rules, only connections from the frontend subnet are allowed. The outbound rule for the backend is the same as the outbound rule for the frontend—it blocks all outbound Internet traffic.

Figure 3-18 shows the updated topology with NSGs.

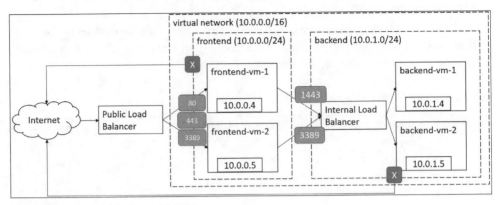

FIGURE 3-18 Network topology with NSGs

In the following exercise, you'll implement the NSG described in Table 3-3 using the Azure management portal. This exercise assumes you've already implemented the network topology in Figure 3-7.

1. Logon to the Azure management portal.

2. In the left navigation bar, click on the Resource groups icon. And then, in the Resource Group List, click on your resource group name to open the resource group.

3. On the resource group Overview blade, click on the +Add icon at the top of the screen.

4. On the Everything blade, search for "network security group." Then, click on the Network Security Group entry.

5. On the Network Security Group blade, click on the Create button.

6. On the Create Network Security Group blade, enter a name for your NSG. Leave all other boxes at default values, and click on the Create button.

7. Once the NSG is created, the NSG blade should open. If the blade doesn't open, click on the notification icon at the top of the portal (see Figure 3-3) and click on the latest notification to bring the blade up.

8. On the NSG blade, click on the Inbound Security Rules link.

9. Click on the +Add icon to add a new inbound rule.

10. On the Add Inbound Security Rule blade, select Service Tag in the Source field. Then, select Internet in the Source service tag field. Change the Destination port ranges to 80, and Protocol to 80. Then, click on the OK button to create the rule, as shown in Figure 13-9.

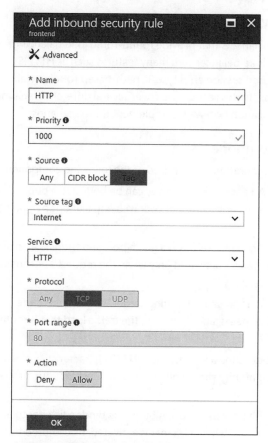

FIGURE 3-19 Define an inbound rule

11. Repeat the above step and create rules for HTTPS and RDP. The result NSG is as shown in Figure 3-20 (you can toggle default rules visibility by clicking on the Default Rules icon).

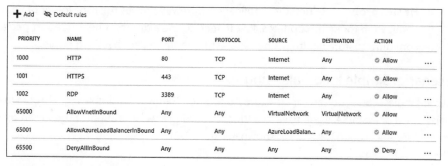

PRIORITY	NAME	PORT	PROTOCOL	SOURCE	DESTINATION	ACTION	
1000	HTTP	80	TCP	Internet	Any	⊘ Allow	...
1001	HTTPS	443	TCP	Internet	Any	⊘ Allow	...
1002	RDP	3389	TCP	Internet	Any	⊘ Allow	...
65000	AllowVnetInBound	Any	Any	VirtualNetwork	VirtualNetwork	⊘ Allow	...
65001	AllowAzureLoadBalancerInBound	Any	Any	AzureLoadBalan...	Any	⊘ Allow	...
65500	DenyAllInBound	Any	Any	Any	Any	⊘ Deny	...

FIGURE 3-20 Frontend NSG

Azure Application Gateway

Azure load balancers are level-4 load balancers that provide round-robin load balancing. Azure Application Gateway is a level-7 load balancer with many features such as HTTP(S) round-robin load balancing, cookie-based session affinity, URL path-based routing, web application firewall, and SSL termination. In this section, we cover several different scenarios, and you'll learn how to use Azure Application Gateway to implement these scenarios.

Azure Application Gateway Components

The Azure Application Gateway configuration is comprised of the following components:

- **Frontend IP configurations**   An application gateway can be bound to a public IP, a private IP, or both. This address is the entry point of your web applications behind the gateway.
- **Listeners**   A listener listens to incoming traffic on a given port and triggers associated routing rule. For a multi-site listener, it's activated only when the request's host name matches with its host name property.
- **Backend pools**   A backend pool represents a routing target. VMs added to the same backend pool are treated as equal peers, and they share the traffic load that is routed to the pool.
- **HTTP settings**   HTTP settings describe a specific set of HTTP characteristics of a backend pool such as if cookie-based affinity should be enabled, request timeout, protocol, and port.
- **Rules**   A rule binds a listener with backend pools. A basic rule binds a listener to a single backend pool. With a basic rule, when a listener is activated, its captured traffic is routed to the backend pool. A path-based rule binds a listener to multiple backend pools. Once a listener captures a request, the request is analyzed, and the request path is retrieved. Then, different backend pools are selected based on the patterns in the request path.
- **Health probes**   By default, Application Gateway probes the root folder of your web application for health updates. If you need to use a different health report page, configure custom health probes and assign them to your backend pools.

Scenario: Simple load balancing

In the simplest case, you can set up Azure Application Gateway for simple round-robin load-balancing. For example, if you have two VMs supporting a website at port 80, you can set up your Azure Application Gateway as shown in Figure 3-21.

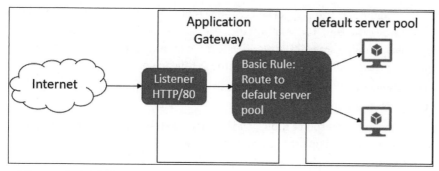

FIGURE 3-21 Basic load balancing

Scenario: Serving contents from different servers

In this scenario, you host a media website. You are hosting regular website artifacts such as web pages and images from a pool of regular web servers. You have also configured specialized media server that can serve up video clips efficiently. What you need in this case is URL path-based routing. Specifically, when a request with a "/video" path segment in the URL comes in, it will be routed to your special media server pool instead of the default server pool that serves up the rest of the web content. Figure 3-22 shows the architecture of such a deployment.

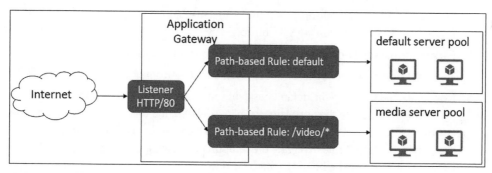

FIGURE 3-22 URL path-based routing

To implement the above scenario, use the following walkthrough.

1. Add a new subnet named "gateway" with CIDR 10.0.2.0/24 to your virtual network. Application Gateway needs to be put into an empty subnet.

2. Click on the + icon at upper-left corner of the portal. Then, select Networking, Application Gateway.

3. On the Basics blade, enter a name for the gateway. Leave the tier operation as Standard. We'll introduce Web Application Firewall (WAF) later in this chapter.

4. Select the Medium SKU size. Application Gateway is offered in three sizes: Small, Medium and Large (VM sizes). The small instance size is intended for development and testing scenarios only. Larger SKU sizes provide more throughput. For example, a large instance can provide 50Mbps to 200Mbps with SSL offload enabled.

5. Set Instance count to 2. To ensure gateway availability, it's recommended to have at least two gateway instances for a production environment.

6. Select the subscription, resource group, and location you want to use. For this exercise, use the same resource group used to host the topology in Figure 3-9. Then, click the OK button to continue.

7. On the Settings blade, select the virtual network you've been using. Then, select the subnet you created for the gateway in Step 1.

8. Set the IP address type to Public for Frontend IP configuration. Then, click on the Choose a pubic IP address link, and then click on the Create new link. Give a name to the public IP, and click on the OK button to continue.

9. Set Listener configuration to HTTP at port 80. Then, click the OK button.

10. On the Summary blade, click on the OK button to create the gateway.

11. Once the gateway is created, open its blade and click on the Backend pools link. You'll see there's already an empty backend pool created. Click on the pool name to open it.

12. Click on the Add target button. Select the Virtual machine option. Then, pick one of the frontend VMs. And, click on the Save button.

13. Back to the backend pools list, click on the +Add button to add another backend pool.

14. Name the new pool "videobackendpool." Add the other frontend VM to the new pool.

15. Now, you need to delete the default basic rule and replace it with a URL path-based rule. However, because the portal doesn't allow deleting the default rule because it's the last rule associated with the gateway, you need to create a temporary rule so that you can delete the default rule. To create the temporary rule, create a temporary listener, because a listener can be bound to only one rule.

16. Back to the gateway blade. Click on the Listeners link.

17. Click on the +Basic button to add a temporary listener. On the Add basic listener blade, set the name as "temp," and the Frontend port and name to 88. The exact port doesn't matter, as long it's not 80, which has been used by the default listener. Click on the OK button to create the temporary listener.

18. Back to the gateway blade. Click on the Rules link.

19. Click on the +Basic button to add a temporary rule. On the Add basic rule blade, set the rule's name to "temp," select the temp listener, and then click on the OK button to create the temporary rule.

20. Now back to the rule list. Click on the default rule (rule1), and then click on the Delete button to delete it.

21. Back to the rule list again. Click on the +Path-based button to add a new path-based rule.

22. On the Add path-based rule blade, enter rule name as **pathbased**. Choose the default HTTP listener. Set the Default backend pool to the default backend pool in Step 12. Then, add a new row to the path-based rule with name "video", paths " /video/*" and backend pool "videobackendpool", as shown in Figure 3-23. Click on the OK button to create the rule.

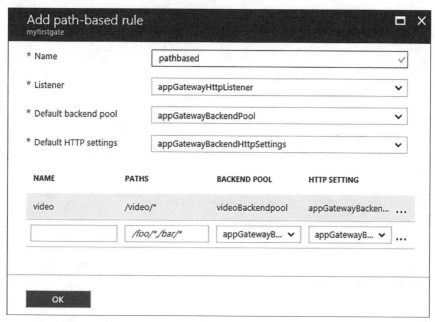

FIGURE 3-23 Path-based rule

23. Now you can delete the temp rule and the temp listener.

NOTE **THE UNIFORM ARM OPERATION PARADIGM**

ARM provides a consistent operation model for managing all types of Azure resources. Creating, updating, and deleting resources via the Azure management portal follows the same operation path regardless of resource types. Interacting with resources via Azure CLI also follows a consistent az <resource type> <action> <options> paradigm. Once you've learned to manipulate one type of resource, you can apply similar operation steps to managing other types of resources. Both the CLI and portal use the same backend API, so they provide functionality parity in most cases. ARM also provides a unified, JSON-based resource templating language called ARM template. You can use ARM template to describe a group of related Azure resources and treat them as an integrated deployment unit.

Scenario: Protecting against common web vulnerabilities

The Internet is a hostile environment. Hackers and malicious users are like sharks swimming around to find victims that have exploitable vulnerabilities. Web Application Firewall (WAF) is an Application Gateway feature that protects your web applications from common exploits and vulnerabilities such as SQL injection and XSS attack. Figure 3-24 shows how WAF can block malicious requests before they reach your sites.

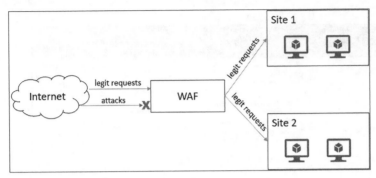

FIGURE 3-24 WAF protects your sites

WAF provides protections against the following attacks:

- SQL injection
- Cross site scripting
- Common web attacks such as command injection, HTTP request smuggling, HTTP response splitting, and remote file inclusion
- HTTP protocol violations
- HTTP protocol anomalies such as missing host user-agent and accept headers
- Bots, crawlers and scanners
- Common application misconfiguration (Apache and IIS etc.)

WAF provides such protections by implementing the OWSAP Core Rule Set (3.0 and 2.2.9). OWSAP Core Rule Set is a collection of generic rules for WAFs written in a SecRules language. These rules are used by WAF to provide in-depth protections against common attacks on web applications.

> **NOTE DEFENDING AGAINST DDOS**
>
> A Distributed Denial of Service (DDoS) attack is a continually rising threat. To define the massive-scale DDoS attack, significant infrastructure needs to be deployed to detect and disrupt such attacks. Microsoft Azure provides global-scale, built-in DDoS protection across all Azure datacenters that prevents common DDoS attacks such as UDP floods, SYN-ACK attacks and reflection attacks. Azure has also been investing in intelligent monitoring and analysis across Internet environments using advanced technologies such as machine learning. The collected intelligence is then used to identify and mitigate potential risks and attacks, making Azure an ever stronger and more secure cloud platform.

Scenario: End-to-end SSL

Azure Application Gateway terminates SSL connections and sends unencrypted data to back-end servers. This relieves the backend servers from the burden of encryption and decryption. However, for some customers, sending unencrypted data is unacceptable. For these customers, Azure Application Gateway supports end-to-end SSL. After it terminates the SSL connection and uses decrypted data to decide packet routes, it encrypts the data again using whitelisted backend server certificates to ensure secured communication with the backend servers. Figure 3-25 shows a sample deployment of the end-to-end SSL scenario.

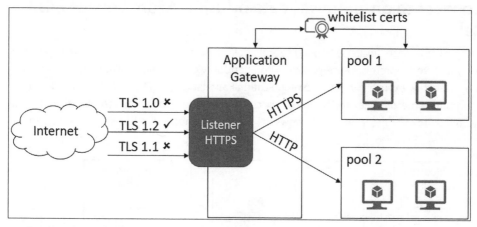

FIGURE 3-25 End-to-end SSL

Figure 3-25 also shows how you can configure SSL negotiation policies:

- SSL 2.0 and SSL 3.0 are disabled by default. These policies are not configurable.

- You can disable any of the three protocols: TLSv1_0, TLSv1_1 and TLSv1_2.

- If no SSL policy is defined, then all three protocols are enabled.

Skill 3.4: Design connectivity for hybrid applications

Skill 3.2 has introduced Azure's hybrid networking capabilities in detail. However, for applications to thrive in a hybrid environment, additional hybrid supports are needed at higher levels. Additional services are required to facilitate accessing data across cloud and on-premises datacenters.

Connect to on-premises data by using Azure Service Bus Relay

You can use Service Bus Relay to build hybrid applications that run in both an Azure datacenter and your own on-premises enterprises environment. Service Bus Relay facilitates this by enabling you to securely expose Windows Communication Foundation (WCF) services that reside within a corporate enterprise network to the public cloud. And it does this without requiring additional incoming firewall rules. Figure 3-26 shows the data flow using Service Bus Relay to access an on-premises WCF service.

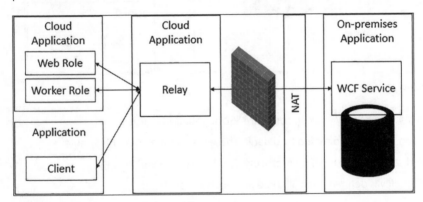

FIGURE 3-26 The Service Bus Relay architecture

Using Service Bus Relay, you can host WCF services within your existing enterprise environment. You can then delegate the task of listening for incoming sessions and requests to these WCF services to the Service Bus Relay service running within Azure. This makes it possible for you to expose these services to application code running in Azure or to mobile workers or extranet partner environments though outbound connections only. With Service Bus Relay, you can securely control who can access these services at a detailed level. It provides a powerful and secure way to expose application functionality and data from your existing enterprise solutions and take advantage of it from the cloud.

Hybrid Connections

Hybrid Connections provides an easy and convenient way to connect Azure App Services to on-premises resources. Hybrid Connections is a feature of App Services. You must config minimal TCP ports to access your network. Using B Hybrid Connections, you can make connections to on-premises resources that use static TCP ports, such as SQL Server, MySQL, Web APIs, and most web services. As of this writing, Hybrid Connections does not support services that use dynamic ports, such as SQL Express. Figure 3-27 shows the setup of a Hybrid Connection.

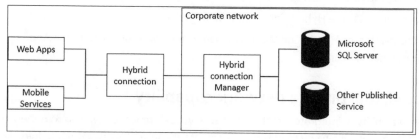

FIGURE 3-27 BizTalk API App Hybrid Connections

You can use Hybrid Connections with all frameworks supported by App Services (.NET, PHP, Java, Python, and Node.js). A feature of using Hybrid Connections to work with resources that are on-premises is that when you move an application such as a website from on-premises to Web Apps, you do not need to change the connection string. Connecting to on-premises resources is exactly the same as if the website were running locally. This makes it possible for Web Apps to be moved to Azure faster because there are no changes required to access the needed data.

Enterprise administrators can keep control over what resources are available to the applications in Azure and can have access to other tools to help them monitor that access. Administrators can set up group policies to determine what resource applications can be accessed through the Hybrid Connections. Event and audit logs can provide visibility into what resources are being accessed. Administrators also do not need to make changes to incoming firewall rules, because the traffic for the Hybrid Connections requires only outbound TCP and HTTP connectivity. Many administrators are reluctant to open up additional ports for security issues. Table 3-7 lists the ports that Hybrid Connections use.

TABLE 3-7 TCP ports used by Hybrid Connections

Port	Usage
80	HTTP port; used for certificate validation.
443	HTTPS port.
5671	Used to connect to Azure. If TCP port 5671 is unavailable, TCP port 443 is used.
9352	Used to push and pull data. If TCP port 9352 is unavailable, TCP port 443 is used.

To configure Hybrid Connections, follow these steps:

1. Sign in to the management portal.

2. On the left side, go to App Services.

3. Select the App Service instance you want to configure.

4. Click on the Networking link.

5. On the Networking blade, click on the Configure You Hybrid Connection Endpoints link under the Hybrid connections section.

6. Download and install the Hybrid Connection Manager.

7. Follow the step for the Hybrid Connection Manager setup and connect it to the App Services instance in Azure.

Web Apps virtual private network capability

Web Apps have the ability to integrate directly into Azure Virtual Network as well as to Hybrid Connections. This does not allow you to put the website into the Virtual Network, but it does allow for the website to reference other services in the Virtual Network. If the Virtual Network is connected to an on-premises network with a site-to-site virtual private network, the website can access all of the on-premises systems such as databases.

Azure ExpressRoute is another option that you can use to connect resources in Azure to the corporate network. This is a feature that uses an ExpressRoute Partner to set up a direct connect between your corporate WAN and Azure. This is the fastest connection to create a Hybrid Connection.

Identifying options for domain-joining Azure Virtual Machines

You can add Virtual Machines to a domain in several different ways. First, you can set up your own domain controllers (also as Virtual Machines) on your Virtual Network in Azure. Once you have your domain controllers configured, additional virtual machines on the Virtual Network can join your domain, like how local services join the on-premises domain. Second, if you have ExpressRoute or VPN configured, you can join an Azure virtual machine back to the on-premises domain. Third, Azure Active Directory Domain Services provides a managed domain service on the cloud with Windows AD compatible domain services such as domain join, group policy, Kerberos/NTLM authentication. You can join your VMs into managed domains backed by Azure Active Directory Domain service.

You also can synchronize your on-premises directories with your cloud-based directories using Azure AD Connect, which will be introduced in Chapter 4, "Design Security and Identity Solutions."

Thought experiment

In this thought experiment, demonstrate your skills and knowledge of the topics covered in this chapter. You can find answer to this thought experiment in the next section.

Using isolated security zones is an effective way for enterprises to reduce many types of risks on their networks. For example, many enterprises use a perimeter network to isolate their Internet-facing resources from other parts of their internal network. You can implement the same level of protection in Azure Virtual Network as well. In this case, you have a number of VMs that will be exposed to the Internet. And you have a number of application servers and database servers on the same virtual network.

With this in mind, answer the following questions:

1. What technologies would you use to implement a perimeter network in Azure Virtual Network?

2. How would you design your network topology?

Thought experiment answers

This section contains the solutions to the thought experiment.

1. You can use NSGs to control network traffic to VMs. Alternatively, you can use UDR to route traffic through a virtual network appliance that implement a firewall or advanced packet filtering.

2. One possible way to design the topology is to put Internet-facing resources, application services, and database servers into different subnets. The Internet-facing resources can communicate only to application servers through specific ports. And only application servers can access database servers governed by another set of rules.

Chapter summary

- Azure provides rich virtual network features that simulate what you've been familiar with in on-premises datacenters. This helps you to lift-and-shift your existing on-premises services to cloud without redesigning your network topology.

- Azure uses Software Defined Network (SDN) to enable multi-tenant virtual networks on top of Azure datacenter infrastructures.

- You can use a combination of Azure-provided DNS and custom DNS to achieve different name resolution scenarios.

- Virtual machines added to an availability set are distributed across fault domains and update domains to reduce probability of total failure.

- You can use Internal load balancers and public load balancers to provide entry points to scaled-out services.

- Traffic Manager is designed to support cross-region, cross-site, high-available service endpoints.
- CDN is an effective way to improve response time by serving cached data directly from edge servers.
- Azure provides rich hybrid connectivity options for you to bridge your on-premises resources with your cloud-based resources.
- You can use Point-to-Site VPN, Site-to-Site VPN, ExpressRoute, vNet-to-vNet VPN, and Network Peering to bridge different networks.
- NSG rules are used to allow or deny network traffics between sources and destinations.
- Application Gateway provides level-7 load balancing for web applications.
- Azure Service Bus Relay and Azure App Service Hybrid Connections allow you to connect your cloud services with on-premises services.

Design security and identity solutions

The Internet is a hostile environment. When providing services over the Internet, you must only allow authorized users access to your services. When saving data, or saving data on behalf of your customers, the data must be well protected and accessed only by the rightful owner.

Designing and implementing a robust authentication system isn't an easy task, however, since it requires deep knowledge on network security and rich experience in anti-hacking techniques. This chapter covers topics on managed identity, leveraging an external identity provider that manages identities as well as handles authentication requests for you. This chapter covers data security in the cloud, as well as techniques and services to make data storages reliable and available. Microsoft Azure Active Directory is also covered and assists system administrators when designing, evolving, and reinforcing effective security policies across large enterprises.

As a leading cloud platform, Azure provides in-depth resource protections at different levels to ensure that customer data and workloads are safe in the cloud. It's important to understand all of the options Microsoft Azure provides for designing secured cloud solutions.

Skills covered in this chapter:

- Skill 4.1: Design an identity solution
- Skill 4.2: Secure resources by using identity providers
- Skill 4.3: Design a data security solution
- Skill 4.4: Design a mechanism of governance and policies for administering Azure resources
- Skill 4.5: Manage security risks by using an appropriate security solution

Skill 4.1: Design an identity solution

The core idea of using managed identities is to delegate complex identity management and user authentication tasks to a trusted party so that you can focus on developing business logics. Instead of managing identities yourself, you choose a trustworthy party who manages identities and handles user authentication requests for you. Once a user is authenticated, this trusted party issues you security tokens, which contain various claims about the user. And then, you can use these claims to make decisions such as granting or denying access and applying corresponding security rules.

The key to a successful implementation of a system using managed identities is to keep a clear picture of the relationships among the participants of the authentication/authorization workflow. Before going deeper, let's first define some terms and then put them into a complete picture to examine how they interact with each other.

> **This section covers how to:**
> - Understand managed identities and claim-based architecture
> - Use Azure Active Directory (AAD)
> - Use Microsoft Graph

Claim-based architecture

The system design that uses an external party to manage identities is sometimes called a claim-based architecture. The following are some of the key components of this architecture.

Securable entity and its attributes

A securable entity refers to a user, an application, or a service identity that makes service requests. An entity often has one or more associated attributes, such as a user name, telephone number, and security role.

Claim

A claim is an assertion made on an attribute of an entity. For example, the street address printed on a driver's license is an assertion made by an authority (such as a state office) on an individual's home address (attribute). Any party can make assertions. But only claims from a trusted authority should be trusted.

Security token

A security token is a collection of claims. It's often digitally signed, encrypted, and transferred through secured channels to ensure its confidentiality, integrity, and authenticity. A consumer of a security token should trust the claims in the token only if it can validate the token is genuine and has not been altered.

Service Provider (SP) / Relying Party (RP)

A Service Provider (SP) provides requested services. Within the context of claim-based architecture, a Service Provider is also called a Relying Party, because it relies on a third-party to manage identities on its behalf.

Identity Provider

An Identity Provider (IdP or IP) authenticates entities and issues security tokens to Relying Parties. The security token contains the claims the Identity Provider made about the entity. Then, the Relying Party can use claims in the token for authorization. An Identity Provider offers one or a number of ways for an entity to authenticate, such as using a password or a security key, a digital certificate, a security token, or a biometric signature. Some Identity Providers also support authentications with a combination of multiple methods, which is called multi-factor authentication (MFA).

Trust

A trust relationship is what ties an Identity Provider and a Service Provider together. A Service Provider assumes the assertions in a security token to be true because the token is issued by a trusted party. A Service Provider can choose to trust multiple Identity Providers. And an Identity Provider can provide authentication service to multiple Service Providers. These trusted parties form a circle of trust, in which an entity (such as a user) only needs to sign on once with any of the trusted Identity Providers in order to gain access to services provided by any of the Service Providers in the same trust circle. This experience is the so-called Single Sign-On (SSO) experience.

Authentication

The task of authentication is to verify if an entity is indeed what it claims itself to be. In order to authenticate, a user usually needs to provide certain proofs, such as a password, a digital certificate, or an issued security token. Once the user is authenticated, an Identity Provider issues a security token to the requesting Service Provider.

Authorization

Authorization is the process to decide if an authenticated user has access to certain functionalities provided by the Service Provider. A Service Provider uses claims in the security token to decide if certain actions should be allowed or disallowed. For example, certain actions are allowed only when there's a claim stating the authenticated user has a role attribute with a value of System Administrator.

In some authorization protocols, the service who offers protected resources is called a resource provider. A resource provider may ask an authenticated user to provide explicit consensus before granting access to a protected resource.

To help you to remember the difference between authentication and authorization, simply remember that authentication deals with the question of "Who are you," and authorization decides, "What are you allowed to do."

Basic authentication and authorization workflow

Figure 4-1 illustrates the basic authentication and authorization workflow under claim-based architecture. This workflow works in a typical scenario where a user uses a browser to access a web application.

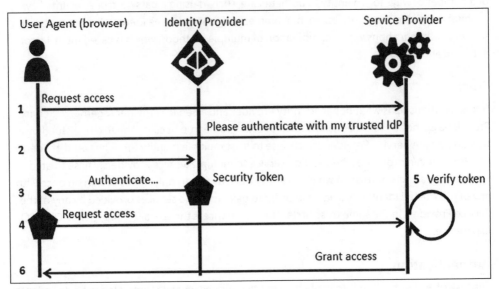

FIGURE 4-1 Basic authentication and authorization process

1. A user (agent) requests access to a service provided by a Service Provider.

2. The Service Provider is configured to use a trusted Identity Provider for authentication. Instead of granting access to the service, it redirects the user agent to the designated Identity Provider to get authenticated first.

3. The user completes the authentication process with the Identity Provider. Once the authentication process is successfully completed, the Identity Provider issues a security token to the user agent.

4. The user agent requests access to the service again, but this time it attaches the security token to the request.

5. The Service Provider verifies the token. And once the token is validated, it retrieves the claims contained in the token.

6. Based on the claims, the Service Provider decides if the access request should be granted or denied.

Working with Native Clients

The previous workflow is based on a browser as the user agent, which is also called a passive client in this context. The workflow relies on URL redirections to carry the process forward. In the case of a native application, such as a Windows Desktop application or a mobile phone application, a different workflow based on OAuth 2.0 specification is often used, as shown in Figure 4-2.

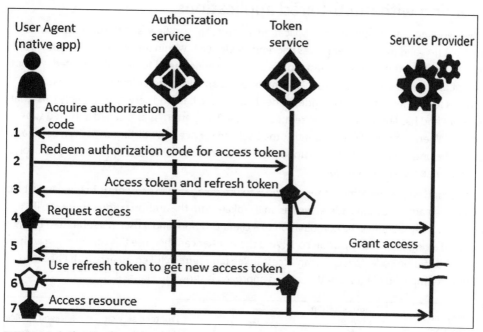

FIGURE 4-2 Authentication and authorization process with native client

1. A user (agent) requests an authorization code from an authorization service. In the request, the user agent identifies itself and specifies which application or service it's trying to access. The authorization service authenticates the user. And if consent is required to use the service or the application, the authorization service also asks for user's consent before continuing with the process. Otherwise, it issues an authorization code to the user agent.

2. The user then redeems the authorization code for an access token from a token service.

3. Once the authorization code, along with the client identification and the service identification, is verified, the token service issues an access token as well as a refresh token.

4. The user agent uses the access token to make service requests.

5. The Service Provider verifies the token and makes authorization decisions before providing the service.

6. When the access token expires, the user agent uses the refresh token it received earlier in step 3 to acquire a new access token. The purpose of the refresh token is to avoid re-authentication, which requires the user to sign on again.

7. The user agent makes additional service requests using the new access token. And the process continues.

Working with multi-tiered applications

When working with a multi-tiered application, a common workflow is that a user signs on to the front tier, and the front tier makes backend service calls within the context of the user's session. In this case, the service requests to the backend service need to be authenticated without explicit user actions. One way to achieve this is to use an application identity, which the front tier uses for authentication as an independent entity. The backend service will simply trust that the front end has authenticated the requesting user. This pattern is also called a trusted subsystem. When using application identity, the backend service can't distinguish which user has issued the original request. And it's up to the tiers to communicate over application protocols when user contexts are needed.

A second way to implement the scenario is to use delegated user identity. In this case, a user requests an authorization code as well as an ID token from the authorization service. An ID token uniquely identifies the combination of a client program and a user. It's submitted to the frontend along with authorization code. And the frontier can then use this token, along with the authorization code, to request an access token (and refresh token) to access the backend service. A simplified diagram of the second approach is shown in Figure 4-3.

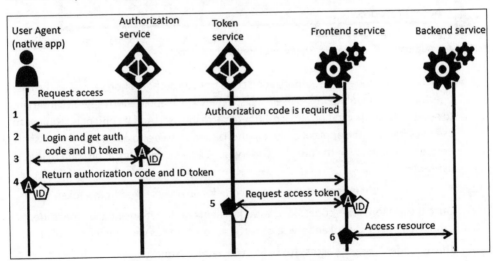

FIGURE 4-3 Authentication and authorization with multi-tiered application

1. A user agent requests access to the backend service via the frontend.
2. The frontend service replies that an authorization code is required to access the back-end service.
3. A user signs on and gets an authentication code along with an ID token.
4. The authorization code and the ID token is returned to the frontend service.
5. The frontend service requests an access token from the token service.
6. The frontend service accesses the backend service with the access token.

Additional scenarios

When a server daemon needs to invoke another service, the daemon has to carry out the authentication workflow without any user interactions. In this case, the daemon needs to have its own identity and credential (such as a digital certificate) so that it can directly request for access token by itself.

When a service needs to call another service, it needs to request an access token for the second service on the user's behalf. This can be done by following the OAuth 2.0 On-Behalf-Of (draft) specification.

Azure Active Directory

Azure Active Directory is a comprehensive managed identity service that provides identity management and authentication services to your applications using standard protocols such as SAML 2.0, ws-Federation, and OpenID Connect. In addition to acting as an identity provider under the claim-based architecture, Azure Active Directory also provides other enterprise-focused services, such as a multi-factor authentication service, a centralized application access panel to manage access to SaaS applications, an application proxy that allows you to enable remote access to your on-premises services, as well as a Graph API that you can use to directly interact with Azure Active Directory objects for scenarios such as user managements and role-based access control (RBAC).

Azure Active Directory is a highly scalable and highly reliable service with redundant deployments in data centers around the globe. It handles billions of authentication requests every day. Some of the most popular SaaS applications such as Office 365 and InTune rely on Azure Active Directory for authentication.

Azure Active Directory supports all of the above authentication/authorization workflows that we've introduced in the previous section. Understanding how the participating parties interact with each other in these workflows will definitely help you to make sure all necessary configurations are in place. However, you don't have to deal with such details because most of them are abstracted away by Azure AD Authentication Library (ADAL). The library facilitates authenticate processes with both cloud and on-premises directories. And it provides additional features, such as automatically refresh expired access tokens, to further simplify the development process. In the sample scenario later in this chapter, you'll see how ADAL and Visual

Studio tooling work together to make implementing common authentication/authorization scenarios a breeze.

Azure Active Directory is offered in three tiers: free, basic and premium. The free tier covers the basic cloud-first application scenarios. The basic tier and the premium tiers are designed for enterprise usages at scale. Both tiers come with a Service Level Agreement (SLA) of 99.9%. In addition, the premium tier also provides advanced features such as machine learning-based security and usage reports, and alerting and multi-factor authentication. For a detailed comparison of feature sets provided by these tiers, please refer to: *http://azure.microsoft.com/ en-us/pricing/details/active-directory/*.

Differences between on-premises AD and Azure Active Directory

Azure Active Directory and on-premises Active Directory Domain Services (AD DS) share lots of similarities. They both provide authentication and authorization services. They both allow managing directory objects such as users and groups. And they both provide a Single Sign-On (SSO) experience to enterprise users. Moreover, you can leverage tools such as Azure AD Connect to synchronize users and groups between your on-premises directories and your cloud-based directories. It's important, however, to realize that there are some key differences between the two.

First, they are designed for different scopes, and they operate in different environments. An on-premises Active Directory is designed to secure on-premises resources. And it usually works within local networks of a single enterprise. Azure Active Directory is designed to protect cloud-based resources. It's a multi-tenant system that works over the Internet.

Second, they use different protocols. On-premises Active Directory uses protocols such as Kerberos and LDAP, while Azure Active Directory uses Internet-oriented protocols such as SAML 2.0, ws-Federation, OpenID Connect, and RESTful Graph API.

Third, although their functionalities overlap in terms of authentication and authorization, they have mutually exclusive features. For instance, only on-premises Active Directory supports constructs such as forests, domains, and organization units. And only Azure Active Directory natively provides features such as Application Access Panel and RESTful interfaces.

On-premises AD and Azure Active Directory working together

Obviously, Azure Active Directory can operate on its own to provide a pure cloud-based identity management solution, which is ideal for companies who have most of their resources on cloud. On the other hand, Azure Active Directory can also be configured as an extension to the existing enterprise on-premises Active Directory. In the second case, an enterprise can project part of its directory to the cloud so that users can use the same set of credentials to access both on-premises resources and cloud resources.

The way to connect Azure Active Directory to Windows Server Active Directory is to use Azure AD Connect. The service provides a downloadable component that you can install on your on-premises Windows Server. And then, you can configure fine-grained object synchronization between your on-premises directories and your cloud-based directories.

Another way to leverage Windows Server AD for cloud application authentication is to use Active Directory Federation Service (ADFS), which we'll discuss in more details in the next skill.

Sample scenario with Azure Active Directory Authentication and Visual Studio

Here we walk you through a simple scenario that implements the basic authentication/ authorization workflow shown in Figure 4-2 to help you to familiarize yourself with common development processes with Azure Active Directory. In this sample scenario, we'll create a simple ASP.NET application and then use Azure Active Directory to provide authentication.

Prerequisites

The following items are needed before following along with the scenario:

- Visual Studio 2015 or 2017 with Azure SDK for .NET 3.0.1 or above.
- An active Microsoft Azure subscription.

Part 1: Provision an Azure Active Directory tenant and a user

1. Sign on to the Microsoft Azure management portal.
2. Click on New, Security + Identity, Azure Active Directory.
3. On the Create directory blade, enter an organization name to identify your directory tenant and the initial domain name. The final domain name of your tenant will be the name you enter plus the onmicrosoft.com postfix. In this example, we use ref70534. onmicrosoft.com, but you'll need a different domain name. Then, pick your country or region, and click on the Create button to continue. This takes a minute. Once the directory is provisioned, a message like Figure 4-4 will appear. Click on the link to manage your new directory tenant.

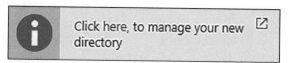

FIGURE 4-4 Directory creation message

4. This takes you to a brand new Azure tenant. If you observe the upper-right corner of your portal, you'll notice that you are in a different tenant now, as shown in Figure 4-5. To switch to a different tenant, click on your email and select the tenant in the drop-down list.

FIGURE 4-5 AAD tenant display on portal

5. Click on the Add A User Link on the Quick tasks tile.

6. On the user blade, enter the user's full name in the Name field. Then, enter a user name for the user in the format of <username>@<AAD tenant>.onmicrosoft.com, for example, haishi@ref70534.onmicrosoft.com. Change the user's Directory role to Global Administrator.

7. Check the Show Password checkbox, copy down the one-time password, and then click on the Create button to create the user.

8. Start a new InPrivate browser window (or incognito window in Chrome). Sign on to the portal again with the new user. You'll be prompted to set a new password, which you must do to complete the sign-on process. You should see a Welcome To Microsoft Azure message. Click on the Maybe Later button to discard the message to continue to the management portal. Close the InPrivate view when you are done.

Part 2: Create and secure an ASP.NET application

1. Launch Visual Studio. Create a new ASP.NET Web Application (.NET Framework).

2. On the New ASP.NET Web Application dialog, select the MVC template, and then click on the Change Authentication button, as shown in Figure 4-6.

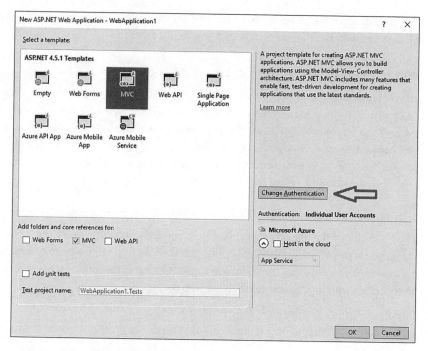

FIGURE 4-6 New ASP.NET Web Application dialog

3. On the Change Authentication dialog, pick the Work And School Accounts option. Then, enter your Azure SD tenant domain name (such as ref70534.onmicrosoft.com). Optionally, you can check the Read Directory Data checkbox to allow the reading and writing of directory data. Click on the OK button to continue, as shown in Figure 4-7.

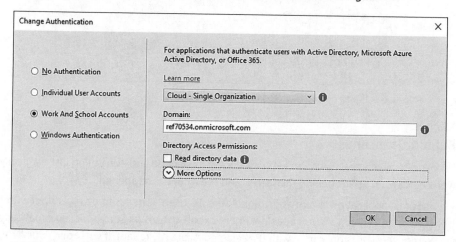

FIGURE 4-7 New ASP.NET Web Application dialog

4. A browser dialog will pop up to ask you to sign on to your Azure Active Directory tenant. Sign on using the user credential that you've just created.

> **NOTE** **USER CREDENTIAL VALIDATION FAILED ERROR**
>
> If you see a "User credential validation failed" error but are certain you user is a global administrator, you should do the following to resolve this issue: 1) Cancel the creation wizard and return to Visual Studio IDE. 2) Select File, Account Settings menu. 3) Under All Accounts section, remove the tenant user account. If you see any warnings with any of the account, either re-authenticate or remove the account. Once all account warnings are resolved, repeat the above steps.

5. Close all of your browser instances. Follow the wizard to complete project creation.

6. Press F5 to launch the application in browser. If you are using Edge, you'll see a This Site Is Not Secure error. Click on the Details link, and then click on the Go on to the webpage to continue. If you are using other browsers, you need to follow similar steps to ignore the certificate warning and continue to the web page.

7. You'll be prompted to sign on. Sign on using the user credential in this exercise.

8. You'll see a consent page for your application to read user profiles. Click on the Accept button to continue.

9. After signing in, you should see your user name displayed on the web page, as shown in Figure 4-8.

FIGURE 4-8 Display of authenticated user name

Behind the scenes

It looks almost magical. You didn't enter a single line of code and everything just magically worked. Now, let's peek behind the scenes and see what has happened.

- For an application to authentication Azure AD users, it needs to be registered with the Azure AD tenant. As you enable authentication, the Visual Studio tool automatically registers your application with the selected Azure AD tenant. If you open your Azure AD tenant in the management portal and examine the App Registrations list, you'll see your web application listed there. Once an application is registered, it's assigned a unique

Application ID, which is used to identify the application within the Azure Active Directory tenant.

- OWIN middleware (Open Web Interface for .NET) is configured to use OpenId Connect authentication—see the ConfigureAuth method in the Startup class. A few NuGet packages, including Microsoft.Owin.Security.OpenIdConnect, Microsoft.Owin.Security.Cookies and Microsoft.Owin.Host.SystemWeb, are added to the project. You'll learn about OWIN in more details in the next section.

- The HomeController class is annotated with a [Authorize] attribute to request users to authenticate before accessing the corresponding pages.

- Once a security token is received, user-related claims are transmitted to the ClaimPrincipal.Current security principal object. The claims are also made available to WebPageRenderingBase.User, which is used in the _LoginPartial.cshtml page to display the user name.

Authentication frameworks

ASP.NET and ASP.NET Core use different authentication frameworks. ASP.NET 5 uses OWIN authentication middleware. ASP.NET Core, on the other hand, uses ASP.NET Core Identity. This section provides a brief introduction to both frameworks.

Open Web Interface for .NET (OWIN) and authentication middleware

OWIN is an open specification that defines an abstraction layer between web applications and web servers. The primary goal of OWIN is to decouple web applications and web servers to stimulate growth of an open source ecosystem for web modules, web hosts, and web development tools.

Katana is Microsoft's implementation of OWIN. It uses a layered architecture that consists of four layers: host, server, middleware and application.

- **Host**   Is responsible of management of the underlying process, selection of the server, and construction of OWIN pipelines.

- **Server**   Manages the application processes. It listens to requests and sends them through an OWIN pipeline defined by the user.

- **Middleware**   Contains layers of components that are chained together into a pipeline. Requests flow through this pipeline before they reach the application. OWIN defines a very simple interface between layers called the application delegate or AppFunc, which takes an IDirectory<string, object> environment and returns a Task. Middleware is where extensions and crosscutting components can be introduced, including authentication middleware.

  ASP.NET uses a cookie authentication middleware for authentication. The middle tier issues cookies and validates cookies on subsequent requests. Katana ships a number of cookie authentication middleware for a number of external identity providers that support the OAuth2 or OpenID protocol, including Microsoft Account, Yahoo!,

Facebook and Google. In addition, ASP.NET templates provide necessary UI and controller constructs for you to choose which external Identity Provider to use.

- **Application** Is where the application logic is implemented. The application is mostly OWIN unware, except for the startup code that sets ups OWIN pipelines based on the application's requirements.

ASP.NET Core Identity

ASP.NET Core Identity is a membership system that allows built-in support for user management and authentication as well as authentication with external Identity Providers such as Facebook, Google, Twitter, Microsoft Account and more. If you choose the built-in user management, you need to configure a user store such as a SQL Server database. If you choose to use external Identity Providers, you need to configure your application to use the OAuth 2.0 protocol to work with selected Identity Provider.

Microsoft Graph API

Microsoft Graph API is a unified graph API that allows you to interact with the data of millions of users in the Microsoft cloud. You can not only access user profiles (with consent), but you can also access various Office 365 resources such as calendars and OneDrive files, all through a single endpoint at *https://graph.microsoft.com*.

> **NOTE   AZURE AD GRAPH API**
>
> Azure AD Graph API provides a REST API endpoint for you to interact with directory data and objects. It's strongly recommended to use Microsoft Graph API instead. Microsoft Graph API is expected to support all functionality that Azure AD Graph API offers.

A lap around Graph Explorer

The easiest way to get acquainted with Microsoft Graph API is to use Graph Explorer (*https://developer.microsoft.com/en-us/graph/graph-explorer*). In the following exercise, you'll give it a try.

1. Navigate to Graph Explorer at *https://developer.microsoft.com/en-us/graph/graph-explorer.*

2. Click on the Sign In With Microsoft button on the left to sign on using the user credential you've created in the previous exercise.

3. Click on the My Profile query under the Sample Queries section. This sends a GET request to *https://graph.microsoft.com/v1.0/me/.* This simple query returns the profile of the authenticated user. In this environment, it returns the following JSON result:

```
{
    "@odata.context":
"https://graph.microsoft.com/v1.0/$metadata#users/$entity",
    "id": "119df…",
```

```
    "businessPhones": [],
    "displayName": "haishi",
    "givenName": null,
    "jobTitle": null,
    "mail": null,
    "mobilePhone": null,
    "officeLocation": null,
    "preferredLanguage": null,
    "surname": null,
    "userPrincipalName": haishi@ref70534.onmicrosoft.com
}
```

4. Now, try a different query that returns your assigned roles. To do so, send a GET request to *https://graph.microsoft.com/v1.0/me/memberOf*. Querying role membership requires an administrator's consent. To grant yourself sufficient access rights, click on the Modify Permissions link to the left of the page. On the Modify Permissions dialog, make sure the Group Read All checkbox and User ReadAll checkbox are checked. This is a right that needs administrator consensus, so click on the Access To Your Entire Organization link instead of the Modify Permissions button, as shown in Figure 4-9.

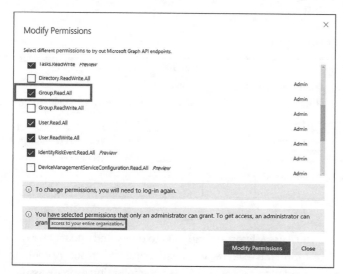

FIGURE 4-9 Modify Permissions dialog

5. Once you click on the Access To Your Entire Organization link, you'll be prompted to log on again. Log in as an administrator. After you log in, return to the explorer page and issue the GET request to *https://graph.microsoft.com/v1.0/me/memberOf*. This query should return something like the following:

```
{
    "@odata.context": "https://graph.microsoft.com/v1.0/$metadata#directoryO
bjects",
    "value": [
        {
            "@odata.type": "#microsoft.graph.directoryRole",
```

```
                "id": "60dbf…",
                "deletedDateTime": null,
                "description": "Company Administrator role has full access…",
                "displayName": "Company Administrator",
                "roleTemplateId": "62e90..."
            }
        ]
    }
```

Querying Office 365 data

You can use Microsoft Graph to query and update various Office 365 data, including Excel workbooks, OneDrive files, OneNote resources, Outlook mails (including attachments), Outlook calendar, and SharePoint sites.

For example, to query emails from hbai@microsoft.com, use query: *https://graph.microsoft.com/v1.0/me/messages?$filter=from/emailAddress/address eq 'hbai@microsoft.com'*. Microsoft Graph API uses query parameters that are compatible with the OData V4 query language. Table 4-1 shows sample usages of some of the common parameters (the *https://graph.microsoft.com/v1.0/* prefix is omitted).

TABLE 4-1 Sample Microsoft Graph API parameters

Parameter	Function	Sample
$count	To include a count of items	contacts?$count=true
$expand	Expand child item	drive/root?expand=children($selected=id,name)
$orderby	Sort items by a field	users?orderby=displayName
$skip	Skip a number of items	me/events?orderby=createdDateTime&skip=20
$skipToken	To request more data pages	users?orderby=displayName&skiptoken=.....
$top	Specify maximum number of items to return	me/messages?top=5

In the following exercise, you'll use Microsoft Graph API to query and update an Excel workbook on your OneDrive. To perform this exercise, you need to use a Microsoft Account that has an Excel workbook already uploaded to a OneDrive folder. The following exercise assumes you have a workbook named Testbook.xslx under your OneDrive folder. The workbook contains one sheet, Sheet1, with a few cells, as shown in Table 4-2.

TABLE 4-2 Sample Excel worksheet

	A	B
1	Price	100.0
2	Quantity	3
3	Total	=B1 * B2

1. Sign on to Graph Explorer.

2. Send query: GET *https://graph.microsoft.com/v1.0/me/drive/root:/Testbook.xlsx*. This returns metadata of the workbook. You'll need the id property for next steps.

3. Next, create an operation session. You can create a session in either persistence mode or non-persistence mode. If you choose the latter, all your edits go into a temporary file and will be discarded as the session terminates. In this exercise, you'll use a persistence session. To create the session, send a POST request to: *https://graph.microsoft.com/v1.0/me/drive/items/{id}/workbook/createSession*, with a JSON payload:

   ```
   {"persistChanges": true}
   ```

4. Once you have the session created, you can start to operate on the workbook. First, query the B3 cell from the default worksheet Sheet1 with a GET request:

   ```
   https://graph.microsoft.com/v1.0/me/drive/items/{id}/workbook/
   worksheets('Sheet1')/range(address='B2')
   ```

5. The above query returns a complex JSON response that contains every single detail about the cell, among which you can see the value of the cell.

   ```
   "values": [
           [
               3
           ]
       ],
       "valueTypes": [
           [
               "Double"
           ]
       ]
   ```

6. To update the cell, send a PATCH request to *https://graph.microsoft.com/v1.0/me/drive/items/{id}/workbook/worksheets('Sheet1')/range(address='B2')* with the following JSON payload:

   ```
   {
       "values": [
           [
               5
           ]
       ]
   }
   ```

7. Now the cell is updated, and formulas on the workbook are reevaluated. If you query cell B3 now (by sending another GET request to address *https://graph.microsoft.com/v1.0/me/drive/items/{id}/workbook/worksheets('Sheet1')/range(address='B3')*), you should get 500, which is the updated amount value.

Power of Graph

The greatest power of Microsoft Graph is to the ability to link related information. For example, you can use an email API to get the sender of an email and then use the calendar API to set up a follow-up meeting with her. You can also find out her organizational chart and share a document on OneDrive with the group. All of these navigations can happen within your application's context, allowing your application to take advantage of the rich Office 365 features.

Microsoft also provides intelligent, dynamic connections. For example, you can find out the most relevant documents a user viewed or accessed. You can also query how a user shares her contents with others to estimate her level of collaboration with others.

In addition to API queries, Microsoft Graph also supports web hooks that can be used to send notifications to clients on events such as new messages, contact changes and file share changes.

Secure resources by using hybrid identities

As large enterprises transit to the cloud era, they are facing the practical challenge of making their existing on-premises resources and their new cloud resources to seamlessly work together. And the key to achieve this goal is to provide a Single Sign-On (SSO) experience across on-premises resources and cloud resources.

As we've introduced in the previous skill, you can make Azure Active Directory and your on-premises AD work together using directory sync. In this skill, we'll dig more into the implementation details.

Before discussing directory synchronization options, let's first review Active Directory Federation Service (ADFS), which has been used to extend the reach of on-premises credentials.

Active Directory Federation Service (ADFS)

Active Directory Federation Service (ADFS) has been long existed before Azure Active Directory, and it has been a proven way to extend the reach of on-premises Active Directories to external network. ADFS is Microsoft's implementation of the ws-Federation Passive Requestor Profile protocol. It allows cloud-based applications to leverage on-premises AD user credentials to authenticate by using standard protocols and SAML tokens.

You can continue to use ADFS as part of your hybrid identity solutions. Consider using directory synchronization to bring your directory objects into Azure Active Directory if you'd like to have a centralized management plane and to take advantage of the new monitoring, analysis, and self-service capabilities provided by Azure Active Directory.

Directory synchronization

Historically, there have been several synchronization solutions provided by Azure Active Directory, including DirSync, Azure Active Directory Sync (AAD Sync), and FIM + Azure Active Directory Connector. At the time when this text is written, the three engines have been replaced by a new Azure AD Connect.

To conceptually understand directory sync, we need to understand three concepts: Connector Space, metaverse and synchronization rules.

- **Connector Space**   Each participating directory is connected to a Connector Space, which caches shadow copy of objects that contain a subset of actual directory objects. Directory object operations, such as additions, deletions and modifications are written to connector spaces before they are synchronized with the actual directories.

- **Metaverse**   A metaverse sits at the center of a directory sync, and it holds a consolidated view of all the objects being synchronized.

- **Synchronization rules**   Synchronization rules define how attributes flow when certain criteria are met. You use synchronization rules to control how objects are synced and optionally transformed across multiple directories.

Figure 4-10 shows a simplified view of a directory sync with two participating directories.

FIGURE 4-10 Directory sync

During synchronization, you can choose if hashes of user passwords are synced as well. If the password hashes are synced, authentications can be carried out by the target directory without involvements of the original directory. Otherwise, the actual authentication operations are passed back to the original directory. For instance, when you sync an on-premises Active Directory with Azure Active Directory, if password hashes are synced, authentications are carried out by Azure Active Directory. Otherwise, the authentication operations are passed back to the on-premises directory.

Azure AD Connect

Azure AD Connect integrates your on-premises directories with Azure AD. By bridging the identities, you can provide single sign-on experience to your users when they use on-premises applications, cloud services, and Office 365 at the same time.

Azure AD Connect has three components: Azure AD Connect Sync, optional ADFS, and Azure AD Connect Health. Figure 4-11 shows how Azure AD Connect components interact with each other and with other participants.

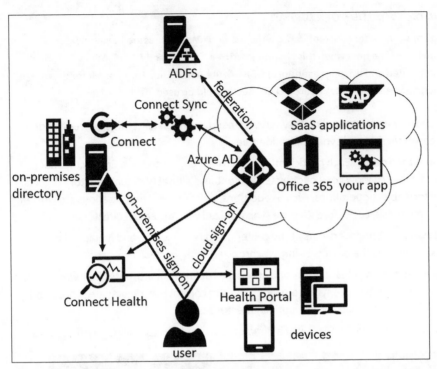

ADFS

Connect Sync

Connect

federation

SaaS applications

Azure AD

on-premises
directory

Office 365 your app

on-premises sign on

cloud sign-off

Connect Health

Health Portal

user

devices

FIGURE 4-11 Azure AD Connect components

Azure AD Connect Sync

Azure AD Connect Sync is the main component of Azure AD Connect. It handles all of the
identity synchronization operations. By default, all users, contacts, groups and Windows 10
computers are synchronized. However, you can set up filters to sync objects based on domains,
OUs, or attributes.

Password hashes can be synced between your on-premises directory and your Azure AD
tenant, with the on-premises directory used as the authority. You can also allow passwords to
be updated on the cloud and written back to the on-premises directory.

Azure AD Connect and ADFS

Azure AD Connect allows you to configure federation between your Azure AD tenant and your on-premises directory via ADFS. With federated sign-in, enterprise users can use their on-premises credentials to sign on to Azure AD-based services. And while they are on the corporate network, they don't need to enter their passwords again.

EXAM TIP

Hybrid identity is one of the commonly asked questions in the exam. You should focus on the scenarios it enables, especially in the scenarios where some services are running on Azure, while some legacy services need to remain in on-premises datacenters. In such cases, hybrid identities can be used to provide single sign-on experience and to maintain single source of password. Configuring end-to-end directory sync scenario requires quite a few steps, so it's a task that is rarely carried out. It's useful to go through a basic scenario to understand how the components work together. However, it's not necessary to consider all customization and advanced configuration scenarios. For example, information on "How to make your ADFS deployment highly available" is more useful than "What Azure CLI commands to use to create a highly available ADFS deployment."

You can configure Azure AD Connect to work with existing ADFS deployments, or you can set up new ADFS deployments on Azure. To ensure high availability, you should set up an ADFS farm instead of a single-instance ADFS deployment.

Azure AD Connect Health

Azure AD Connect Health monitors your on-premises identity infrastructure as well as identity synchronization status. It helps you to maintain your key identity infrastructure components in working states to provide continuous authentication service to your applications.

Information collected by Azure AD Connect Health is displayed on an Azure AD Connect Health Portal (*https://aka.ms/aadconnecthealth*). You can view and respond to warnings and errors in various areas such as Azure Active Directory Connect (Sync), Active Directory Federation Services, Azure Directory Domain Services, and agent configurations, as shown in Figure 4-12.

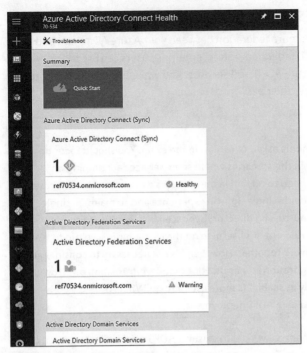

FIGURE 4-12 Azure Active Directory Connect Health

Scenario: Azure AD Connect with Express installation

In this scenario, you'll implement a hybrid identity solution that allows enterprise users to use their on-premises credentials to sign on to cloud services. The scenario assumes you already have an on-premises directory as well as an Azure AD tenant configured.

PART 1: ENABLE CUSTOM DOMAIN NAME ON AZURE AD TENANT

Before you can set up Azure AD Connect to sync to an Azure AD tenant, you are requested to apply a custom domain to your AD tenant.

1. On your Azure AD tenant blade, click on the Domain names link.

2. In the domain list blade, click on the +Add domain name link.

3. On the Domain name blade, enter a domain name that you own, because you'll be requested to add a TXT record with your domain registrar using the provided information. After you create the required TXT record, click on the Verify button to verify the domain (DNS records may take up to 72 hours to propagate).

4. Once your domain is successfully verified, you can see the Download Azure AD Connect link on the domain blade, as shown in Figure 4-13.

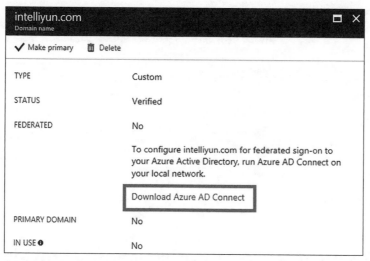

FIGURE 4-13 Domain blade

PART 2: INSTALL AND CONFIGURE AZURE AD CONNECT

1. On an on-premises member server, download Azure AD Connect.

2. On the Welcome to Azure AD Connect screen, check the I Agree To The License Terms And Privacy Notice checkbox, and click on the Continue button.

3. On the Express Settings screen, click on the Use express settings button.

4. You'll be prompted to enter your Azure AD credential. You should provide a user credential who is a Global Administrator of your tenant. Then, click on the Next button to continue.

5. Then, on the Connect to AD DS screen, you need to provide the credential of an Enterprise Administrator for your Active Directory Domain Services. Provide the credential, and click on the Next button.

6. On the Azure AD sign-in configuration screen, click on the Next button to continue.

7. On the last screen, click on the Install button.

8. Once the installation finishes, click on the Exit button to close the wizard.

PART 3: VERIFY USER ACCOUNT SYNC

1. Return to the Azure management portal.

2. Open your Azure AD tenant's blade. Then, click on the Users and groups link.

3. Create a new domain user on your on-premises directory.

4. Once the directories are synced, you should see the users under the All Users blade of your Azure AD tenant. Figure 4-14 shows that a new domain user, He Chen, which has been synced from the on-premises directory to Azure AD tenant.

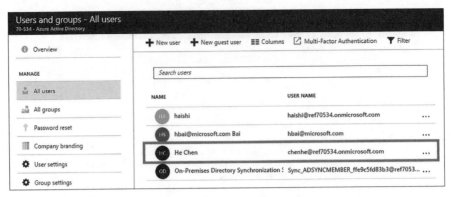

FIGURE 4-14 Synced users

Skill 4.2: Secure resources by using identity providers

An identity provider establishes a circle of trust. Applications join the circle by registering with the identity provider. All of the user accounts from the identity provider will be able to access these applications by authenticating with the identity provider. However, this model doesn't always work.

In some cases, you may want to grant users from a different identity provider to access your applications. For example, you may want a user with a valid Google account to access your application. In this case, the user identity is from a different identity provider; hence, it's not known to your Azure AD tenant. How can you allow that user to access your applications?

A B2B scenario is even more challenging. For example, Company A is using a consulting Company B to collaborate on some project. Company A would like to allow users from its own company, as well as a group of users from Company B, to access the project resources. How do you efficiently manage accesses from many different identity providers?

> **This section covers how to:**
> - Design solutions that use external or consumer identity providers such as Microsoft account, Facebook, Google, and Yahoo
> - Determine when to use Azure AD B2C and Azure AD B2B
> - Design mobile apps using AAD B2C or AAD B2B

Sample scenario with external Identity Provider and ASP.NET Core

This sample scenario walks you through the steps of configuring an ASP.NET Core application to use Microsoft Account as the Identity Provider. This sample uses the plain Azure AD capabilities. Later in this skill, you'll learn how to achieve the scenario using Azure B2C.

Part 1: Create an ASP.NET Core application

1. Launch Visual Studio 2015 or 2017, and create a new ASP.NET Core Web Application (.NET Framework) using the Web Application template.

2. On the New ASP.NET Core Web Application (.NET Framework) dialog, click on the Change Authentication button.

3. On the Change Authentication dialog, select the Individual User Accounts option and click on the OK button.

4. Back to the New ASP.NET Core Web Application (.NET Framework) dialog, click on the OK button to create the application.

5. Next, you'll enable SSL for your application. Although not all Identity Providers mandate SSL, it's a good practice to communicate with Identity Providers with SSL as some sensitive information will be passed over the wire. Open your project Properties window, click on the Debug link in the left pane, and check the Enable SSL checkbox.

6. Copy the URL that appears to the right of the checkbox (using the Copy link) and paste it into the App URL text box.

7. Edit Startup.cs and modify the `services.AddMvc();` line in the ConfigureServices method as the following. Please note the SSLPort should match with your SSL settings in the above step.

```
services.AddMvc(options =>
{
    options.SslPort = 44351;
    options.Filters.Add(new RequireHttpsAttribute ());
});
```

8. Save your project.

Part 2: Configure Microsoft Account authentication

1. Sign on to *https://apps.dev.microsoft.com*.

2. On your Application Registration Portal, click on the Add An App button under the Converged Applications section.

3. On the Register Your Application page, enter an application name, such as MyTest, and click on the Create button to register your application.

4. On your application's registration page, click on the Add Platform button. And then, click on the Web icon on the Add Platform dialog. This adds a Web card into the Platforms section. Enter a Redirect URL in the format of https://<your app URL>/signin-microsoft, and a Logout URL in the format of https://<your app URL>/end-session, as shown in Figure 4-15. Click on the Add URL button to add the URL.

5. Set your application's home URL under the Profile section.

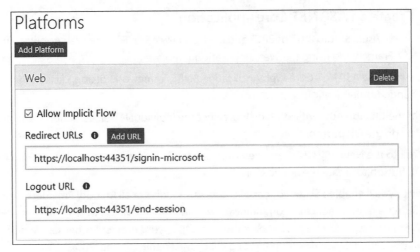

FIGURE 4-15 Platforms section on application registration page

6. Click on the Save button at the bottom of the screen to save changes.

7. Record the Application Id displayed on the page.

8. Click on the Generate New Password button in the Application Secrets section to generate a new password.

9. On the New Password Generated dialog, copy the password, and click on the OK button to discard the dialog box. Note that this is the only time the password is displayed. So please make sure the password is copied before you discard the dialog box.

Part 3: Use the Secret Manager tool

To work with an external Identity Provider, you need to configure your registered application ID and application secret with your application. Obviously, it's not a good idea to save such configurations in your code. Secret Manager tool is a development-time tool that can read and write secrets outside your source code tree. In this part of the exercise, you'll use the Secret Manager tool to store your application id and password.

> **NOTE SECRET MANAGEMENT IN PRODUCTION ENVIRONMENT**
>
> It's recommended to use Azure Key Vault to manage your application secrets and certificates for production environments.

1. Open a Command Prompt window and navigate to your project working folder.

2. Use the following commands to store your application ID and password:

```
dotnet user-secrets set Authentication:Microsoft:ClientId <application id>
dotnet user-secrets set Authentication:Microsoft:ClientSecret <generated password>
```

Part 4: Enable Microsoft Account middleware

1. Add a reference to the Microsoft.AspNetCore.Authentication.MicrosoftAccont NuGet package version 1.1.2. Use 2.0 versions only if your ASP.NET Core project is using .NET Core 2.0 as well.

2. Modify the Configure method in Startup.cs to add the Microsoft Account middleware. Insert the following line before the app.UseMvc() method call.

```
app.UseMicrosoftAccountAuthentication(new MicrosoftAccountOptions()
{
    ClientId = Configuration["Authentication:Microsoft:ClientId"],
    ClientSecret = Configuration["Authentication:Microsoft:ClientSecret"]
});
```

3. Press Ctrl+F5 (instead of F5) to launch the application without debugging.

4. Once the home page loads (ignoring certificate warnings as before), click on the Log In link at the upper-right corner of the page. Then, on the log in page, click on the Microsoft button, as shown in Figure 4-16.

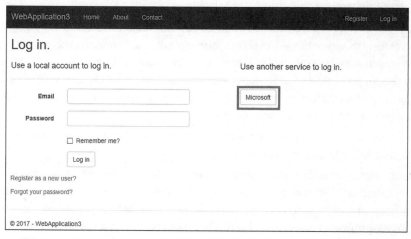

FIGURE 4-16 Login page

5. Follow the log in process and consensus process to log in to the application. If you see an error screen saying, A Database Operation Failed While Processing The Request, click on the Apply Migrations button to migrate your local user store database and then refresh the page.

6. You should be logged in by now. Optionally, you can also register the user account with your local user store.

Azure B2C

Azure B2C is an identity management solution for your applications. It allows users from other identity providers to authenticate and access your applications. It supports social accounts such as Microsoft Account, Google, Facebook, LinkedIn, Amazon, Weibo, QQ, WeChat, and Twitter. It also supports enterprise accounts through standard protocols such as OpenID and SAML. It provides a local account management capability as well so that your users can register accounts directly in your local user account store.

Azure B2C supports not only web applications and Web APIs but also mobile and desktop applications on iOS, Android, and Windows.

Azure B2C supports customizable polices that control various aspects of the authentication process, including look and feel of sign-in pages, attributes (or claims) to be collected during sign-up process, and allowed account types. You can also control how profiles and passwords are managed via policies. For example, Azure B2C supports self-service password reset. You can set up a password reset police that allows user to reset her password using an email address.

To use Azure B2C, you need to create a new Azure Active Directory B2C tenant and then manage your applications and identity providers in the tenant. If you plan to use your B2C tenant for production applications, you'll also need to link your Azure AD B2C tenant to your Azure subscription.

Azure B2B

Azure AD B2B enables your organization to work with other organizations of various sizes safely and securely. As long as your organization has an Azure AD tenant, you can set up a B2B relationship with your partners who may or may not be using Azure AD. If your partner is using Azure AD, a federation between the two tenants is established, and users from both tenants will be able to access resources from each other's tenant based on granted accesses. If your partner doesn't have an Azure AD tenant, Azure AD B2B creates a shadow tenant as an umbrella for your partner's user accounts and then establishes the federation relationship between the two tenants.

Azure B2B is a capability, not a product. You set up the federation with other tenants by simply inviting users from other tenants and identity providers to be a guest user of your Azure AD tenant. For example, to invite a live.com user to join your tenant, follow these steps:

1. Open your Azure AD tenant blade. Then, click on the Users And Groups link.

2. On the Users And Groups blade, click on the All Users link.

3. Click on the +New guest user link.

4. On the Invite A Guest Blade, enter the email you want to invite and an option message. And then, click on the Invite button to set the invite.

5. Once the invitee receives the invitation email (as shown in Figure 4-17), she can click on the Get Started button to accept the invite.

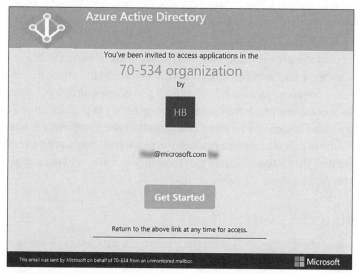

FIGURE 4-17 Invitation email

6. Now the invited user can access applications that have granted access to the user.

Skill 4.3: Design a data security solution

Microsoft is committed to ensuring the security of customer data. Microsoft Azure provides multiple layers of security and governance technologies, rigid compliance policies, and hardened operational practices to ensure data integrity and privacy, while maintaining data availability for rightful users.

Data protection

Data protection involves protecting data at-rest, in-transit, and in-use. At-rest data refers to the data being stored on physical media. In-transit data refers to the data being transmitted between two components, such as between two networks, between a service and a client, and between two services. In-use data refers to the dynamic data used in computation, such as CPU cache and memory state.

As a leading cloud platform provider, Microsoft has heavily invested in Azure data centers to make sure they provide the best protections over customer data. At the physical level, Azure datacenters deploy ISO-compliant safeguards such as 24/7 surveillance, smartcard access, and key-locked racks. At a process level, rigorous operation processes are in place to ensure the datacenters are fully audited and can be accessed only by authorized personnel. For example, a just-in-time policy ensures that Microsoft personnel don't have persistent access to customer data. They may be granted just-in-time accesses to resolve urgent issues, and the accesses are revoked as soon as the issue is closed.

Data encryption

Data encryption is one of the most important methods to protect data, especially data-at-rest. Azure has three main data repositories: Azure Storage services, SQL Database, and Azure Active Directory. Azure provides different encryption supports for these repositories.

Azure Storage

Azure Storage is a scalable, durable, and highly available data storage service provided by Azure. It offers blob storage for storing any type of text or binary data, table storage as a NoSQL key-value data store, and queue storage for reliable messaging between two components. In addition, it also provides file storage that can be shared by multiple applications and services using the SMB 2.1 protocol.

Azure Storage is one of the fundamental services of Azure. It provides data storage capability for many other Azure services. For instance, the OS disks and data disks used by Azure Virtual Machines are based on Azure Blob storage.

Azure provides out-of-box encryption support on Azure Storage services. Azure also allows you to bring your own data encryption keys instead of using Azure managed keys.

At an application level, you can use .NET cryptography API or cryptography libraries provided by other programming languages. You can also encrypt data using SDKs provided by on-premises Active Directory Right Management Services (AD RMS) or Azure Right Management Services (RMS).

At a platform level, you can leverage Azure StorSimple service, which provides primary storage, archive, and disaster recovery. When configuring StorSimple, you can specify a data-at-rest encryption key for data encryption. StorSimple uses AES-256 with Cipher Block Chaining (CBC), which is the strongest commercially available encryption. Encryption keys can be managed using your own Key Management System (KMS) or Azure Key Vault service, which we'll introduce later in this section.

At a system level, you can leverage Windows features such as Encrypting File System (EFS), Azure Disk Encryption that supports BitLocker for Windows, and DM-Crypt for Linux, or third-party volume-level encryption to protect the data on your guest OS disks and data disks (VHDs). System-level encryptions are often transparent to the OS and the applications, so no application changes are needed to adopt such protections.

Microsoft Azure provides an Import/Export service that allows you to transmit a large amount of data to Azure by shipping physical data disks. BitLocker is mandatory when you use the service. For data import, you need to enable BitLocker before you send the data disks to Azure. The BitLocker key will be communicated separately. For exports, you need to send empty disks to Azure, and the service will load the data onto these disks and then encrypt the data before shipping the drives back to you.

SQL Database

You have two options to run SQL Server databases on Azure. First, you can use Azure SQL Database, which is a PaaS service provided by Azure that gives you hosted SQL database instances. Because the database instances are managed by Azure, you don't need to worry about database availability or low-level data protection, as Azure takes care that for you. On the other hand, you can set up your own SQL Server instances on top of Azure Virtual Machines. In this case, you own every aspect of the database instances, including ensure high availability of database instances as well as implementing appropriate data protection solutions. For both options, you can configure Transparent Data Encryption and Column-Level Encryption to configure at-rest data encryptions.

SQL Server Transparent Data Encryption (TDE) provides protections over at-rest data by performing real-time I/O encryption and decryption of the data and log files. TDE allows developers to encrypt data by using AES and 3DES encryption algorithms without application changes. TDE provides protection over physical or logical breaches when underlying file systems are compromised and data files are exposed.

For a more granular encryption, SQL Server Column-Level Encryption (CLE) can be used. CLE ensures that data remains encrypted until it's used. When a data page is loaded in memory, sensitive data is decrypted only when SQL Server is processing it. However, using CLE has a couple of downsides. First, applications need to be changed to invoke encryption/decryption. Second, there can be performance impacts, not only because of the extra processing time but also because of the negative effects on query optimizations.

By default, SQL Server keeps encryption keys in its master database. However, SQL Server also provides an extensible key management (EKM) provider architecture to delegate key management to an independent key management service (KMS) such as Azure Key Vault.

Access Control

Access Control ensures that data is accessed only by authorized users. Azure employs multiple levels of access controls over customer data.

Azure Storage

First of all, customer data is segmented by Azure subscriptions so that data from one customer can't be intentionally or accidentally accessed by another customer. Within a subscription, Azure Storage provides container-level and blob-level access controls for Blob storage, and table-level and row-level access controls for Table storage. Each Azure storage account has two associated keys: a primary key and a secondary key. Having two keys allows you to perform planned and unplanned (such as when the primary key is comprised) key rotations as needed.

In addition, Azure Storage also supports URL-based access with Shared Access Signatures (SAS). SAS allows you to grant direct access to storage entities (blobs, queues, tables, or table rows) with a specified set of permissions during a specified time window. For example, when you share a file, instead of sharing your storage account key, you can create a SAS signature with read privilege that allows users to read the specific file within a time window. You don't need to revoke the access because the SAS address automatically becomes invalid once the time window closes.

Listing 4-1 shows how to generate a SAS signature using Azure Storage Client Library for .NET. The code specifies the time window to be 4 hours (line 4 of the function) and grants read privilege (line 5). The code specifies the time window to be open at -5 minutes (line 3) to make sure the policy is active immediately, even if there were some time differences in server time because of clock drifts.

LISTING 4-1 Generating SAS signature using Azure Storage Client Library

```
string GenerateSASURL(CloudBlobContainer container, string blobName)
{
        CloudBlockBlob blob = container.GetBlockBlobReference(blobName);
        SharedAccessBlobPolicy policy = new SharedAccessBlobPolicy();
        policy.SharedAccessStartTime = DateTime.UtcNow.AddMinutes(-5);
```

```
    policy.SharedAccessExpiryTime = DateTime.UtcNow.AddHours(4);
    policy.Permissions = SharedAccessBlobPermissions.Read;
    string signature = blob.GetSharedAccessSignature(policy);
    return blob.Uri + signature;
}
```

The above code generates a URL that looks like this:

```
https://storageaccount.blob.core.windows.net/sascontainer/myfile.txt?
sv=2012-02-12&st=2013-04-12T23%3A37%3A08Z&se=2013-04-13T00%3A12%3A08Z&sr=b
&sp=rw&sig=dF2064yHtc8RusQLvkQFPItYdeOz3zR8zHsDMBi4S30%3D
```

SQL Database

Azure SQL Database uses an access security model very similar to on-premises SQL Server. Since Azure SQL Database instances are not domain-joined, you can use standard SQL authentication by user ID and password, or use Azure Active Directory authentication. For SQL Server instances running on Azure Virtual Machines, they can also authenticate using Kerberos tokens if the VMs are domain-joined.

Azure Active Directory

Azure Active Directory provides a number of built-in roles with different administrative rights. For a simple deployment, a *Global administrator* can take on all administrative responsibilities. For a more complex deployment, different administrators can be assigned to manage specific areas of the tenant. Azure Active Directory provides the following roles:

- **Global Administrator**   Has access to all administrative features. Only Global Administrators can assign other administrative roles.

- **Billing Administrator**   Can make purchases and manage subscriptions. A billing administrator also manages support tickets and monitors service consumption and health.

- **Service Administrator**   Manages requests and monitor health of designated service.

- **User Administrator**   Manages groups, user accounts, and service requests. However, a user administrator has limited capability in managing administrative accounts. For more details please see Table 4-3.

- **Password Administrator**   Can reset passwords for users and other password administrators.

- **User**   Can sign on and access directory objects when granted access. Azure Active Directory Basic tier and Premium tier also support user self-service password reset. This can be enabled by changing the Users Enabled For Password Reset option to All on the Configure page of the Azure tenant.

Table 4-3 summarizes the administrator roles and their associated permissions (data source: *http://msdn.microsoft.com/en-us/library/azure/dn468213.aspx*).

TABLE 4-3 Administrator roles and associated permissions

Permission	Billing admin	Global admin	Password admin	Service admin	User Admin
View company and user information	Yes	Yes	Yes	Yes	Yes
Manage Office support tickets	Yes	Yes	Yes	Yes	Yes
Reset user passwords	No	Yes	Yes	No	Yes[1]
Perform billing and purchasing operations for Office products	Yes	Yes	No	No	No
Create and manage user views	No	Yes	No	No	Yes
Create, edit, and delete users and groups, and manage user licenses	No	Yes	No	No	Yes[2]
Manage domains	No	Yes	No	No	No
Manage company information	No	Yes	No	No	No
Delegate administrative roles to others	No	Yes	No	No	No
Use directory synchronization	No	Yes	No	No	No

1. Yes; with limitations. He or she cannot reset passwords for billing, global, and service administrators.
2. Yes; with limitations. He or she cannot delete a global administrator or create other administrators.

Access Control in Other Azure Services

In addition to providing access control mechanisms for data storages, Azure also provides ways to control accesses to other Azure resources. This section provides a couple of examples of several different access control mechanisms that exist in Azure.

VIRTUAL NETWORK

A Network Security Group (NSG) is a subscription-level object that can be associated to one or more virtual machines in regional virtual networks. Each Azure subscription is allowed to have 100 NSG rules, and each NSG rule can contain up to 200 rules, which can be either inbound rules or outbound rules. You can apply an NSG to either a NIC associated with a virtual machine, or a virtual network subnet. When applied to a virtual machine, an NSG controls all traffic that goes in and out the virtual machine. And when applied to a virtual network, an NSG applies to all traffic going through all virtual machines on that subnet.

SERVICE BUS

Azure Service Bus provides a reliable messaging system for system integration and Internet of Things (IoT) scenarios. Service Bus supports Shared Access Signature (SAS) authentication on various Service Bus entities, such as queues, topics, and Event Hubs.

You can manage SAS keys using Azure management portal, programmatically using Service Bus client SDK, or using scripts. Figure 4-18 shows an example of configuring SAS for a Service Bus queue on Azure Management Portal. The sample shows that three SASs have been created, one for administrators with all access rights, one for receiving messages only, and the last one for sending messages only.

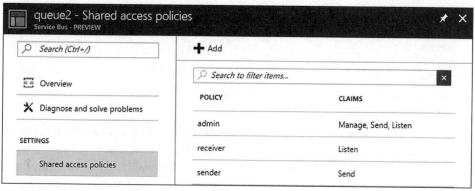

FIGURE 4-18 Service Bus shared access policies

Data reliability and disaster recovery

Cloud platforms are built on commodity hardware. With tens of thousands of servers running in a data center, hardware failures are unavoidable. A critical mission of a cloud platform is to ensure service availability regardless of these failures. And a key technique to achieve availability is to use redundancy.

In addition to built-in redundancy, Azure also provides a comprehensive set of services for backups and disaster recovery.

Data reliability

When you save your data on Azure, Azure automatically makes multiple copies of the data for redundancy. When a single copy of the data is lost, your original data can be restored from the redundant copies.

AZURE STORAGE

When a piece of data is saved to Azure Storage service, the data is replicated multiple times for availability. Azure Storage service provides the following data replication options to ensure reliable storage of data:

- **Locally Redundant Storage (LRS)** Maintains three copies of your data within a single facility in a single region. LRS protects from common hardware failures, but not from facility-wide failures.

- **Zone Redundant Storage (ZRS)** Maintains three copies of your data across two or three facilities, either within a single region or across two regions.

- **Geo Redundant Storage (GRS)** Maintains six copies of your data, with three copies residing in the primary region, and another three copies residing in a backup region that is hundreds miles away from the primary region.

- **Read-access Geo Redundant Storage (RA-GRS)**   Provides all benefits of GRS, plus allowing read access to data at the secondary region when the primary region becomes unavailable.

SQL DATABASE

When you use Azure SQL Database, you automatically take advantage of many built-in fault tolerance features of Azure SQL Database.

Each Azure SQL Database has three database replicas running at any given time. If the primary replica fails, Azure SQL Database automatically fails over to a secondary replica to ensure continuous data access. And if a replica fails, a new replica is automatically created to bring the number of replicas back to three.

In addition, Azure SQL Database provides an automatic Point in Time Restore feature, which automatically backs up your SQL database and retains the backups for seven days for Basic tier, and 35 days for both Standard tier and Premium tier. The feature is on by default, and it accumulates no additional charges, except when you use the restore capability.

Another fault tolerance feature you get automatically is Geo-restore. When backing up your databases, Azure stores the most recent daily backup of your database in a different geographical location. And in the case of a large scale outage in a region, your data can be restored within 24 hours.

If you have more aggressive recovery requirements, you can use Active geo-replication. Active geo-replication (available to Premium) provides the most rapid recovery time by keeping 4 geo-replicated live secondaries.

On top of these features, you can also manually back up your databases. First, you can create transactional consistent copies of your databases to the same or different servers in the same or different regions. Second, you can use Azure SQL Database Import and Export Service to export BACPACK files, which contain a logical copy of the schema as well as the data of a database. You can then import the file back to your database for disaster recovery.

AZURE ACTIVE DIRECTORY

Azure Active Directory is a highly available, geo-redundant service that handles billions of authenticate requests daily. It's deployed across a number of data centers around the globe, and it stores hundreds of millions objects securely in its store. These objects are saved in different partitions for scaling. And each partition has multiple replicas for high availability.

Azure Backup

Azure Backup is a simple yet powerful service that allows you to back up your files to the reliable storage on Azure. Your data is saved in Azure storage with Geo-redundancy, and the data is encrypted at-rest.

To back up your files, you need first create a Backup Vault on Azure and then deploy a Backup agent. Finally, you can configure which files or folders to be backed up and backup schedules. The following sample scenario shows you the basic steps to use Azure backup service.

1. On Microsoft Azure Management Portal, click on the More Services link at the bottom-left corner of the window.

2. Search for "recovery" and click on the star icon to the right of the Recovery Services vaults entry.

3. Click on the +Add link. Enter a name for the vault. Select the subscription and resource group you want to use and then click on the Create button.

4. Once the vault is created, click on its name in the vault list to open it.

5. Click on the +Backup link to create a new backup.

6. On the Backup goal blade, select your workload as running on on-premises, and select Files and folders to be backed up. Click on the OK button to continue. If the OK button is disabled, try to click on the info box that says Click Here To Prepare Your Infrastructure For Backup To Azure.

7. On the next blade, click on the Download button first to download your vault credentials file.

8. There are two versions of Azure Backup Agent. One for Windows Server Essentials, and one for Windows Server or Windows Clients. Click on the corresponding link to download and install the agent.

9. Follow the install wizard screens to complete the installation process. At the last step of installation, click on the **Proceed To Registration** button to continue.

10. On the *Register Server Wizard* dialog, pick your vault credential file, and then click on the **Next** button to continue.

11. Enter a passphrase, or use the **Generate Passphrase** button to generate one. Pick a folder where you want the passphrase to be saved and then click on the **Finish** button.

12. Then, you can schedule, manage, and restore from your backups using the installed agent. For instance, Figure 4-19 shows backups scheduled at 10 PM every Monday.

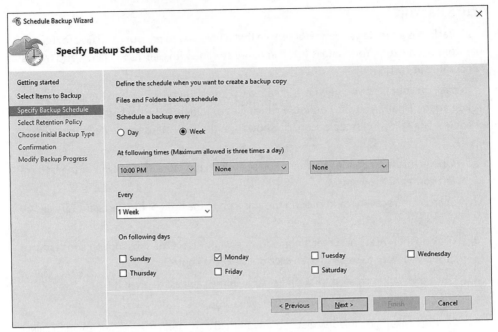

FIGURE 4-19 Service Bus shared access policies

You can also use the agent to configure data retention policies. Once you have file snap-shots stored in your backup vault, you can restore to any archived versions at any time when needed.

StorSimple

StorSimple and Microsoft Azure provide a unique hybrid storage and backup model. An enterprise can deploy physical StorSimple appliance on local networks to provide performant storage. And A StorSimple appliance is paired with a virtual appliance on Azure for backup and disaster recovery.

StoreSimple and Azure provides a balance between performance and scalability. On one hand, because data is stored on a local appliance, you get best performance provided by the high-performance local hardware. On the other hand, multiple snapshots can be created on the cloud for backups so that you are not constrained by local hardware capacity.

Furthermore, because you can configure and monitor multiple local hardware appliances remotely through Microsoft Azure Management Portal, you can effectively control backup and data restore of multiple on-premises sites at the same time.

Site Recovery

Azure Site Recovery helps you protect important applications by coordinating the replication and recovery of physical or virtual machines. These machines can be replicated to a different on-premises datacenter, a hosting service provider, or Azure as the target site. Then, Azure Site

Recovery works with existing technologies such as SQL Server AlwaysOn, Hyper-V Replica, and System Center to coordinate ongoing replications.

Azure Site Recovery allows you to create comprehensive recovery plans to make sure resources are brought back online in an orderly fashion. For instance, you probably want to bring back the machines running the data tier before you attempt to bring back machines running the application tier, which have dependency on the data layer. You can also include scripted and manual steps in your recovery plan to ensure established processes are followed during the recovery process.

Last but not least, Azure Site Recovery also allows you to test your disaster recovery solutions by running planned failovers. You can run these planned tests at your own convenience to ensure everything is in place for unexpected disastrous events.

Azure Rights Management Services

In modern workspaces, data is often shared across different services, applications, users, organizations and devices. Azure Rights Management Services (RMS) allows encryption and access policies to travel with your data so that your data is protected regardless of how it's accessed. RMS enables:

- Data encryption and decryption
- Manage and track encryption key distributions
- Manage key management and data access policies

RMS is comprised of three components: an RMS server, RMS-aware applications, and RMS SDKs. RMS provides SDKs for Windows, iOS, and Android environments so that you can write RMS-aware applications for all popular mobile devices.

Microsoft provides three different RMS server implementations: *Microsoft Rights Management for Individuals*, which is a free hosted service; *Microsoft Rights Management Service* or *Azure RMS*, which is a hosted premium service; and *Active Directory Rights Management Services*, which is an on-premises implementation.

Azure Key Vault

Key management is a very important aspect of cloud security solutions. If your security keys are not properly protected, data-encryption is useless as data can be easily decrypted by using comprised keys. Azure Key Vault allows customers to protect and control keys and secrets using Hardware Security Module (HSM) in the cloud. The service is hosted, scalable, and available, so it provides an easier and more economical way to manage security keys. For example, in previous sections you read about how SQL Server Transparent Data Encryption (TDE) encrypts SQL data. And now you can manage TDE secrets using Azure Key Vault by using a SQL Server Connector for Key Vault.

To create a key vault with Cloud Shell, use the following command:

```
az keyvault create --name <vault name> --resource-group <resource group name>
--location <location>
```

To use Key Vault to generate a new software-protected key, use the command:

```
az keyvault key create --vault-name <vault name> --name <key name> --protection
software
```

Now, you can reference the key using its URL. You can use https://<vault name>.vault.azure.
net/keys/<key name> to reference the latest value. Or, you can use the *kid* property returned by the above command to reference a specific key version.

To add a secret to a key vault, using the following command:

```
az keyvault secret set --vault-name <vault name> --name <secret name> --value
<secret value>
```

To authorize an application to access the keys and secrets in a key vault, you need to register the application with your Azure AD tenant and use the *set-policy* command to set up access policies for the application id. For example, to allow an application with application id 49f92...
to access keys in a key vault, use the following command:

```
az keyvault set-policy --name <vault name> --spn 49f92… --key-permissions decrypt
sign
```

Skill 4.4: Design a mechanism of governance and polices for administrating Azure resources

Many enterprises need to manage a large number of users with different access requirements spanning many services, applications, locations and devices. And the dynamic nature of modern workplaces calls for an efficient solution that can quickly adapt to changes. This objective discusses some of the proven strategies and Azure services that help large enterprise to manage identities and application accesses.

This section covers how to:

- Determine when to use Azure RBAC standard roles and custom roles
- Define an Azure RBAC strategy
- Determine when to use Azure resource policies
- Determine when to use Azure AD Privileged Identity Management
- Design solutions that use Azure AD Managed Service Identity
- Determine when to use HSM-backed keys

Access control challenges faced by large enterprises

The modern enterprise environment is a very dynamic environment with users, services, resources and devices scattered at different places. System administrators in such environments face new challenges that they haven't been facing in on-premises environments.

Access to SaaS applications

Nowadays, more and more enterprise users rely on various public or private SaaS services to carry out day-to-day business functions. For example, many marketing teams use social networks such as Twitter and Facebook for customer engagements and marketing campaigns. And many users use public storage services such as Box and OneDrive for file storage and sharing. Managing access to these SaaS applications is challenging because identities are scattered in different identity providers, managed by individual users in a self-service fashion. As a matter of fact, many enterprises even don't have a clear picture of what services are being used, much less managing them effectively.

Adapt to dynamic teams

In a dynamic enterprise environment, security policies have to be consistently revised and refined to keep up with the rapid changes in working environments. A static privilege model strategy doesn't work. Administrators have to find a balance between centralized control and appropriate distribution of management responsibilities so that groups of users can manage access to their working resources in a self-service model.

Bring your own devices (BYOD)

The traditional boundaries between work and personal life have been blurred by the explosion of consumer devices. More and more employees bring their personal devices to work environments and use those devices to access corporate data such as emails and files. However, such usages have very little visibility to system administrators, because these devices are personal devices and often not registered with the company.

It's very important for modern system administrators to gain insights of how devices are used and to place controls over device usages.

Role Based Access Control (RBAC)

Role Based Access Control (RBAC) is a proven method to manage access to resources at scale. RBAC has been widely adopted in the industry and is natively supported by most of modern operation systems and many of programming languages.

A detailed introduction of BRAC is out of scope of this book. In this section, we'll go through some of the basic concepts of RBAC and then discuss how RBAC is implemented on Azure.

Groups

A group is an effective way to manage access rights of groups of users. Instead of managing access rights of individual users, these users can be organized into logical groups so that they can inherit access rights assigned to these groups.

A typical usage of groups is for a business unit or a team to create a team-wide group, where everybody in the team shares the same access rights. For example, a test team can create their separate Test Team group to control accesses to all test resources the team manages in the cloud.

Roles

A role defines a collection of permissions. The exact allowed actions are explicitly defined in some systems (such as RBAC for Azure Resources) and are implied in some other systems. For instance, the exact actions what an operator can do are subject to authorization decisions made by particular applications.

A role can be assigned to groups, users, or other identity subjects as needed. And role assignments are often inherited along hierarchies. For example, a user belonging to a group inherits role assignments of the group.

RBAC and Claims

RBAC and claim-based architecture work well together. With claims-based architecture, a Relying Party can request trusted Identity Provider to provide a role claim, which reflects role assignments of the user. And then, the Relying Party can use the content of this claim to make authorization decisions.

In the case when a user belongs to too many groups to be returned in a security token, the application needs to issue a separate directory query to verify if the user belongs to a specific group, or groups.

Multi-factor Authentication (MFA)

Multi-factor Authentication (MFA) requires a user to authenticate using multiple authentication methods. The most common variation of Multi-factor Authentication is 2-Factor Authentication (2FA). Common authentication methods use something you know (such as a passwords, SMS, or call-based security codes), something you have (such as hardware or software tokens, smart cards, and mobile applications), or something you are (such as fingerprints and retinas).

Azure supports 2FA for securing Azure Active Directory (included in Azure subscriptions), on-premises resources and Active Directory as well as custom applications. The Azure service that enables MFA is named Azure Multi-factor Authentication service.

RBAC for Azure Resources

In addition to managing access to SaaS services, enterprise Azure users also require fine-grain access control for Azure resources. Microsoft Azure provides built-in Role Based Access Control (RBAC) for Azure Resources at different levels, and all access controls are integrated with Azure Active Directory.

Basic ARM RBAC model

The ARM access control model mostly follows ANSI Core RBAC model (or Flat RBAC in earlier literature). Under the ANSI model, users and groups are assigned to roles, to which permissions are also assigned. Permission is an approval to perform an operation on one or more protected objects. ARM RBAC model is a flat RBAC model because there are no inheritance relationships among roles.

The ARM RBAC model differs from the ANSI Core RBAC model in several ways:

- ARM RBAC supports the concept of scope, which isn't present in ANSI RBAC models. Scopes form an inheritance hierarchy. When a role is assigned to a scope, it's assigned to all descendants of the scope.

- The permission assignments in ARM BRAC roles only specify allowed/disallowed operations. They don't specify applied objects. Although a role definition consists of assignable scopes, the permissions are not bound to a scope until a role is explicitly assigned to a scope.

- There are no per-session role activations. All roles are activated in any sessions.

Roles and resource scopes

Azure has three levels of resource scopes: subscription, resource group, and resource. Azure provides three built-in roles that can be assigned to users, groups or services.

- **Owner** Has complete control over all Azure resources in the scope.
- **Contributor** Can perform all management operations except access management.
- **Reader** Can only view resources. A reader can't read any associated secrets (such as access keys) of resources.

An operation (a.k.a. action) is identified by an object type identifier with an action postfix. For example, the read action on Azure Automation jobs is named as: Microsoft.Automation/automationAccounts/jobs/read where Microsoft.Automation/automationAccounts/jobs identifies the object type, and read is the allowed action on the object type. For a complete list of roles and actions, see *https://docs.microsoft.com/en-us/azure/active-directory/role-based-access-built-in-roles*.

Azure subscriptions

An enterprise often maintains multiple Azure subscriptions for different purposes. For instance, an enterprise may have a subscription for development and another subscription for production. By using RBAC for Azure Resources, administrators can assign different users, or a group of users, to corresponding subscriptions with appropriate roles.

Azure Resource Groups

The next level down is Resource groups. You can have multiple Resource groups under an Azure subscription, and each Resource group can contain a number of Azure resources, such as virtual machines, virtual networks, storage accounts, and websites.

Resources

By default, all resources within a Resource group inherit all access right assignments of the group, so you don't need to explicitly grant access to each individual resource. However, if you choose to, you can override these access rights for each resource as needed.

Custom roles

ARM custom roles allow you to design fine-grained access policies that grant to deny access to specific operations on specific resource types. For example, you can create a VM operator custom role that allows monitoring and restarting VMs, but not provisioning or deleting VMs. The following walkthrough shows you how to set such a role up using the Cloud Shell.

1. Sign on to Azure management portal and open Cloud Shell.

2. To list existing role definitions, use command `az role definition list`. For example, to list all role names, use the command:

    ```
    az role definition list | grep roleName
    ```

3. Now, let's examine a specific "Virtual Machine Contributor" role:

    ```
    az role definition list --name="Virtual Machine Contributor"
    ```

    The above command returns a collection of JSON objects. Each JSON object is a role definition:

    ```
    {
      "id": "/subscriptions/460a7.../providers/Microsoft.Authorization/
    roleDefinitions/
    9980e02c-c2be-4d73-94e8-173b1dc7cf3c",
      "name": "9980e02c-c2be-4d73-94e8-173b1dc7cf3c",
      "properties": {
        "assignableScopes": [ "/" ],
        "description": "Lets you manage virtual machines, but not access to
    them, and not the virtual network or storage account they're connected to.",
        "permissions": [
    ```

```json
        {
          "actions": [
            "Microsoft.Authorization/*/read",
            "Microsoft.Compute/availabilitySets/*",
            "Microsoft.Compute/locations/*",
            "Microsoft.Compute/virtualMachines/*",
            "Microsoft.Compute/virtualMachineScaleSets/*",
            "Microsoft.DevTestLab/schedules/*",
            "<additional",
            "permissions",
            "are",
            "omitted",
            "here>"
          ],
          "notActions": []
        }
      ],
      "roleName": "Virtual Machine Contributor",
      "type": "BuiltInRole"
    },
    "type": "Microsoft.Authorization/roleDefinitions"
}
```

4. Create a new vmoperator.json file under your cloud drive:

```json
{
  "Name": "Virutal Machine Operator",
  "IsCustom": true,
  "Description": "Can monitor and restart virtual machines.",
  "Actions": [
    "Microsoft.Storage/*/read",
    "Microsoft.Network/*/read",
    "Microsoft.Compute/*/read",
    "Microsoft.Compute/virtualMachines/start/action",
    "Microsoft.Compute/virtualMachines/restart/action",
    "Microsoft.Authorization/*/read",
    "Microsoft.Resources/subscriptions/resourceGroups/read",
    "Microsoft.Insights/alertRules/*",
    "Microsoft.Support/*"
  ],
  "NotActions": [
  ],
  "AssignableScopes": [
    "/subscriptions/<your subscription id>"
  ]
}
```

5. Then, you can create the custom role using the following command:

```
az role definition create --role-definition vmoperator.json
```

6. Once the custom role is created, you can assign it to users just like assigning default rules. On Azure Management Portal, click on a VM. Then, click on the Access control (IAM) link.

7. On the Access control blade, click on the +Add link.

8. On the Add permissions link, select the new custom role and users you want to assign. Then, click on the Save button to save assignments.

Empowering a user with self-service

Self-service is a great addition to RBAC by bringing flexibility into an enterprise's security policy. By allowing users to take on some of the common access management tasks by themselves, system administrators are freed to focus on more important tasks such as analyzing and improving security policies. Such common tasks include resetting passwords, changing passwords, and managing groups and group memberships.

Inviting external users

As you've seen earlier in this chapter, sometimes an external user requires access to certain resources. When permitted by the tenant administrator, an Azure Active Directory user can invite external users who have Microsoft Accounts to access your Azure resources. These invited users don't need to be on your Directory tenant, and they don't need to have an Azure subscription either.

Furthermore, the tenant administrator can even allow invited users to invite more users. The administrator controls these settings through the user access section of the tenant's configuration page.

Self-Service password reset

Password management, especially recovering a lost password, is a major management burden on system administrators. Enabling self-service password reset can help you to reduce cost, improve user experience, and lower helpdesk volume.

Azure AD Premium allows self-service password reset for users. Tenant owners configure user password reset policy by using the Configure page of the tenant through Microsoft Azure Management Portal. Figure 4-20 shows the page section where the policy is configured. The screen shot shows that self-service password rest is enabled for a *mygroup* security group.

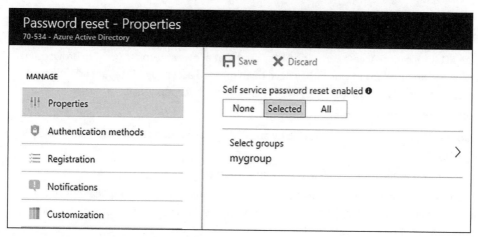

FIGURE 4-20 Password reset policy properties

Self-service group management

Azure AD Premium also allows self-service group management. Users can create security groups and manage group memberships by themselves. A user can also request to join groups, and the group owner can approve/reject these requests without involvements of administrators.

The following sample scenario shows how self-service group management works in an enterprise context.

SAMPLE SCENARIO: REQUESTING ACCESS TO RESOURCES

In this sample scenario, Jack, a new employee has just joined the team, and he needs accesses to a number of Azure resources. The following steps show the process of Jack requesting access to these resources from Jane, the Azure subscription owner.

1. At beginning, Jane has created a group named "Jane's team," which includes all members on her team. Jack has already got his Azure Active Directory credential, but he has not joined Jane's team. Jane's team is using Azure Active Directory Premium.

2. Jack signs on to Azure Portal, at *https://portal.azure.com*, and discovers he doesn't have access to any resources.

3. Jack navigates to the Azure AD Application Access Panel (*https://myapps.microsoft.com*).

4. He clicks on the **groups** link, searches for Jane's team, and then requests to join the group.

5. When Jane signs on to the Azure AD Application Access Panel, she will see Jack's request under Approvals > My Approvals.

6. Jane approves the request, and now Jack inherits all access rights assigned to the group.

7. Later on, Jane can fine-tune Jacks' access rights to specific resources by using the Azure management portal.

Azure AD Application Access Panel

Azure AD Application Access Panel is a web portal that allows enterprise users to browse and launch SaaS applications to which they have been granted access by AD tenant administrators or group owners. You can access the Access Panel through its public URL:

http://myapps.microsoft.com

Or, you can use a tenant-specific URL by appending your organization's domain to the URL. For example:

http://myapps.microsoft.com/ref70534.onmicrosoft.com

Azure AD Application Access Panel supports a large number of SaaS applications out-of-the-box. When you add an application to the portal, you can choose from one of the 2000+ applications, as shown in Figure 4-21.

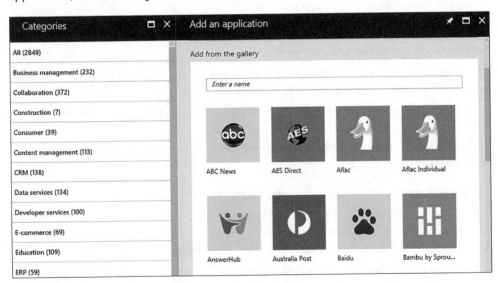

FIGURE 4-21 Add apps screen

Not all SaaS applications support federated authentications with Azure Active Directory. To provide a smooth Single-Sign On (SSO) experience, Azure AD Application Access Panel can securely save user credentials and automatically complete the sign-in process on the user's behalf. The following scenario shows how to enable an SSO experience to Twitter using Azure AD Application Access Panel.

Sample Scenario: Enabling SSO access to Twitter

In this sample scenario, an enterprise uses a company-owned Twitter account to drive marketing campaigns and community awareness. The administrator wants to allow several enterprise users to monitor and contribute to the account. However, the administrator doesn't want to share the Twitter credential with these users, so that when a user leaves the group the credential doesn't need to be reset. This scenario can be easily achieved by using the Azure AD Application Access Panel.

1. Sign on to Azure Management Portal and navigate to your Azure AD tenant.

2. On your tenant's blade, click on the Enterprise Applications link.

3. On the Enterprise Applications blade, click on the +New application link.

4. Click on the Social category and search for "twitter." Click on the Twitter entry and then click on the Add button.

5. Once the application is added, click on the Configure single sign-on link on its Quick Start blade.

6. Select the Password-Based Sign-On option and click on the Save button.

7. Back on the Quick start blade, click on Assign A User For Testing link.

8. On the Users And Groups blade, click on the +Add user link. Select the user you want to assign.

9. Click on the Assign Credentials link. Change the option of Assign Credentials On Behalf Of The User to Yes. Then, enter a Twitter credential you want to assign to the AD account. Click on the OK button and then the Assign button to assign the user, as shown in Figure 4-22.

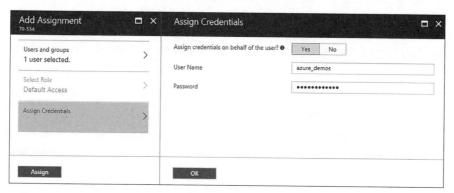

FIGURE 4-22 Assign Credentials blades

10. Open a new browser and navigate to your tenant's application page, for example *http://myapps.microsoft.com/ref70534.onmicrosoft.com*.

11. Sign on with the assigned credential in step 8. You may be asked to verify your phone and your email address and install a browser extension before you can continue to the application page.

12. Click on the Twitter icon, as shown in Figure 4-23.

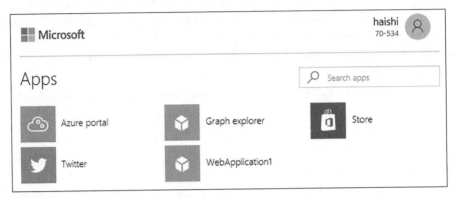

FIGURE 4-23 Application page

13. You are brought to the Twitter page, automatically logged in with the Twitter credential in step 9. Note that the assigned AD user never knows the Twitter password. Once his Azure AD account is disabled or revoked, he loses access to the Twitter account.

Skill 4.5: Manage security risks by using an appropriate security solution

Fighting malicious attacks is a constant battle. As attackers get more tricks and more computing power at their disposal, the landscape of cyber-attacks is filled with dangerous and ever-changing challenges. In order to gain an upper hand against attackers, system administrators must apply smart strategies to shorten the blue team kill chain so the attackers don't meet their goals.

> **This section covers how to:**
> - Identify, assess, and mitigate security risks by using Azure Security Center, Operations Management Suite Security and Audit solutions, and other services
> - Determine when to use Azure AD Identity Protection
> - Determine when to use Advanced Threat Detection
> - Determine an appropriate endpoint protection strategy

A blue team kill chain (in contrast to a red team kill chain, which represents the attacking process) is made by a serious of components, as shown in Figure 4-24. Only when the blue team kill chain is condensed enough can the blue team disrupt the attack process. The blue team (the protectors) needs to first gain awareness, then decide on an action plan, and finally execute the plan ahead of the red team (the attackers).

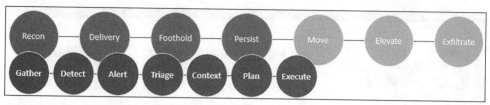

FIGURE 4-24 Blue team kill chain vs. red team kill chain

Azure security solutions

Knowing what's happening is the first step to initiate the blue team kill chain. However, in a dynamic modern enterprise environment, it's not easy to keep a clear picture of existing and emerging threats. To address this challenge, Azure provides a series of services that can help you to identify, access, and mitigate security risks.

Azure Security Center

Azure Security Center provides a unified view of security across all your workloads, regardless if they are on the cloud or on-premises. Leveraging Microsoft's years of experience in security and machine learning, Azure Security Center automatically detects and fixes vulnerabilities before they can be exploited by attackers. Once you enable Azure Security Center, your resources are automatically discovered, onboarded, and monitored. They are constantly evaluated against hundreds of built-in security assessments. And you'll be notified to take prompt actions on the most critical items that are at risk.

You can access Azure Security Center directly from Azure management portal by clicking on the Security Center entry in the left panel of the portal. Once you open the Security Center portal, you can gain a wholistic view over your compute, storage and networking resources. You also get auto-generated recommendations that can help you to improve your security settings. There are also many other features to be covered here.

Operation Management Suite Security and Audit Solution

Microsoft Management Suite (OMS) is a hosted IT management solution for managing both cloud resources and on-premises resources. The core functionalities of OMS are delivered by a group of services, including Log Analytics, Automation, Backup and Site Recovery. Furthermore, specific configuration combinations of these services are packaged into Management Solution that are tailored for specific workloads and scenarios.

OMS provides a Solution Gallery where you can acquire packaged solutions such as Security and Audit, Security and Compliance, Antimalware Assessment, Update Management, Active Directory Assessment and more, as shown in Figure 4-25. To add a solution to your OMS dashboard, simply click on the solution you want to use, and click on the Add button to add a tile to your OMS dashboard.

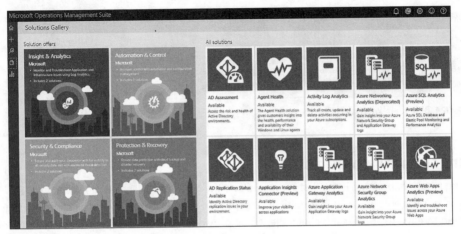

FIGURE 4-25 OMS Solution Gallery

OMS Security and Audit solution provides a comprehensive security view of your IT infrastructure as well as applications. To get your resources monitored by OMS, you need to deploy a customized version of Microsoft Monitoring Agent (MMA). You can choose to install agents individually, or use Azure Automation to deploy agents at scale. If your security policy doesn't allow your on-premises devices to directly connect to the Internet, you can use an OMS Gateway that uses HTTP tunneling to collect and send device data on their behalf.

Managing security risks

The human aspect is always the most elusive part of enterprise security. In modern enterprise environments, workers perform their day-to-day tasks from various contexts, including different network settings such as corporate network, home network, public shared network, different devices such as personal computers and mobile phones, and different office locations such as corporate headquarter and remote branch offices. In such a hybrid environment, enabling worker productivity while ensuring security policies are reinforced is an increasing challenge.

Another human aspect in the security landscape is attackers who look for opportunities to breach your systems to gain access to your private data, to break your services, or to trick your services to gain unfair and illegal financial advantages.

To help you to deal with these challenges, Azure provides a few intelligent services that can help you gain insight and control over such human activities.

Azure Active Directory Identity Protection

Azure Active Directory Identity Protection automatically detects and responds to potential identity vulnerabilities.

For example, if a user logs in from one location and then logs in again from a different location, and If the time difference between the two login attempts is shorter than the travel time by normal means (such as car and flight), the user identity can be identified as at-risk. You can set up policies for identities at different risk levels. For example, you can require two-factor authentication (2FA) for identities with medium or high risks and require periodical password resets for all users.

Azure Active Directory Identity Protection is part of Azure AD Premium P2 edition.

Advanced Threat Protection

Azure Threat Protection (ATP) uses machine learning to detect protentional external and internal security breaches in your environments. ATP analyzes huge amounts of data and automatically learns operation patterns from this data. On one hand, ATP can detect abnormalities that deviate from common patterns. On the other hand, ATP can compare these patterns with known attack patterns to identify potential attacks.

The machine learning–based system has great advantages over traditional, rule-based systems because it's adaptive. It's very hard to capture and update common operation patterns in user workloads with rule-based systems. A machine learning–based system such as ATP can learn common patterns automatically so that is can adapt to workload changes without triggering false positives.

A machine learning–based system can also detect new previously unknown threats. Although it may not understand the mechanism of the attack, it can detect presence of attacks by detecting deviations from known, good patterns.

Thought experiment

In this thought experiment, demonstrate your skills and knowledge of the topics covered in this chapter. You can find answer to this thought experiment in the next section.

Azure Site Recovery is great for setting up disaster recovery for virtual machine–based systems. However, modern cloud applications are often comprised of virtual machines, PaaS services and SaaS services. At this point, Azure doesn't provide an out-of-box solution that covers disaster recovery across all Azure service types.

With this in mind, answer the following questions:

1. What kind of topology can you use to set up a disaster recovery solution for all Azure services?

2. What techniques can you use to ensure consistent deployments?

3. How can you handle data synchronization?

Thought experiment answers

This section contains the solutions to the thought experiment.

1. One possible solution is to use an active primary, standby secondary topology. In normal operations, user traffic is routed to the primary. In case of primary failure, user traffic is routed to the secondary. A secondary can be configured as read-only or read-write. The read-only secondary provides downgraded services till the primary is restored. While the primary is running normally, a read-write secondary is not allowed to take user traffic. However, a read-only secondary can serve user traffic if desired. The main benefit of choosing this topology is to reduce RTO and RPO. The downside of the topology is the need to keep the extra secondary resources around.

   Another possible topology is to use a cold secondary. In this case, secondary instances are created only when failover occurs. Cold secondaries save secondary compute costs but prolong RTO.

2. Azure Resource Manager (ARM) template is a great tool to capture your entire application infrastructure as code. Once resources are captures in templates, they can be deployed in different environments and different regions. Containerization is another great way to achieve consistent deployments.

3. In both topologies, data needs to be periodically replicated from the primary to the secondary. The replication interval is decided by your RTO objectives. Not all data services support cross-region replications. In such cases, you'll need to use custom solutions such as automation scripts, scheduled tasks or third-party solutions to replicate the data.

Chapter summary

- Managed identities allow developers to focus on developing business logics, while delegating authentication and authorization to trusted identity providers.
- Trusted Relying Parties and Identities form a circle of trust, allowing Single Sign-On (SSO) experience within the circle.
- Microsoft Azure Active Directory provides managed identity solutions for both cloud and hybrid environments. You can sync your on-premises Active Directories with Azure Active Directory. And Azure Active Directory Application Proxy allows you to securely expose on-premises services to the Internet.
- Microsoft Azure Active Directory B2C allows SaaS ISVs to tap into social network user bases by enabling users to sign on to these services using their social network credentials such as Microsoft Account, Facebook, and Google. Microsoft Azure Active Directory B2B allows users from other directory tenants to authenticate and access your applications.

- Microsoft Azure provides comprehensive protections over customer data. Customer data is replicated multiple times to ensure data is never lost. Zone replication and geo-replication also replicate data into different facilities so that even with large scale outages data can still be recovered.

- Microsoft Azure's disaster recovery services include Azure Backup for backups at file level, StorSimple for backups at volume level, and Site Recovery at machine and whole topology level. Site Recovery allows customers to perform coordinated recoveries to bring back machines in the correct order, following established work processes and compliance requirements.

- Microsoft RMS allows encryption and access policies to travel along with data, regardless of where the data is accessed. Azure Key Vault protects secret keys using HSMs on cloud.

- An effective RBAC strategy helps administrators to face the challenges of managing security policies for a dynamic working environment. Self-service brings in great flexibility into RBAC strategy.

- Azure AD Application Access Panel provides a centralized place to discover and consume SaaS applications with Single Sign-On.

- Azure Active Directory Device Registration Service allows consumer devices to be registered with your Active Directory tenants so that administrators can monitor and design access policies for these devices.

- Azure Active Directory helps administrator to continuously improve security policies by a continuous discover-monitor-react process.

Design solutions by using platform services

The software industry is known for its emphasis on modularity and reusability. People use software to tackle some of the most difficult problems. And once the problem is solved, the solution is shared and reapplied to similar situations. The collective effort of the software engineering community has extended our ability to handle more and more complex problems at larger scales.

The cloud pushes this idea even further. When you use reusable libraries, you are still responsible for operating the libraries. However, operating some complex libraries at scale is not an easy task, especially when the libraries need significant infrastructure, data, and processing power to operate.

Fortunately, modern cloud platforms like Azure provide a rich set of platform services that you can directly consume without worrying about operating these services. Azure provides solutions to some of the most demanding problems. These solutions include artificial intelligence, global messaging infrastructure and massive media processing, and they are ready for consumption through simple APIs.

With the rise of microservices, the idea of reusing existing services and composing them into new applications is taking the center stage of cloud application development. In this chapter, you'll learn about several Azure-provided services that are hard to implement and host by yourself, especially on a global scale.

Skills in this chapter:

- Skill 5.1: Bring AI into your applications
- Skill 5.2: Design scalable, reliable and performant IoT solutions
- Skill 5.3: System integration and reactive systems through messaging
- Skill 5.4: Build large-scale media processing applications

Skill 5.1: Design for artificial intelligence services

Artificial intelligence has been around for decades; however, it has gained tremendous momentum in recent years. There are several driving forces behind this. First, as the amount of data keeps exploding, there are increasing opportunities as well as demands on deriving more value of the data. Although prescriptive, rule-based data processing is still quite powerful in many cases, heuristic and fuzzy inferences have shown great power to extract huge values, many of which are even not well understood or anticipated. Second, some problems such as self-driving cars are so complex that we have failed to develop a fixed algorithm to solve them. Instead, we turn to AI and train computers to find solutions for us. Searching for these solutions require a lot of compute power—and this is exactly what cloud is good at providing. Therefore, the rise of cloud has given AI a great boost after decades of its birth. Third, as compute becomes more and more ubiquitous, the way people consume compute has gone beyond PCs and beyond smart devices. Eventually, there won't be any devices or even applications to use. People will be able to consume compute by simply interacting with everyday objects naturally and carrying out daily tasks without even thinking about using any software. Yet, intelligent cloud and intelligent devices work silently together and enrich our lives with efficiency, safety, convenience, insight and predictability.

> **This section covers how to:**
> - Understand basic concepts of AI and machine learning
> - Identify AI application scenarios
> - Use Azure AI services such as Cognitive API, machine learning and Bot Service

Basic AI concepts

This section provides an intuitive explanation of AI and machine learning. Although understanding these concepts is not mandatory for incorporating Azure AI services into your application, a heuristic understanding of AI goes a long way when you try to identify possible application scenarios and to make choices among different AI tools.

Obviously, this section is by no means a comprehensive introduction or a mathematically accurate account of AI. The goal is to help you build up some intuition in AI. If you are already familiar with AI, please feel free to skip ahead.

What's AI?

Artificial intelligence is about building intelligent machines to solve specific problems. Although simulating or even achieving human-level intelligence is the goal of some researchers, most AI researchers focus on building intelligent programs that can solve specific problems with close-to-human (and in some cases beyond-human) performances.

AI and machine learning

There are many areas of study and different toolsets in AI, including, but certainly not limited to, machine learning, graphical models, planning, knowledge representations, and more. As you can see, machine learning is just one of the toolsets in AI. The reason why many people confuse machine learning with AI is that machine learning has gone through exponential growth in the past years and essentially overshadows other areas, at least from public view.

The fundamental idea of machine learning is quite simple—instead of giving a computer an algorithm to solve a problem, we train a computer with data so it comes up with an algorithm to solve the problem itself. The most commonly seen training method is called *supervised learning*. In supervised learning, humans provide computers both inputs and desired outputs, and computers try to adjust an algorithm so that the algorithm generates outputs that are close to the desired outputs. If desired outputs are not provided, the training process becomes unsupervised learning, where computers try to make sense of input data and generate meaningful results such as clustering and classifications. Another type of training is called reinforcement training. This is different from supervised learning, in which the machine's goal is to reduce errors. In reinforcement training, machines try to maximize rewards provided when demonstrating certain behaviors.

Neural Networks and Deep Learning

There are many mechanisms for a machine to learn, such as linear regression, support vector machines, decision trees and neural networks. Linear regressions are often used for trend analysis and predictions; support vector machines are often used for classification; decision trees are used for both classification and prediction; and neural networks have delivered impressive results in image recognition, natural language processing and many other areas.

Neural networks are made up of layers of artificial neurons. Neurons take weight inputs from lower layers and get activated based on an accumulated input signal and their own thresholds (called bias) to fire. The first layer of neurons is called an *input layer*; the final layer of neurons is called an output layer; and all other layers in the middle are called hidden layers.

During a training process, neuron's input weights and the bias is gradually adjusted through a gradient descent process so that the output layer fires in desired patterns. For example, if every neuron in an output layer represents a possible classification of data, the goal of training is to get only the neuron corresponding to desired classification to fire.

Neuron networks can have different topologies. A shallow network consists of an input layer, a hidden layer and an output layer with fully connected neurons. A deep network often consists of more hidden layers using different topologies. For example, a Convolutional Neural Network (CNN) uses convolution layers to map spatially related neurons into feature maps and pool layers to compress feature maps. A Recurrent Neural Network (RNN) allows neurons to feed their outputs back into their own inputs. A CNN is great to capture spatial features; hence, it's great for image processing. An RNN is great to capture temporal features; hence, it's great for processing sequential signals such as spoken languages.

Challenges of Machine Learning

Machine learning is quite powerful. However, there are many challenges a data scientist must deal with when trying to implement a successful machine learning solution:

- **Data cleansing and feature engineering**   It's estimated that about 80% of effort in a machine learning project is spent on data processing. Before a machine-learning model is trained, data scientists must make sure data is collected and formatted properly. Then, they must extract meaningful features from the data and feed the features to machine learning models. Feature selection is often done through heuristic processes based on experiences and experiments.

- **Selection of network topologies and hyper parameters** A neural network often consists of millions of inputs and billions of weights and biases. In addition, a neuron network is also associated with many hyper parameters that heavily influence how the network behaves. A network can be designed with different topologies. Different choices in network design and hyper parameters have huge impacts on final results. However, because the possible parameter combination space is so vast, a brute-force search for optimal parameters is impossible with current compute architectures.

- **Demands on compute resources** A neural network, especially a deep neural network, takes a lot of compute resources to be trained. Currently, many trainings are conducted in GPUs in a distributed fashion so that complex training processes can be partitioned and parallelized. Once a model is trained, however, using the model for inferences is usually quite cheap and fast. And a trained model can be burned into hardware circuits such as ASICs and FPGAs for even faster inferences.

- **Overfitting** When a model is trained with a given data set, it might get strongly biased towards the specific data set. It will handle the training data set nearly perfectly, but will perform poorly when fed with different data. This phenomenon is called overfitting. Compared with other challenges, overfitting is not a significant challenge because there are many established ways to deal with overfitting. However, it's a common mistake that you must watch out for.

Integrating AI into your applications

For most applications, integrating AI means to reuse trained machine learning models to enhance the application. Azure provides several different ways to locate and consume trained models:

- **Azure Cognitive Services** Encapsulates a rich set of trained machine learning models as easily consumable APIs. It brings capabilities such as face detection, object tracking and text sentiment detection into your applications, enabling fresh user experiences and intelligent features.

- **Azure Bot Services** Enables end users to interact with your applications through conversations. Instead of navigating through pages and menus, users engage with your applications through conversational channels such as Skype, Slack and Facebook Messenger. Azure Bot Services is often used together with Language Understanding Intelligent Service (LUIS), which can map natural language sentences into predefined intentions. For example, you can configure LUIS to translate sentences like "order a pizza," "order some pizzas," and "I want to eat pizza," into an explicit "order pizza" intention for your application to process.

- **Azure Machine Learning** Provides a web-based studio that allows you to design, train, and publish your trained models as a productionized web service. You can design your experiments using many pre-defined models such as Support Vector Machine, Decision Forest, Logistic Regression and Multiclass Neural Network. Then, you can bring in your data to train the model and evaluate the model using test data. Once you are satisfied with the result, you can publish the trained model as a web service that others can consume through REST calls.

Detailed steps to provision and configure these services are best learned through the official Azure documents; hence, they won't be covered here. Instead, the following sections present several sample scenarios that leverage AI in various ways.

Intelligent web app

AI can be used to enhance user experiments in many traditional web applications. Some typical usage of AI in such applications include:

- **Content ranking and automatic recommendations** Quality content is often a key aspect of a successful web application. As the amount of content accumulates, however, the web application needs to be smart with selecting and presenting contents to users so that only contents with the best chance of return can occupy predominant positions on the web pages. Moreover, the web application can proactively propose new contents that its users are more likely to appreciate.

- **Workflow optimization** AI can automate many manual tasks to simply human workloads. For example, a photo album website can use machine learning to automatically tag pictures with recognized individuals, scenes, and objects so that users can easily find pictures.

- **Abnormality detection** Abnormality detection can be used to detect and alert on deviations from regular workflows and data norms. The technique has been proven valuable to avoid attacks and serious user errors.

Figure 5-1 shows a sample photo album web application that uses AI to automatically group pictures by using Cognitive Service face identifications.

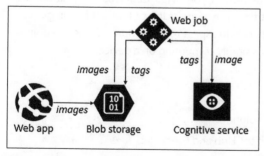

FIGURE 5-1 A web application uses AI for photo classification

Interactive design through conversation

Azure Bot Services allows users to engage with applications through conversational channels. Figure 5-2 shows a bot-assisted system that provides guidance in designing cloud-based applications. The system crawls through Azure Resource Manager (ARM) template sources and converts templates into graph segments. Then, it feeds the graph segments to a machine-learning model to detect common patterns. The patterns are in turn recommended to the end user based on project contexts by a recommendations engine. The user interacts with the system through a chat bot. The chat bot guides you through the design process using conversations. And finally, the architecture is written into a final ARM template.

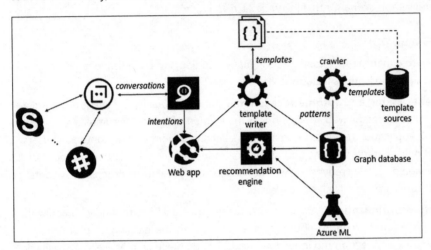

FIGURE 5-2 System design with a chat bot

Skill 5.2: Design for IoT

If you deployed something on a Raspberry Pi and it did something cute (or even useful), does this mean you've deployed an IoT solution? The truth is, you've just deployed some compute tasks on a device, which is far from an IoT solution. The name of IoT, or Internet of Things, suggests that an IoT solution must have a networking aspect to it. An individual device doing something on its own is not an IoT solution; it's simply computing on a device.

> **This section covers how to:**
> - Understand the structure of an IoT solution
> - Connect devices and cloud through IoT Hub and Event Hub
> - Use Azure services to build a scalable IoT data processing pipeline

IoT scatters compute resources into a dynamic and often heterogeneous compute plane to exchange data and to complete coordinate compute tasks. Figure 5-3 shows a generic IoT solution architecture. It's comprised of a control plane and a compute plane. The compute plan is made up by devices that are connected by a mesh.

- **Control Plane**   Responsible for device management, workload management as well as monitoring and reporting. It maintains the compute plane infrastructure through device registrations and device health reports. It manages workloads using a workload scheduler, on top of which is an orchestration engine that provides QoS (Quality of Service) supports such as scaling and failovers. The control plane also provides a single pane of glass monitoring view into the whole system. Finally, a control plane provides business insights and online analytical capabilities to extract business value from collected data.

- **Compute Plane**   Made up of various types of devices, which are connected through device meshes. A device mesh provides connectivity and messaging among devices so that they can exchange data with each other. A device mesh also provides a security and management boundary around a group of devices, such as devices for a specific tenant. Device connectivity can be provided by a local network, such as a WSN (wireless sensor network), a LAN network, or over the cloud. Devices can also communicate with each other through a messaging system such as a centralized message bus. Some of the device meshes also process local orchestration capabilities such as failover, backup, and recovery.

- **Server Pipeline**   A value creation pipeline that extracts, aggregates, infers and generates new business value out of device data. Lots of IOT-related Azure services fall into this category, including Stream Analytics, Time Series Insights, Power BI, machine learning and many other services.

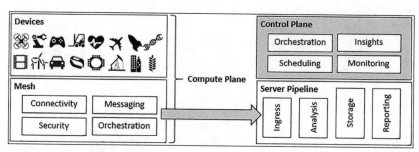

FIGURE 5-3 Generic IoT solution architecture

With the generic architecture in mind, the next few sections map specific Azure services into the overall architecture and provide general guidelines on when to choose which services and how to orchestrate them together.

Microsoft IoT Suite

As shown in Figure 5-3, an end-to-end IoT solution can be complex and involves many services and devices. The goal of Microsoft IoT Suite is to simplify IoT implementation by providing prebuilt packages for typical scenarios such as predicative maintenance, remote monitoring and connected factories. Figure 5-4 shows the architecture of a predictive maintenance solution provisioned by Microsoft IoT Suite. With such preconfigured solutions, you can get up and running in very little time and start to customize the solution towards your needs. Beginning with a working environment is a very powerful tool for building complex systems because a working environment makes it easy to comprehend how things are linked together. Otherwise, you'll have to decompose the system yourself and make a series decision to make sure the parts can interact with each other.

So, Microsoft IoT Suite is a great tool for you to bootstrap your IoT solutions quickly, if your scenario fits into one of the preconfigured scenarios. Once the solution is deployed, however, you still need domain knowledge with each individual service to fine-tune the solution to meet your requirements. One possible way to use Microsoft IoT Suite is to use the auto-provisioned environment as a reference architecture. As you internalize how the architecture works, you can build up your own environment in parallel.

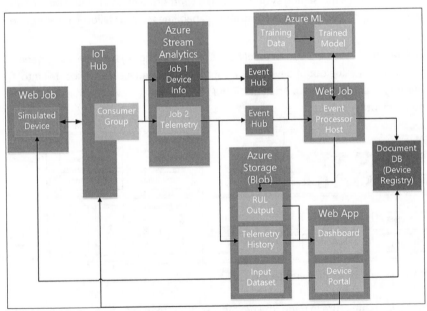

FIGURE 5-4 Predictive maintenance solution by Azure IoT Suite (image source: *https://docs.microsoft.com/en-us/azure/iot-suite/iot-suite-predictive-walkthrough*)

Azure IoT Hub

Azure IoT Hub is part of the IoT Control Plane. It provides several key management capabilities for an IoT solution, including (but not limited to):

- **Bi-directional communication between devices and cloud** IoT Hub provides device management features that allow millions of devices to be registered to send data to cloud. It supports various ingress protocols to ingest device data and send the data to downstream services for further processing.

- **Enterprise scale integration** IoT Hub can handle billions of messages and route these messages to different processing units both inside and outside Azure IoT systems. It's also integrated with monitoring and management services like Azure Monitor, Azure Resource Health, and Configuration Manager.

- **End-to-end security** This part includes device certification, TLS security, and X.509 support, IP-level ACLs and managed device firmware/software patching.

Device twins

In the field of IoT, you often hear the term "device twins." A device twin is a digital representation of a physical device. IoT Hub device management allows you to create device twins for your devices and monitor and manage your devices through these digital twins.

A device twin has a few associated tags and methods. And it also has two sets of states: reported state and desired state. One of the main jobs of a device management is to reconcile the reported state with the desired state so that a device is brought and kept at desired state. The desired state is then replicated and applied to the physical device.

Message routes

With earlier versions of IoT Hub, you need to implement message routing logic solution as part of your IoT solution. The new version of IoT Hub adds the message routing capability to the IoT Hub itself so that you can set up different messages routes based on message headers and/or message body fields and route the messages to different recipients such as event processing queues.

Azure Time Series Insights

Azure Time Series Insights is aimed at reducing the barrier of getting insights from your IoT data. It allows you to explore and analyze time series data fast and at scale with a fully managed service.

IoT sensor data typically consists of time-based measurements. And handling such data is a very common scenario in IoT. However, because of packet losses and retransmissions, sensor data often comes in out of order, with repeats, noises, shews and missed values in between. So, sorting, querying and visualizing this data is not necessarily an easy task. And the problem is complicated further when you must deal with millions of devices.

Azure Time Series Insights provides a highly reliable time-series data store that is designed to handle cloud-scale ingestion and storage of time-series data. You don't need to maintain any data schemas because data schemas are automatically inferred from data and updated as data morphs over time. Azure Time Series Insights automatically index the data and provide powerful and flexible query on top.

Azure IoT Edge

In traditional IoT systems, the role of sensors is primarily to collect and send data to the cloud, and the value of data is extracted only in the cloud. As the IoT landscape expands, more and more complex computes are required on the IoT compute plane instead of the server data pipeline. In other words, new IoT scenarios such as self-driving cars and coordinated drone fleets need us to push intelligence to the edge so that the devices themselves can make complex decisions in real-time without cloud involvements.

Pushing a workload to the edge is not a complex task. However, continuous management of workloads is hard in such a distributed, dynamic compute plane. Azure IoT Edge is designed to solve this problem. To do this, Azure IoT Edge containerizes workloads and sets up container hosts and orchestration engines on the edge to host these workloads. Furthermore, Azure IoT Edge works with other Azure services such as Azure Functions and Azure Machine Learning to package their existing workloads in containers so that these workloads run on both the cloud and the edge with symmetry.

Server-side pipeline

Once device data leaves the edge and arrives at the cloud, it's pumped through a server-side pipeline. To construct such as data pipeline, you can daisy-chain various Azure services together to form an end-to-end pipe, as shown in Figure 5-5.

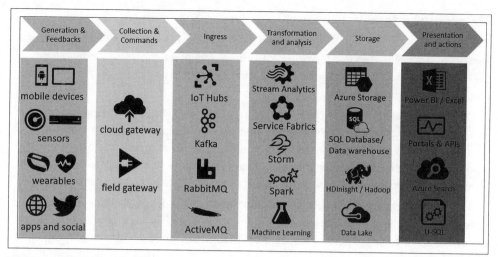

FIGURE 5-5 IoT Server-side pipeline

However, with a microservices oriented view, the above pipeline is transformed into a flat architecture where diverse types of processing units are linked by high-available messaging systems such as the Event Grid. Figure 5-6 shows such a flat architecture based on microservices.

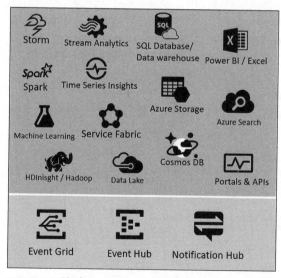

FIGURE 5-6 Platforms section on application registration page

Messaging systems

The starting point of a server-side pipeline is a data ingestion point. Both IoT Hub and Event Hub can ingest device data into the cloud. IoT Hub has additional capabilities to send data back to devices. The Event Hub allows streamed devices data to be directly captured into Azure Blog storage or Azure Data Lake.

Once data enters the cloud, it can be routed in various ways. Azure Event Grid provides a pub-sub data distribution service that allows multiple data publishers to send multiple data subscribers. This design provides a flexible messaging system that supports 1-to-1, 1-to-many, many-to-1 and many-to-many communication patterns. This mesh of data pipelines connects various types of processing units together to form powerful data processing networks.

As data leaves cloud, you can use Notification Hub to rebroadcast data back to many devices running virtually on any platforms. This forms a complete feedback loop back to devices, which leverage the intelligent results created by cloud and in turn generates more meaningful data back to the cloud.

Figure 5-7 shows a fictional photo-sharing scenario. When a user takes a picture, the picture is uploaded and automatically organized into channels (such as an event, a location, or a subject). New data of these channels is automatically pushed to subscribed users. In this scenario, as a new picture is ingested through Event Hub, the Event Hub Capture feature writes data directly into Azure Blob storage. A new blob event fires. And the event is subscribed by an Azure Function through Event Grid. The function code reads the blob data and writes feature data into a Cosmos DB. An application running on Service Fabric listens to the Cosmos DB change feed, queries the data and feeds it to a machine learning model for evaluation. The evaluation result is published as a Web API, which a mobile application backend calls and broadcast the data to mobile devices.

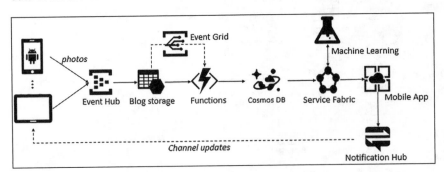

FIGURE 5-7 A fictional IoT scenario

Processing units

Data flows from processing units to processing units in the server-side pipeline. Each processing unit performs various actions on the data, such as transformation, split and aggregation, storage, filtering and sorting. More importantly, these processing units extract business value from the data, making the data flowing through the pipeline a continuous value-creation process.

STREAM ANALYTICS

Stream Analytics is an event-processing engine that runs real-time analysis on data streams. You can connect Stream Analytics to various types of input streams to ingest data, run various transformations on the data, and send the data down the pipeline through output sinks.

A Stream Analytics job topology starts with input streams and reference data. You can attach to data streams from Azure Blog storage, Event Hub, or IoT Hub. You can also attach to reference data stored in Azure Blob storage. Reference data is static or slow-changing, and it's used for correlation and lookups as needed.

The processing logic of a Stream Analytics job is defined by the Stream Analytics Query Language, which is a subset of T-SQL syntax. If you are familiar with T-SQL, understanding Stream Analytics queries should be an easy task. For example, the following query detects fraudulent calls based on streams of incoming calls:

```
SELECT  System.Timestamp as Time,
        CS1.CallingIMSI,
        CS1.CallingNum as CallingNum1,
        CS2.CallingNum as CallingNum2,
        CS1.SwitchNum as Switch1,
        CS2.SwitchNum as Switch2
FROM CallStream CS1 TIMESTAMP BY CallRecTime
        JOIN CallStream CS2 TIMESTAMP BY CallRecTime
        ON CS1.CallingIMSI = CS2.CallingIMSI
        AND DATEDIFF(ss, CS1, CS2) BETWEEN 1 AND 5
WHERE CS1.SwitchNum != CS2.SwitchNum
```

Even without understanding the underlying schema, you can see how the query compares to call streams and detects calls from the same identity (CallingIMSI) within a short time period but from different locations (*SwitchNum*).

Stream Analytics supports many output sink types, including SQL Database, Blob storage, Event Hub, Table storage, Service Bus queue, Service Bus Topic, Cosmos DB, Power BI, Data Lake Store and Azure Functions (in preview as the time when this is written). Output data can be formatted in CSV, Avro, or JSON format.

SERVICE FABRIC

Service Fabric is a microservices platform that is designed to host large-scale microservices on the cloud. Once you implement your data processing logic as a Service Fabric application, you can deploy it to a Service Fabric cluster and scale the application either manually or automatically based on auto-scaling rules.

To link Service Fabric processing units to the server-side data pipeline, you'll need to implement data ingestion logic yourself. There are three ways to implement such logics:

- **Periodical polling** In this case, your application periodically polls a data source for new data and processes the data in batches.

- **Web hooks** In this case, you implement a Web API and configure the endpoint with a data source that support Web hooks such as Event Grid and Blob Event notifications.
- **Custom communication stack** Service Fabric also allows you to implement your own custom communication stack to support protocols of your choice. The custom communication stack isn't available for services on Docker containers.

Service Fabric is also a Docker container orchestration engine that can orchestrate both Windows containers and Linux containers. This capability allows you to bring in your legacy containerized services into Service Fabric and enjoy QoS benefits such automatic failover without code changes.

OTHER PROCESSING UNITS

Theoretically, any compute components hosted on Azure can participate as part of the IoT server-side data pipeline, including Azure Machine Learning, Azure Functions, Azure Web Apps, Azure Batch, and many more. Due to space constraints, these options are not discussed further in this chapter.

 Quick check

There are many choices to host your processing unit. How do you mitigate the risk of choosing a wrong one?

Quick check answer

The choice of which types of processing unit hosts to use is affected by many factors, including scaling factors, pricing, familiarity with the technology, and many more. And some earlier decisions might be proven incorrect as the project. To mitigate the risk of choosing a wrong processing unit host, you should consider containerizing your processing units as Docker containers. Azure is providing increasing support of Docker containers in its services, including Azure Web Apps, Service Fabric, Azure Batch, Azure Container Services and more. Once your processing units are containerized, it will be easier for you to migrate across these services in case you need to switch to a different host. Furthermore, the IoT Edge also uses Docker container to package and distribute workloads. If you need to push some of the computations to the edge, having the workload containerized will allow you to leverage IoT Edge to mobilize your workloads across cloud and edge.

Skill 5.3: Design messaging solution architectures

In the past decades, messaging systems have been effective tools for enterprise system integrations. In recent years, with newer paradigms such as Actor Model and Reactive Programming, messaging systems have found new applications in the microservices world.

Azure provides abundant options in messaging systems. Before we jump into comparing different options, however, let's spend some time to review how messaging systems fit into overall system architectures.

Messaging systems for system integrations

Enterprises often need to integrate applications with their partners. And for larger enterprises, applications from different business units often need to be orchestrated into complete workflows. Such integration projects face some shared challenges:

- **Integration while maintaining application isolation**   The integrated applications often are developed by different teams or even different companies. They will evolve at their own paces. Coordinated changes across applications are hard. Hence, the integration solution shall allow applications to remain independent as they work together.

- **Work across different frameworks and platforms**   Applications are developed using various tools and frameworks. It's impractical to force all applications to use a unified underlying platform. So, an integration solution must work across programming languages, runtime frameworks, and hosting platforms.

- **Compensate for performance differences**   Different systems generate and process data at different rates. And different systems may have different availabilities. An integration system can't assume all systems are online at the same time, nor do all systems work at the same pace.

- **Quality of integration systems**   For cross-application integrations to work, the integration system needs to have high service qualities. The system must be available, reliable, and scalable to maintain reliable message paths across application boundaries. The integration system also needs to have other qualities such as security, auditability, and testability.

- **Adaptive integration topology**   Applications are not affiliated with each other permanently. In an integrated system, applications may get added, updated or removed. If all applications must be manually updated to reflect such topology changes, they will incur significant downtimes and disconnections across application boundaries. Ideally, an integration system should allow new applications to be plugged into the system and old applications to be removed from the system without impacting other running applications.

Messaging systems provides nice solutions to address the above challenges:

- Messaging systems allow loose coupling. Through messaging systems, applications are loosely coupled without direct references to each other. Applications interact with each other by sending and receiving messages at abstract addresses, which can be dynamically bound to different message-handling entities. This additional layer of abstraction allows applications to remain independent—they don't even need to know other systems exist on the other side of a message pipeline.

- Messaging systems provide message buffers between applications so that applications with different processing capacities can work together. Messages from faster applications are queued in the messaging system. This allows the faster applications to proceed without waiting for the slower applications. Message buffers also enable offline communications because an application can be offline when the messages are generated and come online at a later time to drain the message queue.

- A messaging system can support several types of communication patterns, such as 1-to-1, 1-to-many, and many-to-many. And as an application topology changes, new applications can join the community without affecting existing applications. For example, an application A publishes to a topic T. Any subscriber to the topic gets a copy of the message when A pushes a new message. When a new application joins, it simply subscribes to the same T topic and start to interact with application A and other applications without needing any reconfiguration of application A.

- A message system often supports common communication channels and protocols such as REST, AMQP, MQTT, XMPP, WCF, and more. These protocols are widely supported by different languages and frameworks, allowing them to work across platform boundaries to connect systems on different technological stacks together.

System integration patterns

Over the years, the software industry has accumulated tens of proven integration patterns, many of which have been built into Azure messaging services. These patterns help you to address the most common challenges in system integration. These patterns enrich your system design tools and reduce the risk of incorrect designs. So, it's worthwhile to study how to recognize opportunities to apply these patterns when possible.

It's obviously impossible to cover all possible message-based integration patterns. The following sections provide brief descriptions of some of the most commonly used patterns.

Competing consumers

In most systems, generating work items is much faster than processing work items. Hence, it's very common for a system to recruit multiple work item processors to share the workload.

Some architects use a centralized message dispatcher that maintains a list of processors and dispatches messages to these processors. However, this approach suffers from several shortcomings. First, a centralized message dispatcher introduces a Single Point of Failure (SPoF) into the system. When it fails, the message dispatching stops, and the whole system breaks down. The centralized component is also a potential bottleneck, because all messages need to be funneled through it. Second, a centralized message dispatcher adds unnecessarily complexity. For the dispatcher to dispatch messages to processors, it needs to maintain a list of registered processors. It also needs monitor health states of these processors so that it doesn't send messages to a broken processor or an overloaded processor. Third, error handling is complex. When a processor fails to process a message, the message needs to be somehow returned to the dispatcher so that it can be dispatched to another processor.

The Competing Consumer pattern provides an elegant solution without requiring a centralized component. With the pattern, several processors subscribe to a message topic and compete to drain the work item queue, as illustrated by Figure 5-8.

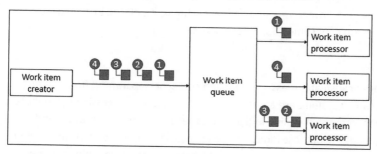

FIGURE 5-8 Competing Consumer pattern

The Competing Consumers pattern has server advantages over a centralized message dispatcher solution. First, there isn't a centralized a component. Any number of item processors can join the workforce by subscribing to the same work item queue. This allows the system to be horizontally scaled at any time without centralized coordination. Second, the work item processors handle work items and their own paces. This allows these processors to work at their full capacities without overloading themselves. Third, queuing services such as Azure Service Bus queue allows a work item processor to place exclusive but auto-expiring locks on work items. Before a work item processor handles a work item, it places a lock on the work item so that the item won't be picked up by other processors. When the processor finishes with the item, it will remove the item from the queue. However, if a processor crashes while processing an item, the lock on the item will eventually expire so that it can be picked up by another processor.

When using the Competing Consumer pattern, you need to be aware of several characteristics:

- The Competing Consumer pattern ensures a work item to be processed at least once. However, it doesn't guarantee an item be processed only once. For example, a processor A locks on an item, does all the processing, and crashes before it can unlock the item. Then, as the lock expires, the item can be picked up by another processor B and be worked on again.

- The Competing Consumer pattern assumes the messaging system is highly available. Fortunately, Azure-provided messaging systems are all designed for global availability, resilience and scalability. So, this assumption is usually safe in most cases.

- The Competing Consumer pattern doesn't guarantee the order in which the work items are processed. Because different processors can move at different speeds, work items are likely to be processed out of order.

- A malformed or misconfigured work item may cause great damage. A bad work item may trigger a bug in the work processor can cause the work processor to crash. As the work item gets unlocked and tried by other work processors, the same error will take down other work processors. Depending upon how fast the work processors can recover, a bad item might bring down the whole processing pipeline. A dead letter queue can be used in this case; once a work item fails a few times, it's placed in a dead letter queue so that it doesn't consume additional resources.

Messaging gateway

The messaging gateway encapsulates message-handling code and separates it from the rest of the application. Messaging systems are asynchronous by nature. And accessing to a remote messaging system needs common handling logics such as security, message creation, and retries for failed connections. All of these logics can be encapsulated into a generic messaging gateway that enables a system for messaging-based integrations without requiring too many changes to existing applications.

The messaging gateway pattern is shown in Figure 5-9. Message gateways enable messaging-based integrations across applications that haven't been designed with asynchronous messaging in mind. The messaging gateways handle all of the complexity of reliable communication with the messaging system, providing a synchronous API to the application if needed.

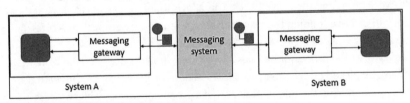

FIGURE 5-9 Messaging gateway pattern

Other than intrusive ways to integrate a messaging system to an existing system, there are a few nonintrusive ways to connect a messaging gateway to an existing system. First, if the system already supports remote calls, the messaging gateway can implement the remote call API to communicate with the existing system. Second, a messaging gateway can tap into the logging system of an existing system to extract and send messages. This method is suitable only for messaging-sending (such as notifications to other systems).

Regardless of implementations, a Message Mapper is often needed to translate between domain objects and messages. When multiple systems are expected to work together, a Message Translate can further translate between a canonical message format and system-specific message formats. When translating to canonical message formats, you should constrain yourself from sending default values to unrecognized/unsupported fields, even if the other party requires you to do so, unless there's an agreed upon specification that clearly states specified default values. Null values are clear indications that the field is not supported by your system. Filling it with any values may cause confusions down the road.

Event sourcing

Event sourcing is not an integration-specific pattern. However, because event sourcing allows you to play back system event sequences, it's often used as an integration or cross-region backup and failover solution.

The basic idea of event sourcing is to initiate all domain object changes through event objects. If all system events are recorded and persisted, you can in theory rebuild system state from scratch at any point of time. Event sourcing provides some quite powerful features. For example, if you found a wrong transaction in the event history, which has led to a series rippling errors across the system, this could be difficult to be tracked down and fixed. With event sourcing, you can rewind the system back to the transaction, fix it, and play back all events afterwards to bring the system up-to-date again.

Of course, playing back events from the very beginning of the system isn't efficient and often impractical. Many event sourcing systems implement periodical checkpoints. The events before the checkpoint are discarded, which means when you try to recover a system, you can only rewind back to the earliest archived checkpoint.

When used as a disaster recovery solution, events in an event sourcing system is periodically shipped to a secondary site based on the system's Recovery Point Objective (RPO) and Recovery Time Objective (RTO). More aggressive RPO and RTO goals require more frequent shipments of events. And to recover a failed primary, the primary is first brought back to the last known checkpoint. Then, events from the secondary since the checkpoint are shipped back to the primary for playback.

When used as an integration solution, events from one system are sent to a secondary system. However, because the events in an event sourcing system usually have fine granularity, some additional messing patterns are needed to reduce the amount of transmission. For example, a message filter can be used to filter out unrelated events; a message aggregator can be used to aggregate related events into fewer events.

Azure Messaging Services

Two of the most common messaging paradigm are queues and pub/subs. A message on a message queue usually has only one consumer. Once a message is retrieved from the queue, it's not available to other consumers. Pub/sub, on the other hand, allows a message to be sent to multiple recipients at the same time. This section first compares queuing options provided by Azure messaging services and then compares pub/sub options.

Queuing options

Table 5-1 presents a comparison between of two queuing services provided by Azure: Azure Storage Queues and Azure Service Bus Queue. Then, some of the key characteristics will be compared to help you make informed decisions.

Table 5-1 Azure Queuing services

Comparison Criteria	Azure Storage Queues	Azure Service Bus Queues
Ordering guarantee	No	FIFO guarantees within session
Delivery guarantee	At least once	At least once or at most once
Atomic operation	No	Yes
Receive behavior	Non-blocking	Blocking with/without timeout or non-blocking
Push-style API	No	Yes
Receive mode	Peek & lease	Peek & lock or Receive & delete
Exclusive access mode	Lease-based	Lock-based
Lease/lock duration	30 seconds (default)/7 days (maximum)	60 seconds (default)
Lease/lock precision	Message level	Queue level
Batched receive	Yes	Yes
Batched send	No	Yes

(data source: https://docs.microsoft.com/en-us/azure/service-bus-messaging/service-bus-azure-and-service-bus-queues-compared-contrasted)

■ Both storage queue and service bus support peeking the queue without de-queuing messages. When a message is de-queued, the client holds a time-based lease or lock. The message is invisible to other clients as long as the lease/lock is valid. Once the lease expires, the message becomes visible to other clients for consumption. Peek & lock is the key mechanism to enable reliable message processing in the Competing Consumer pattern. However, if you don't need such high reliability, you can use the Receive & Delete model, which de-queue the message immediately when you get the message from the queue.

■ Both queuing services support at-least once delivery, which means a message is guaranteed to be delivered but can be delivered multiple times. Service Bus queue also supports at-most once delivery, which guarantees a message won't be delivered multiple times.

Service Bus Queue is designed for generic messaging scenarios, while Azure Storage Queue is suitable for storage-related messaging. The two messaging systems have different limits and quotas on message sizes, queue lengths and concurrent clients. For example, Storage Queue supports messages up to 64KB in size, while Service Bus Queue supports larger message sizes up to 1MB. For a specific system, you may need to do some measurements in terms of latency and throughput before you can decide which messaging systems to use.

You can also use batched delivery to balance between latency and throughput as needed. Batched delivery can usually increase overall system throughput, but individual message latency is sacrificed. In most of the integration scenarios, batched delivery is usually preferred.

Pub/sub options

The pub/sub pattern allows a message publisher to publish messages to multiple subscribers. You can implement the pattern on Azure by using Azure Service Bus Topics, Event Hub, and Event Grid.

All three services support message publication and subscription. And there aren't definitive rules on which service to choose. However, they do have their corresponding suitable scenarios. Service Bus is designed for high-reliable messaging across systems. If your system doesn't allow lost messages or needs strong transactional supports, you should consider Service Bus. Event Grid is designed for the reactive programming model where processing units (or functions) are linked by reactive event streams. Event Hub is designed for IoT scenarios and telemetry delivery.

Service Bus doesn't support pushing messages to subscribers. Instead, message subscribers need to monitor the subscribed topics to get new messages. Event Hub supports pushing message through AMQP. Event Grid supports built-in messaging connectors from and to many Azure services, as shown in Figure 5-10.

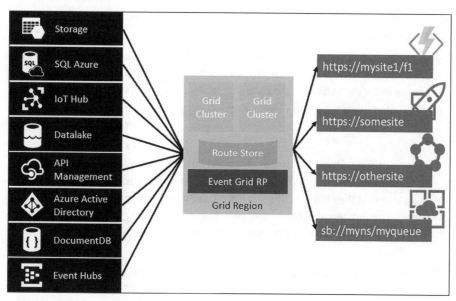

FIGURE 5-10 Azure Event Grid

Reactive systems

The Reactive Manifesto (*https://www.reactivemanifesto.org/*) defines four key characteristics of a Reactive System: Responsive, Resilient, Elastic, and Message Driven. A well-designed microservices system should assume all the characteristics. However, responsiveness and message driven are not mandatory to a microservices system. On the other hand, a reactive system on cloud is practically a microservices system that provides responsiveness and message-driven characteristics.

Responsive

Responsiveness requires a system remain responsive and consistent under all conditions, even when the system is under heavy load or is experiencing errors.

In a reactive system, handling processes are triggered by arrivals of new data. As soon as new data arrives, the corresponding processing units are triggered. And because these processing units run in parallel, there are no centralized scheduling or locking to slow them down. The processing units are also isolated and can be confined within resource consumption boundaries. This isolation ensures consistency by avoiding busy processing units stealing resources from others.

Resilient

Component isolation also limits the blast radius of an error so that a system doesn't lose significant amount of processing power because of a few errors.

The overall resiliency of a system is often achieved by redundancy. For example, data high availability can be achieved by data replications; service high availability can be achieved by multiple service instances behind a load balancer; and cross-system availability can be achieved by integration patterns such as Circuit Breaker.

Elastic

Elasticity means a reactive system can horizontally scale out and scale in as its load changes. A system with centralized components is often hard to be scaled out because these components tend to assume that they have visibility to the entire system state, or they have complete control over all working processes in the system. When multiple copies of such components are launched, they will step onto each other can cause confusions and sometimes-catastrophic failures.

Isolated, stateless services are very easy to scale. As the workload increases, additional instances of stateless services can be initiated to share the workload. When the workload dries out, extra instances can be taken down to conserve compute resources. Stateful services are harder to scale because the stickiness of data forbids these components to be launched, relocated and destroyed freely. A common way to scale stateful service is to use partitions. However, dynamic repartitioning can still be challenging. In many systems that need stateful services, the scope of the stateful service is minimized to ensure mobility of the stateful layer.

For example, in many IoT solutions, a digital twin of a device is only responsible for state management of a single device, making it easier to be replicated, backed up, and restored.

Message-driven

Message-driven is a key component of a reactive system. Microservices decouple components in space. And Message driven components are decoupled in time. Decoupling in space allows services to evolve independently. It also allows flexible service deployment topologies, including foundation of mobility, distribution, resource balancing, scaling, and failover. Decoupling in time allows services to operate independently. It allows concurrency, streaming, batching, resiliency, isolation, and elasticity.

Reactive systems and serverless

A reactive system is made up by processing units and reactive streams connecting them. To satisfy the elastic and reliance requirements of a reactive system, processing units need to be isolated and mobilized. Moreover, compute resources need to be dynamically recruited as the system load changes. Dynamic compute resource management is a generic problem that many elastic systems would like to delegate to the underlying hosting platform. Because the serverless concept promises completely offloading resource management concerns to the hosting platform, it's an ideal paradigm to host reactive systems.

Azure Functions

Azure Functions is one of the key Azure offerings for serverless compute. Azure Functions allows you to write your reactive logics in the language of your choice, such as JavaScript, C#, F#, PHP, Bash, Batch, and PowerShell. Then, you simply hand the code to Azure Functions, configure inbound and outbound connections, and Azure Functions takes care of the rest.

SAMPLE SCENARIO: BLOB NOTIFICATIONS AND AZURE FUNCTIONS

In this sample scenario, you create a system that automatically reacts to new blob events on your storage account and sends a tweet about the new blob to your subscribers. The system architecture is as shown in Figure 5-11. To set up the environment, you need to follow these high-level steps:

1. Create a new storage account with a public blob container.

2. Create a new Azure Functions application with a function that reads the incoming blob event and sends out a tweet to Twitter. Set the trigger of the function as a web hook.

```
public static HttpResponseMessage Run(HttpRequestMessage req, TraceWriter log)
{
    // Get request body
    var jsonString = req.Content.ReadAsStringAsync().Result;
    var events = JsonConvert.DeserializeObject<GridEvent[]>(
        jsonString, new JsonSerializerSettings { ContractResolver = new
CamelCasePropertyNamesContractResolver() });
    TwitterData twitterData = new TwitterData();
    twitterData.Initalize(events[0]);
```

```
    var consumerKey = GetEnvironmentVariable("consumerKey");
    var consumerSecret = GetEnvironmentVariable("consumerSecret");
    var accessToken = GetEnvironmentVariable("accessToken");
    var accessTokenSecret = GetEnvironmentVariable("accessTokenSecret");
    Auth.SetUserCredentials(consumerKey, consumerSecret, accessToken,
accessTokenSecret);
    Tweet.PublishTweet(twitterData.ToString());
    log.Info("Tweeted event!");
    return req.CreateResponse(HttpStatusCode.OK, "");
}
```

3. Create a new Event Grid subscription to a Storage Accounts topic. Set up the event type to be "Blob Created" and the event target endpoint to be the function's endpoint. Optionally, you can also set up prefix filters or postfix filters. For example, you can set up a ".jpg" filter to trigger only on new *.jpg* files.

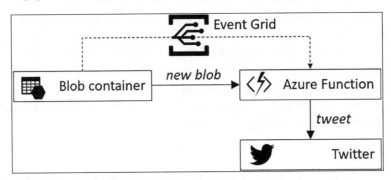

FIGURE 5-11 Blob Notification with Azure Functions

Logic Apps

Azure Functions provides individual processing units. Logic Apps provides complete, distributed workflows. Logic Apps is serverless because as a developer, you don't need to need to manage any underlying infrastructures supporting your workloads. Logic Apps is reactive because your workflows respond to various triggers, execute in parallel and integrate with other systems via messaging.

SAMPLE SCENARIO: INTELLIGENT CUSTOMER ENGAGEMENT

The best way to appreciate the power of Logic Apps is to see it in action in a real scenario. In this scenario, the system monitors tweets with specific hashtags (such as a product name or a company name). When new tweets with the hashtag are detected, the system runs these tweets through Azure Cognitive to detect sentiment of the tweets. If it finds a negative tweet, it will look the sender up in the company's CRM system. If the sender is a managed account, it will then extract the business email address from the CRM system and look for email interactions between an executive and the specific customer. If the executive has communicated with the customer a few times before, the system automatically sends an email to the executive with tweet details and reminds the executive to engage with the customer directly. The overall workflow is as shown in Figure 5-12.

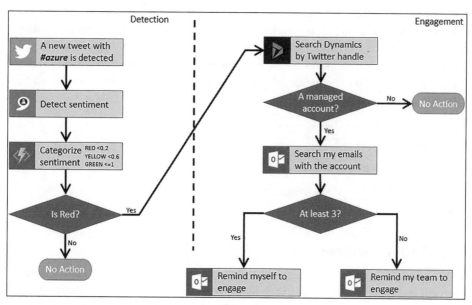

FIGURE 5-12 Intelligent customer engagement workflow

Push notifications to mobile devices

To complete an end-to-end scenario from intelligent cloud to intelligent edge, you sometimes need to push notifications to mobile devices. However, pushing to mobile devices is not an easy task, because different devices use different mechanisms for push notifications, such as APNs (Apple Push Notification services) for iOS, GCM (Google Cloud Messaging) for Android, and WNS (Windows Push Notification Service) and MPNS (Microsoft Push Notification Service) for Windows.

Azure Notification Hub hides all of the platform details, allowing you to push millions of messages to all major platforms. You can also set up sophisticated policies to tailor your messages by customer, language, and location. Using push notifications is a great way to engage with your customer to provide better user experiences. For example, after a user submits a long-running job, she doesn't need to wait around by the computer. Instead, a notification on job completion will push to her once the task has been completed. Push notifications are also great for proactive engagements with customers to trigger new business opportunities. For example, you can push recommendations based on time and user's location so that you can recommend merchandises relevant to the environment.

Skill 5.4: Design for media service solutions

Building and hosting a dedicated, large-scale media service is not a common project for most architects and developers. And for occasional video publications to the public, existing public video services suffice in most cases. However, for enterprise internal multimedia content management that requires media content to be captured, streamed, and archived in an isolated environment, you'll need something like Azure Media Services to build an end-to-end media hosting and management solution.

> **This section covers how to:**
> - Understand Azure Media Services
> - Use Azure Media Indexer
> - Monitor media services

Azure Media Services

Azure Media Services is an extensible PaaS offering that you can use to build scalable media management and delivery applications. With Media Services you can securely upload, store, encode, and package video or audio content for both on-demand and live streaming delivery to various device endpoints (for example, TV, PCs, and mobile devices).

You can build entire end-to-end workflows using Media Services. You can also choose to use third-party components for some parts of your workflow. For example, you can encode using a third-party encoder and then upload, protect, package, and deliver using Media Services. Figure 5-13 shows the major components in Media Services in the typical order in which they are used in a standard workflow.

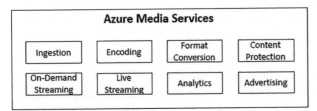

FIGURE 5-13 Azure Media Services

Key components of Media Services

Media Services is a set of many components that function together to create workflows to serve your media. You can create workflow to provide video on demand, video streaming, or the ability to monitor the work being done. Figure 5-13 shows the various components that comprise Media Services.

Typically, video is encoded and stored in the format in which it will be streamed or downloaded. This means that more storage and processing is needed when the assets are uploaded to Media Services because they might be packaged with HLS for users on iOS and Android, but they might use Smooth Streaming on Xbox and Windows. Dynamic packaging is a feature of Media Services by which you can skip the pre-packaging process and package the asset on the fly, based on the platform that is requesting it.

For many companies, security of the media they are streaming is very important. Companies such as Netflix charge people to view its content, and it wants to prevent piracy, as well. For other companies, such as one providing a web broadcast of a free event, piracy is not as big of a concern. In either case, there needs to be protection from man-in-the-middle attacks. With this type of attack, malicious individuals can inject their own data into what is being sent or modify the original content. Media Services supports two types of security models: an AES Clear Key dynamic encryption, and a Digital Rights Management (DRM) technology.

AES Clear Key dynamic encryption is a basic "lite" encryption. This is done on-the-wire and is widely known as *symmetric AES encryption*. When using AES, there can be authentication restrictions in place. The first type is an open restriction. With an open restriction, the client asks for a clear key, and that is what is sent to the player and used to decrypt content. This means that this is a player and a client that is trusted. The second way is to use a token restriction. Media Services does not provide its own token system; instead, it uses other Secure Token Systems (STS) providers. Tokens can be in the Simple Web Token (SWT) format or the JSON Web Token (JWT) format. You can create a custom STS or use Azure AD to create the tokens. The tokens are then sent to Media Services, and the delivery service will then provide an encryption key if the token is valid for the content.

The second security option is to use a DRM technology, PlayReady. With DRM technology, you can define a restrictive licensing agreement to manage user access rights to the content. This can then support additional business models, such as a paid video streaming service. Before content is uploaded to Media Services, it is pre-encrypted by the PlayReady system using your license, content keys, and a Key ID. This is all done before the file is moved into storage. This client then asks for a license from the PlayReady server to allow the user access to the content. Media Services just serves up the encrypted file to the clients; it is decoded using the license from PlayReady. This security method uses common encryption scheme (CENS) to encrypt to the smooth streaming content.

Live Streaming

Another feature that Media Services supports is the live streaming of content. This feature was used to stream the 2014 Sochi Winter Olympic games and the 2016 Rio Summer Olympic games. This included live video encoding and streaming, access from web and mobile devices, and capacity for more than 100 million viewers for the Sochi event, and over 3 billion minutes for the Rio event. One problem that many companies have when trying to create a live-streaming system is the capital expenses to purchase servers and other supporting systems. Media Services facilitates this without the crushing capital expenses, and companies can ramp up to a global scale quickly. There is yet one more benefit: When the need is over, the system can be removed from your Media Services platform immediately.

The first step to set up live streaming is to configure a channel to use to ingest the live stream. When a channel is created, it will provide two URLs to be used in the next step. The first is an ingest URL. You can set the protocol on this URL to either RTMP or to Fragmented MP4. The second URI is a Preview URL. With the Preview URL, you can preview what the stream is before it is published.

After the channel is set up, you must add a program to it. The program will specify the duration of an archive window as well as the encryption method for the streaming. When the program is configured and published, the live streaming can be viewed. The setting for the name of the asset for the live stream in the program will be created in the Content section of Media Services.

Azure Media Indexer

An additional service that is available in Media Services is the Media Indexer. Using the Media Indexer, you can make content of your media files searchable and generate a full-text transcript for closed captioning and keywords. You can also index files that are publicly available on the Internet by specifying URLs of the files in the manifest file. You can run the Media Indexer on a single content file or you can batch it to handle a large number of files.

An indexing job generates various output files, which include a score for the indexing job based on how recognizable the speech in the source video is. You can use the value to screen output files for usability. A low score means poor indexing results due to audio quality. Background music is something that can reduce how well the speech is recognized.

Monitor Services

To monitor the data and the Media Services, you first need to turn on monitoring for the Blob container. After you do this, you can use Media Service dashboard to keep an eye on information such as Encoder Data In, Encoder Data Out, Failed Tasks, Queued Jobs, Streaming Data Out, Streaming HTTP Errors, and Streaming Requests. You can view the last six hours up to the last seven days of data.

Thought experiment

In this thought experiment, demonstrate your skills and knowledge of the topics covered in this chapter. You can find answer to this thought experiment in the next section.

Azure provides a rich set of platform services that you can use in your application. It's great that you have many flexible options to choose from. However, this also means you may need to accumulate and refresh on tremendous amount Azure knowledge so that you can make informed choices when you design your own systems.

With this in mind, answer the following questions:

1. What strategies you can use to reduce the risks of make wrong choices?

2. How would you design a cloud-native application?

Thought experiment answers

This section contains the solution to the thought experiment.

1. Although projects have very different requirements and different functional and non-functional goals, there are some common strategies that can help you to control the risk when you navigate through the complex cloud world. First, you should try to decompose your application into smaller, controllable pieces that are largely independent from each other. This allows you to control the impacts of wrong decisions and gives you more flexibility to correct wrong choices. Independent services also give you flexible hosting options so that you can adjust your system capacity to meet workload demands. Second, recognizing opportunities to reuse proven patterns is a very important strategy for architects to reduce the risks of wrong designs because these patterns have been repeatedly reused and tested over the years. Third, when you make design decisions, you should try your best to base your decisions on data. Please note here "data" doesn't refer to what's stated in documentations but to what you can measure based on your own workloads. For example, there are many techniques you can use to tune system throughput and latency, such as caching, partitioning, batching, and resource balancing, etc. You need to perform representative measurements that can guide you to an optimum balance for your specific workloads. Data-driven decisions also help you to avoid illogical decisions such as ones made based on personal preferences. What's listed above are just a few strategies that have been proven to be useful. This is obviously not a complete list. But hopefully this list can give you some ideas to come up with your own methodologies.

2. Using microservices is an effective way to design and operate applications on the cloud. Instead of building monolithic applications, you should design your applications as independent services. Only when your services become mobilized components, your application can enjoy the QoS offerings from cloud. For example, to dynamically scale your application, the cloud platform needs to create and tear down service instances as needed. This requires your services to be designed so that they can be deployed quickly and be torn down at any time without side effects. Stateless services are easier to be moved and scaled. So, when you design your applications, you should try to constrain a number of stateful services that you use. You should also pay close attention to inter-dependencies among your services. Centralized services form bottlenecks and possible single point of failures in your system, so they should be avoided. Last but not least, you should try to minimize direct coupling among your services. Instead, you should use messaging systems to loosely couple your services.

Chapter summary

- Azure provides a rich set of platforms that you can incorporate into your applications to help you realize common scenarios with high availability, reliability and scalability.

- Azure provides a comprehensive, end-to-end solution for AI workloads. You can use Azure machine learning to develop and train your models; you can use Azure Bot Services to bring conversations to your applications; you can use prebuild AI models in Azure Cognitive Services; and you can use Azure hardware such as GPUs to speed up your model trainings.

- An end-to-end IoT solution spans cloud and edge. IoT Edge schedules workloads to a compute plane on the edge. When data reaches the cloud, it goes through a data pipeline on the server.

- Azure IoT Suites provides prebuild, end-to-end IoT solutions for typical scenarios such as predictive maintenance and remote monitoring.

- Azure provides a comprehensive IoT data pipeline. Azure IoT Hubs manages device registrations and ingests data to Azure. Then, the data flow through a pipe made up by various processing units, streaming and storage services. For example, IoT Time Series Insights helps you to gain insights of your time series data. Azure Stream Analytics allows you to use SQL-like queries to aggregate and analyze your data. Azure Power BI allows you to present your results.

- Message-based integration is a proven solution for system integration. There are many reusable patterns you can use to address common needs, such as the Competing Consumer pattern, Message Gateway pattern, and event sourcing pattern.

- Azure provides queuing services such as Azure Storage Queues and Azure Service Bus Queues. It also provides global-scale pub/sub options such as Azure Service Bus Topics, Event Hub, and Event Grid. And finally, you can use Notification Hub to push notifications to devices on any platforms.

- Azure provides serverless-hosting options such as Azure Functions and Azure Logic Apps. Azure also provides messaging systems that can be used as reactive streams in reactive systems. Azure Logic Apps allows business users to assemble complex workflows using prebuilt processing units such as email sender, image analyzer, and CRM searchers.

- You can use Azure Media Service to provide enterprise-scoped or public media solutions that cover media streaming, encoding, hosting, publishing and security.

Design for operations

Maintaining the availability of our infrastructure is an important aspect of IT operations. To maintain availability, design and deploy with requirements and scope in mind. Monitor systems for issues and potential issues, which need to be mitigated and logged. Issues can be related to an element of the system or even, in the case of a major disaster, the complete outage of the entire data center. Fortunately, you can design strategies and processes and deploy tools to take the most of this massive burden off you and put it on automated systems.

In this chapter, you will learn how you can use tools to deploy an effective strategy to monitor and manage systems and even automate systems deployment and the remediation of issues. You will learn about automation tools that will help ensure that when systems are deployed or changed, they maintain best practices or even company preferences. There are three different angles to understand: application monitoring, platform monitoring, and automation. There are many tools to support this effort. System Center, Azure PowerShell, the Azure Management Portal and Azure services, and other capabilities can be designed to keep systems maintaining uptime. As we look at the different components and tools you can use, you will learn about what design elements you should deploy in various situations.

Skills in this chapter:
- Skill 6.1: Design an application monitoring and alerting strategy
- Skill 6.2: Design a platform monitoring and alerting strategy
- Skill 6.3: Design an operations automation strategy

Skill 6.1: Design an application monitoring and alerting strategy

Application monitoring is analyzing data collected from the application and systems that run the application and then acting on that data as needed to ensure performance, health, and the availability of the application. To design an application monitoring and alerting strategy for Azure, you need to understand the tools and capabilities for monitoring. You need to learn how to analyze logs, analyze performance metrics, monitor services including deep application insights, and how to enable alerts. Microsoft Azure has a monitoring platform built-in as several cloud services. These services allow you to visualize, query, route, archive, and monitor metrics and logs coming from resources in Azure. Azure has many services that provide this capability. These services provide visibility into the application along with anything that the application relies on to sustain function and availability. All of these systems and capabilities are important, and all provide different depths of monitoring. Using Azure monitoring services you can determine if the application is accessible from the web, and the services can provide deep application insights such as how long it takes to retrieve a dataset from a database call.

This section covers the following topics:

- Determine the appropriate Microsoft products and services for monitoring applications on Azure
- Define solutions for analyzing logs and enabling alerts using Azure Log Analytics
- Define solutions for analyzing performance metrics and enabling alerts using Azure Monitor
- Define a solution for monitoring applications and enabling alerts using Application Insights

---

Determine the appropriate Microsoft products and services for monitoring applications on Azure

Azure monitoring services used for monitoring applications on Azure include:

- Azure Monitor
- Azure Advisor
- Azure Service Health
- Azure Activity Log
- Azure Dashboards
- Azure Metrics Explorer
- Azure Alerts
- Azure Log Analytics
- Azure Application Insights

Other tools and services are leveraged to visualize and remediate issues. Some of these include the Azure Portal, PowerShell, Azure CLI, REST APIs, Analytics, Automation, and Scheduler. All tools and services can be used together to effectively monitor and remediate issues.

Azure Monitor

Azure Monitor has three basic categories of data: activity logs, metrics, and diagnostic logs. More on metrics and diagnostics logs later in this section. The activity log will give many insights. Using the Activity Log, you can determine when things happened, what happened, who did it, and when it happened for any create, update, or delete operations on resources in your subscription. The Activity log collects logs for errors, alerts, outage, notifications and more. In the portal NAV bar, click More services (or All services), type in **monitor**, and click Activity Log. See Figure 6-1.

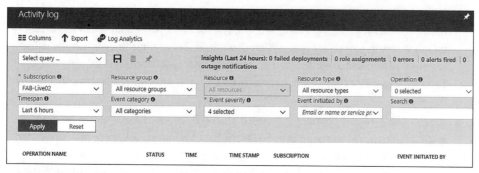

FIGURE 6-1 Activity Log

When a web application is stopped, the Activity Log tells when it happened and by whom. Storage of the details of Activity Log events is maintained on the platform and available to query for 90 days. You can limit the timespan of logs you look at through the filter. Other filter mechanisms are also available to help visualize individual services and groups. Once you set a filter, you can save the filter and then pin it to your dashboard.

In the list view, you can change the columns that are displayed by clicking Columns at the upper-left corner of the application, as shown in Figure 6-1. If you click to drill down on an activity log, you can get additional information. There are two tabs of information. A list of basic information is available in the summary tab; the same information is available in JSON format on the JSON tab.

> **NOTE   CLASSIC SERVICE MODEL RDFE**
>
> RDFE (Red Dog Front End) is the service endpoint that Windows Azure Pack for Windows Server and API installs and uses. This endpoint forwards and validates calls to Service Provider Foundation. It is the foundation of Classic resources in Azure.

EXAM TIP

The Azure Activity Log is primarily for activities that occur in Azure Resource Manager. It does not track resources using the Classic/RDFE model. Some Classic resource types have a proxy resource provider in Azure Resource Manager (for example, Microsoft.ClassicCompute). The operations appear in the Activity Log if you interact with a Classic resource type through Azure Resource Manager using these proxy resource providers.

The categories of data in the Activity Log include:

- **Administrative** This category contains the record of all create, update, delete, and action operations performed through Resource Manager. Examples of the types of events in this category include "create virtual machine" and "delete network security group."

- **Service Health** This category contains the record of any service health incidents that have occurred in Azure. An example of the type of event you would see in this category is "SQL Azure in East US is experiencing downtime." Service health events come in five varieties: Action Required, Assisted Recovery, Incident, Maintenance, Information, or Security, and only appear if you have a resource in the subscription that is impacted by the event.

- **Alert** This category contains the record of all activations of Azure alerts. An example is "CPU % on myVM has been over 80 for the past 5 minutes." A variety of Azure systems have an alerting concept. You can define a rule of some sort and receive a notification when conditions match that rule. A record of the activation is also pushed to this category of the Activity Log each time a supported Azure alert type "activates," or the conditions are met to generate a notification.

- **Autoscale** This category contains the record of any events related to the operation of the autoscale engine based on any autoscale settings you have defined in your subscription, such as "Autoscale scale up action failed." Using autoscale, you can automatically scale out or scale in the number of instances in a supported resource type based on time of day and load (metric) data using an autoscale setting. Start, succeeded, and failed events are recorded in this category when the conditions are met to scale.

- **Recommendation** This category contains recommendation events from certain resource types, such as websites and SQL servers. These events offer recommendations for how to better use your resources. You only receive events of this type if you have resources that emit recommendations.

- **Security** This category contains the record of any alerts generated by Azure Security Center, for example, "Suspicious double extension file executed."

- **Policy and Resource Health** These categories do not contain any events; they are reserved for future use.

Azure Portal, PowerShell, Azure CLI, or REST API can evaluate Activity Logs. The logs can also be ingested or streamed into Azure Log Analytics for deeper analytics.

Define solutions for analyzing logs and enabling alerts using Azure Log Analytics

Log Analytics is a service that ingests logs from Azure Monitor and on-premises or other systems. Log Analytics correlates logs from multiple sources allowing you to perform additional analysis on the collection of logs, which are then viewed, queried, or further analyzed for insights on the entire system. Logs can be accessed and presented through the Azure Portal using standard views allowing search or dashboards. The search is a built-in capability that allows for saving searches that can be run and refreshed in the portal or leveraged in automation to act on the result of differences in the search results over time.

Exporting data to Excel or PowerBI allows for analyzing and visualizing the log data outside of Log Analytics. It allows for connectivity to alerts and dashboards. There is also a Log Search API to integrate with other systems or build custom solutions for reading or integrating Log Analytics data. Log Analytics can be expanded to add logic, visualization, and data acquisition rules to provide insight around a particular area or set of systems. Management Solutions provide additional functionality, including metrics and alerting capabilities. The Azure Portal is used to install management solutions.

There are many management solutions available in Azure. One management solution, Network Performance Monitor (NPM), is a cloud-based hybrid network monitoring solution that helps you monitor network performance between various points in your network infrastructure. It also helps monitor network connectivity to service endpoints and monitor the performance of your Azure ExpressRoute. This management solution adds metrics for monitoring endpoints, network performance, and more. It also provides network discovery, as well as dashboard visualizations.

The first step to analyze logs and metrics is to create an Operations Management Suite (OMS) Log Analytics workspace. The workspace includes a data repository and other management and configuration capabilities to ingest and visualize logs from many different sources such as:

- Azure resources (Azure Monitor and Azure Diagnostics)
- On-premises computers monitored by System Center Operations Manager
- Device collections from System Center Configuration Manager
- Diagnostic or log data from Azure Storage
- Countless External Sources including:
    - Windows and Linux server logs (virtual machines or hosts)
    - HTTP Data Collector API can be used to write data to the repository from a REST API client.

Let's create a workspace while adding a Network Performance Monitoring management solution.

1. In the Azure portal, click **Create A Resource** > **Monitoring + Management** > **See All** > click **More** to the right of Management Solutions.

2. Scroll down and click the **Load More** link. This link displays more Management Solutions. In the list of management solutions continue to scroll down and click **Load More** until Network Performance Monitor is visible. Click **Network Performance Monitor**, then click **Create**.

3. Click **OMS Workspace**, then **Create New Workspace**. This is where we create the OMS workspace. On the OMS Workspace blade fill in additional details as follows:

   A. **Create New**   Leave Create New turned on.

   B. **OMS Workspace**   Type in a workspace name such as **535BookWorkspaceXXXxxx** (where XXXxxx are any unique characters used to make your selection unique in all of Azure OMS).

   C. **Subscription**   Select a subscription from the drop-down list.

   D. **Resource group**   Click **Use Existing**, then select your resource group. You may also create a new Resource Group if you prefer.

   E. **Location**   Add **Select A Location Of Your Choice** from the location drop-down list.

   F. Optionally turn on **Pin To Dashboard** then click **OK**. The OMS workspace will go through validation, and then deployment.

4. Once the OMS workspace is created, click Create on the Network Performance Monitor blade. Creating both the OMS workspace and the Network Performance Monitor is usually quick. Once complete, we will need to configure additional options on the Network Performance Monitor.

5. Click **All Services** > **Monitoring + Management** > **Log Analytics**, then click your workspace name (535BookWorkspaceXXXxxx). This will open the OMS Workspace Log Analytics blade. Click **OMS Portal** at the top of the blade. This will open a new web tab or page with your OMS Portal. The Network Performance Monitor will be available on a tile with a note *Solution requires additional configuration*.

6. Click the **Network Performance Monitor** tile from the OMS Workspace to open up the Overview > **Network Performance Monitor** > **Network Performance Monitor configuration blade**. On the first tab, *Common Settings*, you can download OMS agents or download a PowerShell script to configure agents for monitoring using PowerShell and the TCP protocol.

7. Click the **Performance Monitor** tab. There are two protocols that can be used for near real-time monitoring of network performance, TCP and ICMP. Use TCP for synthetic transactions is already turned on. TCP is not supported on Windows Client based nodes where the OMS agent is installed.

8. Select **Use ICMP** for synthetic transactions to avoid manual deployment steps. This setting can be easily changed at any time. Click **Save & Continue** to advance to the Service Endpoint Monitor (Preview) tab.

9. On the Service Endpoint Monitor (Preview) tab you can turn on Office 365 monitoring and Dynamics 365 monitoring. Azure PaaS Monitoring will be available soon. Click **Save & Continue** to advance to the ExpressRoute Monitor setup.

10. On the **ExpressRoute Monitor** tab you can download a PowerShell script to run on all agents using an ExpressRoute connection.

11. Once you install agents for the network performance monitor the setup will be complete.

MORE INFO **CREATING AN OMS WORKSPACE WITHOUT ADDING A MANAGEMENT SOLUTION**

1. Click **All services** > **Monitoring + Management** > **Log Analytics** > **Add**. The Create New option should already be selected.

2. Enter an OMS workspace name. The OMS workspace name is used as a base public URL so it must be unique in all of OMS.

3. Select a resource group and subscription then select Location. Notice not all locations are available under the Location drop-down; select the nearest location.

4. Click Pricing Tier to expand the pricing tier blade. The cost of your workspace depends on the pricing tier and the solutions you use. Notice all components are available in free or per node tiers. The differences are in capabilities such as retention. For now, choose the Free tier. You can change pricing later in the GENERAL settings of the Pricing Tier on the Log analytics settings blade. For more information on pricing see: *https://azure.microsoft.com/pricing/details/log-analytics/*.

5. Click OK to start building the workspace. Azure automatically opens the Log Analytics Management Solution after it is deployed. You can always get back to Log Analytics by finding it in all resources or under the resource group you created or selected when you built it.

There are four different ways to collect logs and metrics from Azure services. These include:

- Azure diagnostics direct to Log Analytics
- Azure diagnostics to Azure Storage to Log Analytics
- Connectors for Azure services
- Scripts to collect, then post data into log Analytics

The collection method used depends on the service type. For additional information on the services and collection methods see *https://docs.microsoft.com/en-us/azure/log-analytics/log-analytics-azure-storage#connectors-for-azure-services*. Exporting logs into the OMS workspace enables analysis capabilities on those logs. Exporting can be done through the Set-AzureRmDiagnosticSetting PowerShell command or the Enabling Diagnostics With Resource Manager templates using Microsoft.Automation/automationAccounts/providers/diagnostic-Settings. For step-by-step instructions for any of the four collection methods see *https://docs.microsoft.com/en-us/azure/log-analytics/log-analytics-azure-storage*. You can search your Log Analytics data from the Azure portal under **Log Analytics** > **General** > **Log Search**. Under **Log Analytics** > **Settings** > **Advanced Settings** > **Data**, you can add events, other logs, and performance counters. Learn how to see view or analyze data collected with Log Analytics Log Search at *https://docs.microsoft.com/en-us/azure/log-analytics/log-analytics-tutorial-viewdata*. You can also learn how to visualize data at *https://docs.microsoft.com/en-us/azure/log-analytics/log-analytics-tutorial-dashboards* and alert on data at *https://docs.microsoft.com/en-us/azure/log-analytics/log-analytics-tutorial-response*.

EXAM TIP

Use Azure Performance Diagnostics VM extension for monitoring Azure virtual machines (both Linux and Windows). The agent provides the insights collected from within the virtual machines. You can also use the extension for virtual machine scale sets.

> **NOTE QUICK START STEP-BY-STEP FOR COLLECTING DATA**
>
> There are Quick Start step-by-step instructions in Azure Docs to help get started with collecting data for:
>
> - **Azure VMs** *https://docs.microsoft.com/en-us/azure/log-analytics/log-analytics-quick-collect-azurevm*
> - **Linux Computers** *https://docs.microsoft.com/en-us/azure/log-analytics/log-analytics-quick-collect-linux-computer*
> - **Windows Computers** *https://docs.microsoft.com/en-us/azure/log-analytics/log-analytics-quick-collect-windows-computer*

Searching and visualizing Logs are very helpful in managing and monitoring systems. Monitoring and managing systems and evaluating performance and metrics are all parts of a DevOps process. However, like with other aspects of DevOps, automatically responding and applying an action to what is DevOps practices strive to deliver. Alert actions carry out automation. Alert rules can automatically run log searches on the Log Analytics repository at a predefined interval. Alerts trigger the creation of a new alert log record and the automation for taking action. An alert can be any number of actions, including sending an email, kicking off automation, exporting, or posting to a custom app. An alert can even integrate with a third-party IT Service Management (ITSM) system such as ServiceNow, as shown in Figure 6-2.

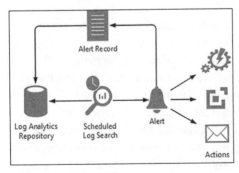

FIGURE 6-2 Alert workflow

It is important to consider the timing of data written to logs, the synchronization of the logs, and the frequency of the alert query. If, for example, you create an alert log search and have it executed every 10 minutes, you may not be alerted within 10 minutes of the incident. The OMS agent on the machine needs to send the data to the repository before the query can find it in the log search. When a machine collects information (the server creates a log), that log is stored locally on that server. The OMS agent on that machine sends the data to Log Analytics based on a frequency. Let's say you configure that frequency to 10 minutes. It also takes time to transfer the logs from the server to the OMS data repository. The log data collected on the server is packaged and sent, and depending on the size, frequency, and the network latency, can add even more time. The log is not in the OMS repository and available for search results, until the batch process completes. Given the variables and settings identified in this example, it can take 20–25 minutes after a server has an incident and the alert is triggered. The creation of the alert and execution of the action are also susceptible to latency or runtime, which could add even more time. When planning alerts, the frequencies and intervals of the entire cycle time should be considered. The reliability of alerts and the responsiveness of an alert, as well as the usefulness of the alert, are important factors, but these often compete with each other. To fully understand alerts and everything that impacts alerts you need to understand some definitions:

- **Alert**   Performing an action.
- **Alert rule**   A rule specified to trigger an alert based on the results of a log search.
- **Alert action**   An action automatically performed and executed by an alert rule. It can, for instance, send an email, invoke an external process through HTTP POST request, or start a Runbook and Azure automation.
- **Log search**   A query that is run every time an alert rule fires. The resulting records determine if an alert is triggered.
- **Time window**   Used to query records based on log creation date/time. The time window can be 5 minutes to 24 hours from the current time. This window should be long enough to accommodate ingestion delays. It should be two times the length of the longest delay you can accept. For instance, if you want alerts to be reliable for 30-minute delays, the time window needs to be one hour.
- **Missing alerts**   They are sometimes triggered if the time range is too small. Missing alerts can happen because the data may not be available when running the search due to congestion.
- **False alerts**   These are sometimes triggered if the ingestion delay (based on Time window) is too small. If your query is looking for the absence of data and you do not have a long enough delay, false alerts can result. As an example, if you are querying the availability of a system through heartbeat logs and there is an ingestion delay, the resulting heartbeat records may not have been processed yet.
- **Frequency**   This determines how often the query should run, ranging between 5 minutes and 24 hours. The frequency should be equal to or less than the time window. It is used to make alerts more responsive. If the value is too large and thus greater than the time window, then you risk missing records in the query.
    - If the reliability goal for the delay is up to 30 minutes and the normal delay is 10 minutes, the time window should be one hour, and the frequency value should be 10 minutes. The configuration triggers an alert with data that has a 10-minute ingestion delay, which is between 10 and 20 minutes from the creation of the alert.

- Suppress alerts is an option that allows for suppressing for at least as long as the time window that reduces noise caused by multiple alerts triggering within the time window.
- **Threshold** The limit evaluated to determine if an alert is triggered.
- **Number of results** An alert created when the number of records returned by the log search exceeds a specified number.
- **Metric measurement** An alert created for each object for which a log search returns a record with values that exceed the specified threshold.

> *NOTE* **DIAGNOSING AN ALERT NOT TRIGGERING**
>
> Trying to diagnose why an alert is not triggering can be difficult. For example, in the frequency case above, the data is written to the repository 60 minutes after the alert query executes. If the next day you notice an alert did not trigger and the next day the query is executed over the correct time interval, the log search criteria would match the result. It appears that the alert should have triggered. In fact, the alert did not trigger, because the data was not yet available when the alert query executed.

EXAM TIP

The Number Of Results alert rule always creates a single alert, while Metric Measurement alert rules create an alert for each object that exceeds the threshold. The Number Of Results alert rules creates an alert when a threshold is exceeded a single time. The Metric Measurement alert rules can create an alert when the threshold is exceeded a certain number of times over a particular time interval.

Saved log searches can be scheduled through alert rules and have alerts triggered based on the results. REST API, Resource Manager Templates, or OMS portal can all create alert rules. To create an alert rule in the OMS workspace from Log Analytics in the Azure Overview, click the OMS Portal. Click Log Search (magnifying glass). From here you can click Favorites to see searches that were already created based on the services you deployed. You can also create your own searches. Log Analytics lists your saved alert rules under Favorites. Next is to create or select a query, and here are some examples:

- Query errors writing to diagnostic logs

```
AzureActivity

| where ( OperationName == "microsoft.insights/diagnosticSettings/write" )

| where ActivityStatus == "Failed"
```

- Query of systems where Windows updates executed in the last seven days. If the count resolves to zero, create an alert to evaluate the machine or trigger a Windows update.

```
Event
```

```
|where EventID == "44"

|where TimeGenerated >= ago(7d)

|count
```

- Query Event Logs for errors and warnings (list up to 100 error and warning messages)

```
search in (Event) "error" | take 100
```

For information on the query language see *https://docs.loganalytics.io/docs/Learn/Getting-Started/Getting-started-with-the-Analytics-portal* and *https://docs.loganalytics.io/docs/Language-Reference*. Once you open a saved search or create your own and save it, click the menu option to Alert, which allows you to create an alert rule based on the query. Then from the Create Rule page, configure the alert details, as shown in Figure 6-3, and click Save. Upon saving the Alert Rule, the Alert Rule starts running immediately. You can edit, disable, or remove an alert from **OMS console** > **Settings** > **Alerts**. For more information on alerts see *https://docs.microsoft.com/en-us/azure/log-analytics/log-analytics-alerts*.

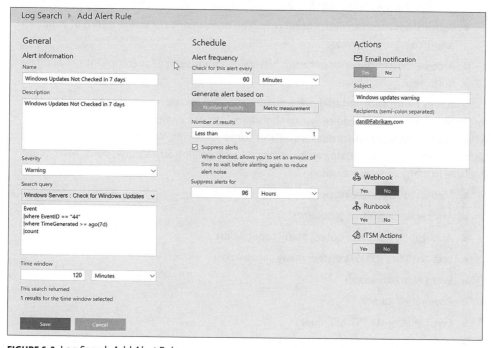

FIGURE 6-3 Log Search Add Alert Rule

EXAM TIP

The OMS workspace has a maximum limit of 250 alert rules.

Define solutions for analyzing performance metrics and enabling alerts using Azure Monitor

Azure Monitoring Metrics allows for consuming telemetry to gain additional insights into your applications and systems. All Azure resources provide metrics. Under Azure Monitor, click Metrics, and select a resource by using the filtering options. This view brings together all metrics in a single pane so you can easily visualize how your resources are performing. You can chart multiple metrics at once by selecting metrics and modify the graph type and time range. You can also view all metric alerts set on a particular resource. Metrics, or performance counters, enable you to:

- Track performance of your resource (such as a VM, website, or logic app) by plotting its metrics on a portal chart and pinning that chart to a dashboard.

- Get notified of an issue that impacts the performance of your resource when a metric crosses a certain threshold.

- Configure automated actions, such as autoscaling a resource or firing a runbook when a metric crosses a certain threshold.

- Perform advanced analytics or reporting on performance or usage trends of your resource.

- Archive the performance or health history of your resource for compliance or auditing purposes.

Resources Metrics are updated every minute allowing for the near real-time visibility of resources. Metrics do not require pre-configuration and are immediately available to query. A history of 30 days of metrics data is available for all resources. When more than 30 days of history is required, metrics data can be archived to Azure Blob Storage. Resource Metrics are available in many services including:

- Metrics (query, alert, respond)
- Any service > Metrics (visualize)
- Application Insights (routed, many capabilities)
- Log Analytics (OMS) (routed, many capabilities)
- Event Hub (streamed)
- PowerShell (query)
- Cross-Platform REST API (query)
- Azure Monitor REST APIs (consume)
- View Designer (display)

Any service in Azure provides the capability to view basic metrics of that service using the Overview blade. Click on any of the metrics in the Overview blade to display the detailed Metrics blade. From here you can also add metric alerts. You can also access Alerts under **Monitoring** > **Alerts**.

With the View Designer, you can create custom views of your logs or metrics data. View Designer is an excellent way to create a customized dashboard for different apps, metrics, administration roles, or anything else. Learn more about the View Designer at *https://docs. microsoft.com/en-us/azure/log-analytics/log-analytics-view-designer*.

Let's create a simple Web App and configure metrics and alerts to look deeper at the performance and alerting capabilities, see Figure 6-4. Perform the following steps from the Azure Portal:

1. Click **+ Create A Resource** > **Web + Mobile** > **Web App**

2. Give your app a name such as *My535AppXXXxxx* (where Xx are unique values; the name must be unique in all of Azure)

3. Select your subscription from the drop-down list.

4. Create a resource group or select an existing resource group.

5. Select **Windows OS**.

6. Click **App Service plan/Location** > **Create new**. If you already have a plan, you may select it instead of creating a new plan.

   A. Enter **App Service** plan name (e.g., 535AppPlan).

   B. Select **Location And Pricing** tier (e.g., S1 Standard).

   C. Click **OK** to close out of New App Service Plan blade.

7. Turn on Application Insights (we use it in the next lesson), then select a Location from the dropdown list.

8. Click Create and then wait for the Web App creation to complete.

9. Navigate to **All Services** > **Web + Mobile** > **App Services** > click on the name (*My-535AppXXXxxx*) of your App Service.

10. On the Overview blade, click the link to browse to the page. This will launch your new web app in a browser window. Enter data into the application and then click the magnifying glass. The search submission will trigger a web request, which is logged. Continue to play with the app for a minute to collect more data.

11. Navigate to **All Services** > **Web + Mobile** > **App Services** > click on the name of your App Service (My535AppXXXxxx) > **Overview.**

12. You will see charts including counts and metrics of the requests as well as Errors, Data In, Data Out, Requests and Average Response Time. Click the **Average Response Time** chart to see more metrics that can be displayed. Notice at the top there is a link to + Add metric alert.

13. Navigate back to the App Service, scroll down the app service navigation pane to Monitoring and select **Alerts**. Click **Add Alert** > Fill in the details of the Alert rule.

    A. **Resource**   Select your Web App (My535AppXXXxxx)

    B. **Name**   Avg Response over 10ms

    C. **Description**   Avg Response over 10ms

D. **Alert on** Metrics

E. **Metric** Select Average Response Time then fill in the additional fields.

F. **Condition greater than**

G. **Threshold** 0.01

H. **Period** Over the last 5 minutes

I. **email owners, contributors and readers** turn on

J. Optionally, add other administrator email addresses separated by semicolons

K. **OK**

14. Click Create.

FIGURE 6-4 Create Web App

Browse to the *My535AppXXXxxx* website again and submit a query from the web app. This will trigger a web response. When the average response time goes over 10ms, the alert fires. It takes at least 5 minutes for the site to collect enough data to activate the alert since it is a rolling average. You can navigate to the website and run queries many times, to collect data quickly in an attempt to push the latency over the 10ms threshold, which will generate the alert. No data is generated if there are no hits to the site because the trigger is on an average of the response time. It also means you can hit the site many times for 30 seconds and then do nothing. After five minutes your average is calculated by the Sum of ResponseTimes / # of responses.

Once you confirm the alert is working properly, it would be wise to change the alert to a higher number such as 100ms. To do this, edit the alert rule from **App Services** > **My535App-pXXXxxx** > **Alerts** > **App Responses GT 10ms**. Change the name to **100ms** instead of 10ms and change the **Threshold** to **0.1** and then click **Save**.

To view all metrics, select **Monitor** from the navigation pane, and then click on **Metrics**. Select **Subscription** > **Resource Group** and the name of the resource from the drop-down lists. Notice that you have many more available metrics. As you select from available metrics, some of the items become disabled. Disabling prevents you from selecting metrics that have different chart unit axes. If selecting a percentage metric, you can only add other percentage metrics to the same chart. You can add additional metrics, pin any metrics you create to the dashboard, and add metric alerts if desired.

EXAM TIP

You can access host-level metrics from VMs (Azure Resource Manager–based) and virtual machine scale sets without any additional diagnostic setup. These host-level metrics are available for Windows and Linux instances. You can access Guest-OS-level metrics when you turn on Azure Diagnostics on your VMs or virtual machine scale sets.

Define a solution for monitoring applications and enabling alerts using Application Insights

Application Insights is an extensible Application Performance Management (APM) service for web developers, building and managing apps on multiple platforms. It can perform a deep monitoring of applications, their frameworks, dependent services, remote calls, database calls, and more. It integrates with DevOps processes to provide monitoring, analytics, and connection points to many development tools that can be used for continuous improvement. Application Insights works on multiple platforms including .NET, Node.js, and J2EE hosted on-premises, or in the cloud. It can also integrate with Visual Studio App Center and Hockey-App giving deep telemetry for mobile apps.

Application Insights integrates at the framework level, meaning developers do not have to rewrite code for deep insights. The overhead is small because tracking calls are non-blocking, batched, and sent in a separate thread. To enable Application Insights when you create a resource such as a web app, simply turn on Application Insights and then select a location. If you would like to create Application Insights for external resources, you can do that from the portal at **Create A Resource** > **Developer Tools** > **Application Insights**, then enter the details.

Availability alerts and Metric alerts for your application can be added from **All services** > **Web + Mobile** > **App Services** > **My535AppXXXxxx** > **Application Insights**. Application

Insights can test availability and responsiveness of your website from any Azure datacenter around the world. A request is sent to the application, and if the application does not respond quickly enough an incident is raised. There are two types of availability tests: a URL ping test that is a simple test you can create in the Azure portal, and a more advanced multi-step web test, which you create in Visual Studio Enterprise and upload to the portal. From an availability test result, you can:

- Inspect the response received from your server.
- Diagnose failure with server-side telemetry collected while processing the failed request instance.
- Log an issue or work item in Github or VSTS to track the problem. The bug contains a link to this event.
- Open the web test result in Visual Studio.

EXAM TIP

Items can be added to the Azure Portal main navigation pain by clicking on All services, clicking the service you wish to add to navigation, clicking the star next to the service. The star will turn gold showing that it is enabled and now visible from the main navigation menu. It can be turned off by repeating the steps to turn it off.

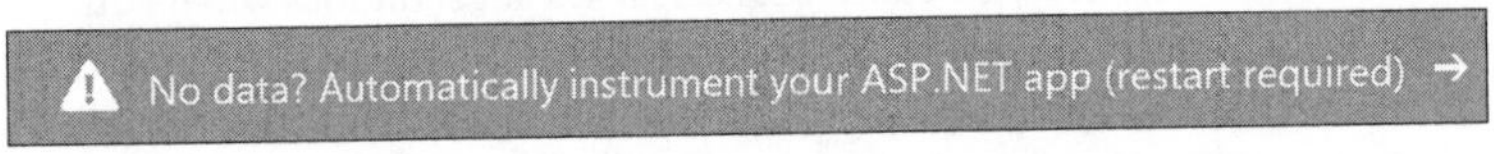

⚠ No data? Automatically instrument your ASP.NET app (restart required) →

FIGURE 6-5 Automatically instrument

Let's configure an availability test for the app (*My535AppXXXxxx*) we created above. An availability test will configure multiple Azure locations to connect to your web app periodically to confirm it is up and running. If there are any issues, an alert will be raised.

1. Navigate to **All Services** > **Web + Mobile** > **App Services** > **My535AppXXXxxx** > **Application Insights** (under Monitoring). Application Insights monitoring will not be enabled by default.

2. Click the link at the top of the right detail page to instrument the Application Insights into your app (see Figure 6-5). Notice that a restart will be required. Once the restart is completed, continue to **All Services** > **Monitoring** > **Application Insights**.

3. Click on your app My535AppXXXxxx, and then scroll down in the Application Insights navigation and click **Availability**.

4. Click **+ Add Test** > fill out the details and then click **Create**.

   A. **Test name**   My 535 App Ping Test

   B. **Test type**   URL ping test

   C. **URL**   Leave the default URL as it will be the URL for your WebApp

   D. The remaining details can be kept as the default values; click **Create**

After the tests run, click the Refresh button to monitor the results in the scatter plot chart. This could take many minutes to complete the tests and report back to Application Insights. You can add additional URL tests to test other parts of the application, such as a search URL, which would also test the database or logic parts of the app. If you scroll down on the chart display, you will see the percentage results from the various locations over time.

Failures will show up as a red dot on the scatter plot. You can click on the dot to get additional insight into any of the scattered dots. You can edit the rule using the edit button at the top of the blade. There is also a More button all the way to the right of the Edit button that provides additional options like disabling, enabling, and deleting the availability test. For additional information on availability tests, including multi-step web tests, see *https://docs. microsoft.com/en-us/azure/application-insights/app-insights-monitor-web-app-availability.* In this post you will learn how to go beyond login screens to get very deep insights into the performance and availability of all aspects of your app.

In many cases, you not only want to track and see the health of your application, but you also want to be alerted if there are changes in performance or usage metrics in your web app. This is what Application Insights alerts are designed to provide. It can alert you when a metric exceeds a threshold, alert you when a web test fails (your site is not available or hitting performance targets), and alert you through proactive diagnostics, which identify unusual performance patterns.

1. Navigate to **Application Insights** > select your app > **Configure** > **Alerts**. From here you can add an activity log alert or add a metric alert. You can set alerts if you have owner or contributor access to this application resource. If you do not have access, take a look at the Access Control blade. For this example, assume you want to know if your app is being hit more than 1000 times in any five-minute period so you can check on it to make sure it can handle the load. For this example, let's use 10 instead of 1000, so you can easily trigger the alert.

2. Click **+Add Metric Alert** then provide the details for the alert rule:

   - **Name**   *My535AppXXXxxx* Page Views
   - **Description**   Exceed 10 Page Views in last 5 minutes
   - **Subscription**, **Resource Group**, and **Resource** should already be selected for the app
   - **Metric**   Page views (notice all the options, take a few minutes to evaluate the various metric options)
   - **Condition**   Greater than
   - **Threshold**   10
   - **Period Over**   The last 5 minutes
   - **Email owners, contributors, and readers**   Turn on
   - Optionally, add other administrator email addresses separated by semicolons
   - **OK**

The Activity Log and Applications Insights will list alerts after they have been triggered. A notification is sent when the status changes. An email will be triggered each time an alert is triggered, and the status is changed. Activated means the threshold was hit. Resolved means the app is now under the threshold. The period used when configuring the alert determines how long of a time period will be used to aggregate results. An event can only be changed once the result status changes. If your app is constantly in an overloaded status, it will stay that way, and no future alerts will be sent out until the status changes back to healthy. If your app is constantly sending out alerts, it is likely due to operating at or near the threshold, where it is bouncing over and under the threshold.

Some of the best metrics to evaluate on your app are browser metrics such as page load times and browser exceptions, which require web page monitoring. If you are running apps on servers, server response time and server exceptions are good alerts to set. You can use PowerShell to automate setting up alerts: *https://docs.microsoft.com/en-us/azure/application-insights/app-insights-powershell-alerts*. You can also use webhooks to automate responding to alerts: *https://docs.microsoft.com/en-us/azure/monitoring-and-diagnostics/insights-webhooks-alerts*.

EXAM TIP

You can create up to 100 availability tests per application resource

Skill 6.2 Design a platform monitoring and alerting strategy

There are many tools and services that can monitor Azure platform services and applications. There are many advanced Azure monitoring capabilities. System Center also has a set of tools that are designed to monitor and alert for platform systems.

> **This section covers the following topics:**
>
> - Determine the appropriate Microsoft products and services for monitoring Azure platform solutions
> - Define a monitoring solution using Azure Health, Azure Advisor, and Activity Log
> - Define a monitoring solution for Azure Networks using Log Analytics and Network Watcher service
> - Monitor security with Azure Security Center

Determine the appropriate Microsoft products and services for monitoring Azure platform solutions

Platform solutions are made up of any number of services running on Azure. To understand monitoring of full solutions you have to know all of the different tools available for monitoring the different components.

Basic Monitoring

Basic monitoring provides fundamentally required monitoring across Azure resources. These services require minimal configuration and collect core telemetry that's leveraged by the premium monitoring services.

Azure Monitor enables basic monitoring for Azure service by allowing a collection of metrics, activity logs, and diagnostic logs. For example, the activity log will tell you when new resources are created or modified. Metrics are available that provide performance statistics for different resources and even the operating system inside of a virtual machine. The Azure Monitor is a platform of services that allow for a single source for monitoring applications running in Azure. You can find a walkthrough of the Azure Monitor at: *https://docs.microsoft.com/en-us/azure/monitoring-and-diagnostics/monitoring-get-started*. With Azure Monitor data you can:

- View with one of the explorers in the Azure portal
- Send logs to Log Analytics for trending and detailed analysis
- Send notifications proactively with alerts

Azure Service Health identifies any issues with Azure services that might impact your application and also helps you plan for any scheduled maintenance.

Azure Advisor constantly monitors your resource configuration and usage telemetry to provide you recommendations based on best practices. Recommendations will help improve the performance, security, and high availability of your resources while looking for opportunities to reduce your overall Azure costs.

Premium Monitoring Services

Premium Azure services provide rich capabilities for collecting and analyzing monitoring data. They build on basic monitoring and leverage common functionality in Azure and provide powerful analytics with collected data to give you unique insights into your applications and infrastructure. They present data within the context of particular scenarios targeted to different audiences.

- **Application Insights** Allows you to monitor availability, performance, and usage of your application whether it's hosted in the cloud or on-premises. By instrumenting your application to work with Application Insights, you can achieve deep insights, allowing you to quickly identify and diagnose errors without waiting for a user to report them. With the information that you collect, you can make informed choices on your application's maintenance and improvements. In addition to the extensive tools for interacting with the data it collects, Application Insights stores its data in a common repository to leverage shared functionality such as alerts, dashboards, and a deep analysis with the Log Analytics query language.

- **Log Analytics**   Plays a central role in Azure monitoring by collecting data from a variety of resources into a single repository where it can be analyzed with a powerful query language. Application Insights and Azure Security Center store their data in the Log Analytics data store and leverage its analytics engine. This, combined with data collected from Azure Monitor, management solutions, and agents installed on virtual machines in the cloud or on-premises, allows you to form a complete picture of your entire environment.

- **Service Map**   Provides insight into your IaaS environment by analyzing virtual machines with their different processes and dependencies on other computers and external processes. It integrates events, performance data, and management solutions in Log Analytics so that you can view this data in the context of each computer and its relation to the rest of your environment. Service Map is similar to the application map in Application Insights but focuses on the infrastructure components supporting your applications.

- **Network Watcher**   Provides scenario-based monitoring and diagnostics for different network scenarios in Azure. It stores data in Azure metrics and diagnostics for further analysis and works with the following network monitoring solutions for monitoring various aspects of your network:

    - Network Performance Monitor (NPM) is a cloud-based network monitoring solution that monitors connectivity across public clouds, data centers, and on-premises environments.

    - ExpressRoute Monitor is an NPM capability that monitors the end-to-end connectivity and performance over ExpressRoute circuits.

    - Traffic Analytics provides visibility into user and application activity on your cloud network.

    - DNS Analytics provides security, performance, and operations related insights, based on DNS servers.

- **Management solutions**   Are packaged sets of logic that provide insights for a particular application or service. They rely on Log Analytics to store and analyze the monitoring data they collect. Management solutions are available from Microsoft and partners that provide monitoring for various Azure and third-party services. Examples of monitoring solutions include Container Monitoring, which helps you view and manage your container hosts. Another example is Azure SQL Analytics, which collects and visualizes performance metrics for SQL Azure databases.

> *MORE INFO*   **ELASTIC SCALE**
>
> You can scale out your SQL database with Elastic Scale. You can learn more about Elastic Scale at: *https://docs.microsoft.com/en-us/azure/sql-database/sql-database-elastic-scale-introduction.*

Shared Functionality

The following Azure tools provide critical functionality to monitoring services. They are shared by multiple services allowing you to leverage common functionality and configurations across multiple services.

- **Azure Alerts**   Proactively notifies you of critical conditions and potentially takes corrective action. Alert rules can leverage data from multiple sources including metrics and logs. They use Action Groups, which contain unique sets of recipients and actions in response to an alert. Based on your requirements, you can have alerts launch external actions using webhooks to integrate with your ITSM tools.

- **Azure Dashboards**   Provides visual representations of monitoring data. Dashboards allow you to combine different kinds of data into a single pane in the Azure Portal and share with other Azure users. For example, you can create a dashboard that combines tiles showing a graph of metrics, a table of activity logs, a usage chart from Application Insights, and the output of a log search in Log Analytics. You can also export Log Analytics data to Power BI to take advantage of additional visualizations and also to make the data available to others within and outside of your organization.

- **Metrics Explorer**   Provides visualizations of metrics. Metrics are numerical values generated by Azure resources that help you understand the operation and performance of the resource. You can send metrics to Log Analytics for analysis with data from other sources.

- **Activity Logs**   Provide data about the operation of Azure resources. This includes such information as configuration changes to the resource, service health incidents, recommendations on better use of the resource, and information related to autoscale operations. You can view logs for a particular resource on its page in the Azure portal, or view logs from multiple resources in Activity Log Explorer. You can also send activity logs to Log Analytics so they can be analyzed with data collected by management solutions, agents on virtual machines, and other sources.

System Center

System Center can monitor systems regardless of their location. They can be on-premises, in a private cloud, in a partner data center, or in a public cloud such as Azure. It is an entire suite of tools with which administrators can manage and monitor many different aspects of your systems. System Center components include the following:

- **Operations Manager** (SCOM)   Monitoring, alerting and logging.
- **Configuration Manager** (SCM)   Server, client, device and application management for on-premises and cloud-based infrastructure.
- **Virtual Machine Manager** (SCVMM)   Provision and manage resources to create and deploy virtual machines (VM). SCVMM provides a dashboard for on-premises and cloud virtual machine infrastructure.

- **Orchestrator** (SCOR)   Automate the creation, monitoring, and deployment of resources.
- **Data Protection Manager** (SCDPM)   Back up and recover data for workloads, applications, and services.
- **Service Manager** (SCSM)   Manage incidents and control asset lifecycle management.
- **Service Management Automation**   Service Management Automation is an IT process automation solution. It enables you to automate the creation, monitoring, and deployment of resources in your Windows Azure Pack environment.
- **Service Provider Foundation** (SPF)   As a service provider, you can use SPF to offer infrastructure as a service (IaaS) to your clients. Your clients can request IaaS resources managed by VMM through your front-end portal.

Each of these components has a unique job. Some of the components have integration points with others, and most components directly integration with Azure. For additional information on System Center and each of the tools see *https://docs.microsoft.com/en-us/system-center/*.

Define a monitoring solution using Azure Health, Azure Advisor, and Activity Log

When defining a monitoring solution, it is important to understand not only the application or service being monitored but also all the platform and services that are needed to keep the application running. As discussed earlier, the activity log and other monitoring tools do a great job of letting you see what is going on in your environment. If you add to that functionality the ability to apply best practices and you are also leveraging information about the underlying platform, you can truly get a world-class monitoring solution.

Azure Advisor is accessible through the Azure Portal under All services > Advisor. The advisor is a great addition to your DevOps processes as it helps you constantly improve the performance of all systems. It will evaluate services you have running in your subscription and make recommendations for how you can improve. These recommendations include:

- **High Availability**   Ensure and improve the uptime of applications.
- **Security**   Detect threats and vulnerabilities that might lead to security breaches.
- **Performance**   Improve the speed of your applications.
- **Cost**   Optimize and reduce your overall Azure spending.

Azure Health informs you of upcoming planned maintenance through alerts. Service Health can be accessed through All Services > Service Health or on a tile in your default dashboard. The Service Health evaluates what services you have, where they are located, and cross-references that with known issues within the platform. It has a world map showing location status that you can pin to your dashboard. Within Server Health you can filter and create service health alerts so when issues are reported to the platform you and your team can be better prepared to limit exposure or remediate issues generated by the disruption.

If you want to define a comprehensive monitoring strategy, leveraging logs, Azure Advisor and Azure Health together is the best approach. If, as an example, you have a VM scale set as well as some web apps running in the EAST US datacenter, you will want to monitor the Azure health of that datacenter as well as implement suggestions from Azure Advisor. When defining this monitoring strategy, you should consider all aspects of the application, application services, and infrastructure leveraged by those servers. In our example, we not only have the web apps and VM's, but we also have storage, networking, logging, diagnostics, backup and more. DevOps tells us we need to emphasize the performance of the entire system. In this case, the entire system encompasses all of the resources in multiple data centers across the country. As a best practice, the backup will be in a different datacenter than the production data so the backup and storage from the second data center will need to be monitored as well. Setting up logging, monitoring and alerting on all components, and then integrating best practices from Advisor and platform monitoring with Service Health, will give you a complete solution. For more information on Azure Service Health see: *https://docs.microsoft.com/en-us/azure/service-health/service-health-overview*. For Azure Advisor see *https://docs.microsoft.com/en-us/azure/advisor/advisor-overview*.

> **NOTE AZURE ADVISER DASHBOARD OWNER**
>
> To use Azure Advisor with a subscription, a subscription Owner must launch the Advisor dashboard. This action registers the subscription with Advisor. From that point on, any subscription Owner, Contributor, or Reader can access the Advisor recommendations for the subscription.

Define a monitoring solution for Azure Networks using Log Analytics and Network Watcher service

Azure monitoring provides the capability of monitoring services, including networking services such as VNET, load balancers, VPNs and more. Monitoring networks and all the complexities of interactions between resources really requires more than just service level monitoring. This is where Log Analytics can help. Network Watcher is built-in to the Azure platform, which performs scenario-based monitoring. It can do much deeper analysis such as IP flow, next hop, packet capture and more. Here is a list of capabilities:

- **Topology** Provides a network level graphic view showing the various interconnections and associations between network resources in a resource group.
- **Packet capture** Captures packet data in and out of a virtual machine. Advanced filtering options and fine-tuned controls, such as being able to set time and size limitations to provide versatility. The packet data can be stored in a blob store or on the local disk in .cap format.

- **IP flow verify** Checks if a packet is allowed or denied based on flow information and five-tuple packet parameters (Destination IP, Source IP, Destination Port, Source Port, and Protocol). If the packet is denied by a security group, the rule and group that denied the packet are returned.

- **Next hop** Determines the next hop for packets being routed in the Azure Network Fabric, enabling you to diagnose any misconfigured user-defined routes.

- **NSG Flow logging** Flow logs for Network Security Groups enable you to capture logs related to traffic that are allowed or denied by the security rules in the group. The flow is defined by five-tuple information: Source IP, Destination IP, Source Port, Destination Port, and Protocol.

- **Virtual Network Gateway and Connection troubleshooting** Provides the ability to troubleshoot Virtual Network Gateways and Connections.

- **Network subscription limits** Enables you to view network resource usage against limits.

- **Configuring Diagnostics Log** Provides a single pane to enable or disable Diagnostics logs for network resources in a resource group.

- **Connection Troubleshoot** Verifies the possibility of establishing a direct TCP connection from a virtual machine to a given endpoint enriched with Azure context. It checks for and detects direct TCP connection from a virtual machine using FQDN, URI, or IPv4 address.

- **Network Security Group View** A view of connected devices and device connections by a network security group. It assesses vulnerabilities by viewing open ports, compares configured with effective security rules, and even defines prescriptive rules for governance for auditing. Get the effective and applied security rules that are applied on a VM.

Network Watcher provides a diagnostic logs view that contains all networking resources and gives you an easy way to enable or disable. You can enable Network Watcher from:

1. **All services** > **Monitor** > **Network Watcher** or from **All Services** > **Network Watcher**.

2. **Overview** > click the "**...**," **ellipses** to the right of your subscription.

3. Select **Enable Network Watcher.** A new NetworkWatcherRG resource group will be created, and the services will be deployed. The status of your subscription will then be set to enabled.

4. Click **Topology**.

5. Select **Subscription**.

6. Select **Resource Group**.

7. Select **Virtual Network** to see the topology. If you do not have a network yet, you can create one from the **Azure Portal** > **Create A Resource** > **Networking** > **Virtual Network**.

8. Click back to **Network Watcher**.

9. Click **NSG Flow Logs**; by default NSGs are disabled.

10. Click on an **NSG**:

   A. Set status to **On**

   B. Select a **Storage Account**

   C. Set **Retention** (days) (zero saves forever)

   D. Optionally turn on **Traffic Analytics** status then select an **OMS workspace**

   E. Click **Save**

   F. Close the **Flow Logs Settings** blade

   G. Take a look at other options that can be turned on for the **Network Watcher**.

For more on Network Watcher see: *https://docs.microsoft.com/en-us/azure/network-watcher/network-watcher-monitoring-overview* and *https://docs.microsoft.com/en-us/azure/network-watcher/*.

Monitor security with Azure Security Center

Azure Security Center gives you the data you need to understand your security posture across on-premises and cloud workloads. It allows you to easily identify and mitigate risk, limiting your exposure to security threats. Security Center provides:

- **Centralized policy management** Ensure compliance with company or regulatory security requirements by centrally managing security policies across all of your hybrid cloud workloads.

- **Continuous security assessment** Monitor the security of machines, networks, storage and data services, and applications to discover potential security issues.

- **Actionable recommendations** Remediate security vulnerabilities before they can be exploited by attackers with prioritized and actionable security recommendations.

- **Advanced cloud defenses** Reduce threats with just-in-time access to management ports and whitelisting to control applications running on your VMs.

- **Prioritized alerts and incidents** Focus on the most critical threats first with prioritized security alerts and incidents.

- **Integrated security solutions** Collect, search, and analyze security data from a variety of sources, including connected partner solutions.

These capabilities are provided through monitoring and analyzing data about systems. The resulting information is rolled up and exposed in a very impressive security dashboard, as shown in Figure 6-5. Additionally, this data can be used to alert and create automation. Automation can often be used to do the remediation of the risk. See the Azure Security Center planning and operations guide at *https://docs.microsoft.com/en-us/azure/security-center/security-center-planning-and-operations-guide* for a quick understanding of how to plan for implementing Azure Security Center.

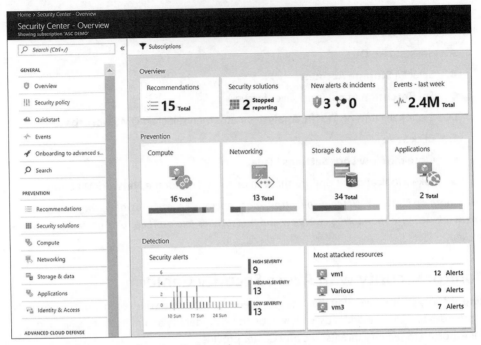

FIGURE 6-6 Security Center Overview Dashboard

The first time it will likely take a bit longer than usual. There are two tiers of pricing for Security Center. The Free version is for Azure resources only and does not include some of the more advanced features such as Just in Time VM Access and Adaptive Application Controls. The pricing is by node (e.g., VM) per month. To fully integrate with on-premises you will need to upgrade to the Standard pricing tier. One of the first things you will need to do is set up centralized policy management. A security policy defines what system-wide policies should be enacted. By enabling a policy, any systems that do not meet the standard will be tracked as an incident. Let's take a look at Security Center.

1. Click **All services** > scroll down.

2. Under **SECURITY + IDENTITY** click **Security Center**. It may be easier to find Security Center if you type **security** into the filter box. When you open Security Center, it will go out and evaluate logs and systems to expose and visualize the data already logged by the systems.

3. From **Security Center**, click **Security Policy**. You will see that **Automatic Provisioning** is turned off.

4. Click on your subscription to expand. You will then have options for Data collection, Security policy, Email notifications and pricing tier.

5. Click **Data Collection**.

A. **Automatic provisioning of monitoring agent**   **Turn On**, which will install a monitoring agent on each VM in the subscription. Data collected is stored in a Log Analytics workspace.

B. **Default workspace configuration**   Select **Use Another Workspace.** We already have a workspace, 535BookWorkspaceXXXxxx, that we created earlier. Select 535BookWorkspaceXXXxxx from the **Connect Azure VMs** to report to select user workspace drop-down list. It is fine to take the default value and have Security center create a dedicated workspace for Security Center if you prefer.

C. Click **Save**. If you already have VMs in your subscription you will get a popup asking *Would you like to reconfigure monitored VMs?* Respond **Yes** to this prompt.

6. Click **Security Policy** to see the many policies that can be turned On or Off.

7. Click **Email Notifications**. The notifications are used in case the Microsoft security team finds that your resources are compromised.

A. **Security contact emails**   Type your email address.

B. **Phone Number**   Type your phone number.

> **NOTE WOULD YOU LIKE TO RECONFIGURE MONITORED VMS?**
>
> If you have existing VMs, you will get a message box that says:
>
> "Would you like to reconfigure monitored VMs?
>
> To apply the default workspace setting on already monitored VMs reporting to ASC managed workspaces, click Yes. To apply only to new agent installations, click No, and to cancel the operation, click Cancel. Please note this process may take up to a few hours. "

8. Click Pricing tier then confirm the Free-pricing tier is selected. If you select the Standard Pricing tier, you can also configure additional capabilities. Without Standard, these features are not available. Capabilities that are not available with the free pricing tier include:

- **Events Dashboard**   Capture all of the log and event data required for a security overview and gain a complete data set in a searchable format. The dashboard displays event collection over time and allows you to quickly view the notable events that you have in your environment.

- **Hybrid Security**   Get a unified view of security across all of your on-premises and cloud workloads. Apply security policies and continuously assess the security of your hybrid cloud workloads to ensure compliance with security standards. Collect, search, and analyze security data from a variety of sources, including firewalls and other partner solutions.

- **Advance Threat Detection**   Use advanced analytics and the Microsoft Intelligent Security Graph to get an edge over evolving cyber-attacks.

  - Leverage built-in behavioral analytics and machine learning to identify attacks and zero-day exploits.

- Monitor networks, machines, and cloud services for incoming attacks and post-breach activity.
- Streamline investigation with interactive tools and contextual threat intelligence.

- **Detecting unprotected resources**   Security Center automatically detects any Azure subscriptions or workspaces not enabled for Security Center Standard. This includes Azure subscriptions using Security Center Free, and workspaces that do not have the Security solution enabled.

- **Just in Time (JIT) VM Access**   Just in time virtual machine (VM) access can be used to lock down inbound traffic to your Azure VMs, reducing exposure to attacks while providing easy access to connect to VMs when needed.

- **Adaptive Application Controls**   Block malware and other unwanted applications by applying whitelisting recommendations adapted to your specific workloads and powered by machine learning. Reduce the network attack surface with just-in-time, controlled access to management ports on Azure VMs, drastically reducing exposure to brute force and other network attacks.

EXAM TIP

You may want to manage your costs and limit the amount of data collected for a solution by limiting it to a particular set of agents. Solution targeting (*https://docs.microsoft.com/en-us/azure/operations-management-suite/operations-management-suite-solution-targeting*) allows you to apply a scope to the solution and target a subset of computers in the work-space. If you are using solution targeting, Security Center lists the workspace as not having a solution.

9. Click on **Compute** in the **Security Center**. If you have a VM in your subscription (created from the prior chapter), then click **VMs And Computers**. You may see that you have some vulnerabilities on the machines. As you click on the machine, and then on the security recommendation, you will see that you have detailed instructions at your fingertips to resolve. The same is also true for the other prevention categories such as networking, storage & data, applications, and identity. Azure Security Center documentation can be found at: *https://docs.microsoft.com/en-us/azure/security-center/*.

Skill 6.3 Design an operations automation strategy

Automation is automatically executing tasks, and is a key foundation of DevOps. It is especially important for the tasks that are: frequently needed, time-consuming, and error-prone. Automation allows for streamlining and ensuring tasks are completed quickly and consistently every time they are run.

Determine when to use Azure Automation, Chef, Puppet, PowerShell, Desired State Configuration (DSC), Event Grid, and Azure Logic Apps define a strategy for auto-scaling

Azure Automation reduces errors and boosts efficiency while lowering operational costs. It also delivers a cloud-based automation and configuration service that provides consistent management across your Azure and non-Azure environments. It includes process automation, update management, and configuration capabilities. Azure Automation provides complete control and automation during deployment, operations, and decommissioning of workloads and resources.

Azure Automation

Azure Automation is a feature integrated into the Azure platform that executes Windows PowerShell or Python scripts as desired. It uses the term runbooks for the scripts, or instructions that you can execute to automate systems in Azure. Automation is designed for Azure systems. However, using Hybrid Runbook Worker (*https://docs.microsoft.com/en-us/azure/automation/automation-hybrid-runbook-worker*), runbooks can run in your local data center to manage local resources. It can also integrate with on-premises systems that are accessible from the public cloud. With Azure Automation, you can perform almost any task on nearly any computer if you can get to that computer and gain access from a Windows PowerShell workflow or Python script from the cloud.

The best use-case for Automation is to automate systems running in Azure if you do not have any other automation system already adopted. Azure Automation allows you to author runbooks graphically. Hybrid Runbook Worker allows you to orchestrate across on-premises and cloud environments. There are many Microsoft and community-contributed scripts available to help you get started quickly. After you create or import existing runbooks into Automation, you can schedule them against the server or servers at a time or times of your choice. It is designed to simplify tedious, long-running, or error-prone procedures and processes. To import or download scripts from the Runbook Gallery or other parts of the TechNet Script Center see the Runbook Gallery: *https://docs.microsoft.com/en-us/azure/automation/automation-runbook-gallery*.

EXAM TIP

It is a best practice in Azure Automation to write reusable, modular runbooks with a discrete function that can be used by other runbooks. You can't convert runbooks from graphical to textual type or vice versa. There are limitations using runbooks of different types as a child runbook. *See https://docs.microsoft.com/en-us/azure/automation/automation-child-runbooks.*

Windows PowerShell for automation

You can use Windows PowerShell by itself for automation. It is best used for automating repeated tasks that are identical. An example of this might be if you were setting up a training room and you want to deploy 15 VMs the same way. You can have Windows PowerShell create these VMs to be identical in every way. After the class is finished, you can use Windows Power-Shell to delete all of the VMs. You could also use Desired State Configuration, but the wrapper is a much more suitable solution for Desired State Configuration. To continue with our training class example, you may not want Desired State Configuration to reconfigure something that a user is doing in a lab. Any tasks that are very time-consuming or prone to error are great examples of use-cases for Windows PowerShell automation.

Chef and Puppet

Chef is a third-party (non-Microsoft) product that you can use for systems management, con-figuration, automation, and for producing analytics. A Chef client is installed on the VM that is being managed, and then that client checks in with the Chef server periodically to see if there are any updates that need to be applied. Chef is a well-known and popular platform built on Ruby, and it enjoys large adoption numbers and familiarity. Chef can manage Windows, Linux, and even Mac computers. Chef is available in the Azure Marketplace, or it can be installed directly on a virtual machine. To configure Chef to integrate with Azure, you can download a certificate that you put on your Chef server so that it can authenticate with Azure to perform various tasks.

Chef *Cookbooks* are a group of scripts or instructions known as recipes that you can run to deploy systems or force compliance with the desired configuration on a system. A *knife* plugin is used to communicate with Azure, so resources on Azure can be fully managed by Chef (think of this as an agent). You can create, modify, and delete resources with it.

Puppet is another option to automate and enforce the consistency of systems. It is like Chef. Chef and Puppet both have a vast open source catalog of modules that you can download and reuse. Azure can automatically add the Chef or Puppet Enterprise Agent as you deploy a new VM. When you deploy the VM, you can add a Puppet or Chef extensions to install the agent and configure the name of your Master Server. You can also deploy an enterprise server (master) using a template in the VM Gallery.

If you have a Linux infrastructure in Azure, Puppet and Chef can both manage and automate the infrastructure. A use-case for Chef is if you already have a Chef-managed infrastructure. A use case for Puppet is if you are already using Puppet for systems management or deployment. You can very easily integrate your new Azure infrastructure and share all of the management scripts with your new cloud capabilities. Another use case for either Chef or Puppet is if you have a broadly diverse infrastructure in many locations with many different operating systems that you want to bring under management. Chef and Puppet both have commands and examples available for Linux and Windows. Each is a versatile and useful tool when you need to prevent configuration drift of Windows and Linux-based systems. They are best used when you already have Chef or Puppet for your configuration management or have a large number of Linux based servers that need to be under management.

Desired State Configuration (DSC)

Desired State Configuration is the automated process of forcing the desired configuration onto a system. This is obtained by inspecting systems and automatically changing the configuration to match that of the desired state. This might be removing something that was added or adding something that was removed. It is used to make deployment easier and dependable, as well as to enforce a particular configuration on a VM or series of VMs. As an example, if you have a bunch of web servers, you need to have PHP support turned on. You can set the desired configuration that forces the installation of Internet Information Services (IIS) and the configuration of PHP. If someone later removes one of these capabilities, Desired State Configuration will reinstall and configure these components.

Some new terms are defined for a special syntax used for Windows PowerShell Desired State Configuration. *Configuration* is a keyword, followed by a set of braces ({}) to delimit the block. Inside the configuration, you can define nodes, which is the computer name. The node has braces ({}) block for action to be performed on that node. Keywords are used to define how the script engine should interpret the instructions. You use the term *Ensure* to make certain that the configuration is met; if it is not, make it so. *Absent* is a term that you use to make sure something is not present; if it is, remove it.

Practical applications of Desired State Configuration include the following:

- Installing or removing Windows roles and features
- Running Windows PowerShell scripts
- Managing registry settings
- Managing files and directories

- Starting, stopping, and managing processes and services

- Managing groups and user accounts

- Deploying new software

- Managing environment variables

- Discovering the actual configuration state on a given node

- Fixing a configuration that has drifted away from the desired state

The best use case for Desired State Configuration is if you want to ensure that newly deployed servers are configured a certain way. Another primary case is when you want to eliminate *configuration drift*, that is, guarantee the servers always maintain their desired configuration. The desired configuration not only monitors for misconfigurations of servers but corrects problems, eliminating configuration drift. DSC can also accomplish configuration changes to many systems that are currently using the same configuration. This is done by simply changing the configuration file to update the configuration, and any machine that is leveraging that configuration will be changed (see Listing 6-1).

EXAM TIP

Make it so and *configuration drift* are key terms that represent desired state configuration.

LISTING 6-1 Desired State Configuration: IIS Installed example configuration

```
Configuration MyWebConfig

{
  # A Configuration block can have zero or more Node blocks
  Node  "Server001"  # set to localhost for any server
  {
    # Next, specify one or more resource blocks
    # This example ensures the Web Server (IIS) role is installed
    WindowsFeature MyRoleExample
    {
      Ensure  = "Present" # To uninstall the role, set Ensure to "Absent"
      Name = "Web-Server" #The name of the IIS feature
    }

    # File is a built-in resource you can use to manage files and directories
    # ensures files from source directory are present in the destination
    File MyFileExample
    {
      Ensure = "Present" # You can also set Ensure to "Absent"
      Type = "Directory" # Default is "File"
      Recurse = $true
      SourcePath = $WebsiteFilePath # This is a path that has web files
      DestinationPath = "C:\inetpub\wwwroot" # Make sure web files are present
DependsOn = "[WindowsFeature]MyRoleExample"
      # Ensures MyRoleExample completes before this block will runs
    }
  }
}
```

In the preceding script example, Listing 6-1, we have two Desired State Configuration resources: *WindowsFeature* and the *File* resource. In this example, the *Name* of the *WindowsFeature* to ensure is *Web-Server*, which is IIS. For the *File*, the *SourcePath* and *DestinationPath* are defined. If the file is not present, it will be copied from the source to ensure that it is present. The reverse can also be established by using *Absent* instead of *Ensure*. As an example, if you want to make certain that default.aspx is removed, set that file and path to *Absent*. There are many other resources available, which you can find at *https://technet.microsoft.com/en-us/library/dn282125.aspx*. Desired State Configuration is a feature of Windows PowerShell, so it is designed for configuring Windows Systems.

EXAM TIP

Azure DSC can configure on-premises servers. It requires an install of the Hybrid Runbook Worker to monitor and execute configuration changes. Read more at: *https://docs.microsoft.com/en-us/azure/automation/automation-offering-get-started*.

Azure Logic Apps

Azure Logic apps are a serverless workflow in the cloud. Logic Apps allow you to build, schedule, and automate processes as workflows. You can integrate apps, data, systems, and services from your own business as well as almost countless other sources. They greatly help with enterprise application integration (EIA) and business-to-business (B2B) communications. Azure Logic Apps are extended through connectors that integrate with many different services such as SQL Server, Microsoft Cognitive Services, SAP, Oracle, SharePoint, BizTalk, CRM, Office 365, Salesforce, social media, other Azure services and much more. A prebuilt connectors list is available at *https://docs.microsoft.com/en-us/azure/connectors/apis-list*. Azure Logic Apps can automate and integrate cloud, on-premises, or both.

Leverage Logic Apps when you want to integrate seamlessly with on-premises and cloud systems, interface with LOB systems with minimal custom code, or integrate with any of the hundred+ systems available through connectors. Logic Apps provides orchestration between systems. As an example, you can monitor a hashtag on Twitter or leverage an app or function that uses Azure Cognitive Service to detect sentiment. When something positive is tweeted about the product, a function can retweet or otherwise act on the data. Here are more examples:

- **Check traffic on a schedule** *https://docs.microsoft.com/en-us/azure/logic-apps/tutorial-build-schedule-recurring-logic-app-workflow*

- **Manage mailing list requests** *https://docs.microsoft.com/en-us/azure/logic-apps/tutorial-process-mailing-list-subscriptions-workflow*

- **Process emails and attachments** *https://docs.microsoft.com/en-us/azure/logic-apps/tutorial-process-email-attachments-workflow*

- **Send X12 messages in batch to trading partners** *https://docs.microsoft.com/en-us/azure/logic-apps/logic-apps-scenario-edi-send-batch-messages*

- **FTP connector** *https://docs.microsoft.com/en-us/azure/connectors/connectors-create-api-ftp*
- **B2B cross-region disaster recovery** *https://docs.microsoft.com/en-us/azure/logic-apps/logic-apps-enterprise-integration-b2b-business-continuity*

Event Grid

Azure Event Grid is a service for managing routing of all events from any source to any destination. It is a fully managed intelligent event routing service that allows for uniform event consumption using a publish-subscribe model. Use Azure Event Grid to react to relevant events across both Azure and non-Azure services in near-real time. Event Grid is the service to use when you have event publishers sending topics and event handlers subscribing to those topics. As Janakiram MSV at Forbes.com puts it, "Azure Event Grid Can Become The Foundation Of Microsoft Serverless Strategy" in *https://www.forbes.com/sites/janakirammsv/2017/08/17/how-azure-event-grid-can-become-the-foundation-of-microsoft-serverless-strategy/*. See Figure 6-6 from *https://docs.microsoft.com/en-us/azure/event-grid/overview* for a sample flow of topic publishers and subscription handlers.

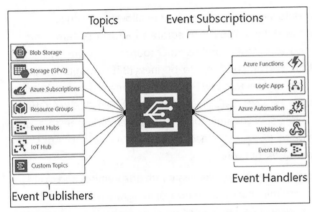

FIGURE 6-7 Event Publisher Topics to Event Handler Subscriptions

Some sample use cases for Event Hub include:

- **Simplify policy enforcement** The Event Grid can notify Azure Automation when a new workload is created (virtual machine, SQL Database, other), then confirm compliance, and add backup or other things that may need to be done.
- **Serverless Computer** An Event Grid can instantly trigger a serverless function to run image analysis each time a new photo is added to a blob storage container.
- **Application Connection** Connect your apps to other services and apps.
- **Message Management** Message advanced routing handling acts on a message that comes in from any of the many sources that can be configured, and then it starts another task based on the type of message or message topic.

- Send email notification about Azure IoT Hub events using Logic Apps.
- Configure Azure functions and a logic app that receive messages based on receiving an event from event grid; send a message to your service bus topic.
- Stream data from event hubs to populate a data warehouse.

Autoscaling

Azure Autoscale allows you to scale resources based on metrics. Autoscale can scale cloud services, mobile apps, virtual machines, and web apps. Autoscale can leverage metrics like CPU, memory, a number of requests or any metric including custom metrics that you can create as part of your monitoring strategy. Autoscaling is used for orchestration of scaling up or down of resources based on demand, or any other metric you decide is an effective method of determining when you need more or fewer resources. There are two different ways to provide autoscaling:

- **Vertical scaling**   Is also called scaling up (bigger) and scaling down (smaller). It is changing the capacity of a resource. For example, you can move an application to a larger VM size. Vertical scaling often requires making the system temporarily unavailable while it is being redeployed. Vertical scaling tends to be more expensive and generally takes more time to execute. Therefore, it's less common to automate vertical scaling.

- **Horizontal scaling**   Is called scaling out (more) and scaling in (less). It is adding or removing instances of a resource. For example, you can add or remove an additional VM to a scale-set or add/remove more instances of a web app. The application continues running without interruption as new resources are provisioned. When the provisioning process is complete, the solution is deployed on these additional resources. If demand drops, the additional resources can be shut down cleanly and deallocated.

Autoscaling is used when you want to change the capacity of an application or workload based on metrics and thresholds or schedules that are predefined. Generally, you scale up/out when you need additional capacity, and you scale down/in when you do not need as much capacity, which will save money by only running the resources you need. Some examples include scaling out or in when you need to:

- Schedule scale out capacity to handle known workload increases always caused when sending a weekly email blast out to customers with the week's product discounts.

- Scale in when your capacity when utilization goes below 50% to save money.

- You want to scale out when your system capacity reaches 80% utilization.

Additional information on auto-scaling best practices can be found at: *https://docs.micro-soft.com/en-us/azure/architecture/best-practices/auto-scaling*.

Define a strategy for enabling periodic processes and tasks

There are a number of ways to enable periodic processes and tasks. Tasks or periodic processes are always triggered by something. We learned earlier about trigger-based tasks, which are event-driven. There are often needs to enable tasks and processes based on a schedule. These are known as a scheduled-driven trigger.

- **Event-driven triggers** Are started in response to an event, such as a message in an event log, a step being triggered by a workflow, or a metric threshold being met.
- **Schedule-driven triggers** Are started based on a schedule such as a timer or recurring schedule. The Azure Scheduler is one way to enable this type of task.

They can be performed for almost limitless reasons. Some of these include:

- CPU-intensive jobs such a mathematical calculations or analysis.
- I/O-intensive jobs such as indexing storage.
- Batch jobs such as data manipulation, moving or archiving.
- Long-running tasks such as reporting, data replication, order fulfillment, or service provisioning.
- Data synchronization such as periodically grabbing data from a Twitter or social media data source.
- Daily/weekly/monthly maintenance jobs (e.g., backup database, run a report).
- Creating a thumbnail of images when an image is added to a storage account or batched every hour.
- Azure system queue jobs such as storage queue, service bus queue, service bus topic and HTTP/HTTPS jobs.

In defining a strategy for enabling periodic processes and tasks you first need to understand a few details about the process or task.

- What will trigger it? A schedule or event?
- How often will it run? Start time, frequency, error/retry action, or recurrence?
- What action will be performed and what system will run it? HTTP/HTTPS, service bus, or queue?

If we want to create a scheduled job to check the availability of our website every hour, monitor the log results to perform any action if there is a problem. We could set up a scheduled, recurring task to trigger the job. To do this from the Azure portal:

1. Click **Create A Resource** > type **Scheduler**, and press ENTER > select **Scheduler** > click **Create**. For this example, we will use: *http://docs.microsoft.com/en-us/azure/architecture/* with a GET request. Fill in the details as follows:
   - **Name** ChkAzureArchetectureSite
   - **Job Collection** Create New
   - **Name** getArchitectureSite
   - **Pricing tier** Free (max Frequency one hour)

- Select or Create **Resource Group And Location**
- **OK**
- **Subscription**   Select your subscription
- **Action Settings**   Configure
- **Action**   HTTP
- **Method**   Get
- **URL**   *http://docs.microsoft.com/en-us/azure/architecture/*
- Notice other settings for headers, authentication settings, retry policy and error action; leave all of these at the defaults and Click **OK**
- **Schedule**   Configure
- **Recurrence**   Recurring
- **Start On**   At a specific time > today's date > one 10 mins from now, UTC offset your time zone
- **Recur Every**   Interval: 1 Frequency: Hours
- **End**   Never
- **OK**
- **Create**

2. Go to the resource to see the schedule and history: **All Services** > **Scheduler** > **Scheduler Job Collections** > **getArchitectureSite**. If you do not want to wait for the job to run, there will be a **Run Now** button at the top of the details page you can click.

3. From the schedule detail, you can see the status of the jobs. Note that since we used the free pricing tier, the job will only run a maximum of 5 times. If you want to run every hour 24 hours a day, you need to upgrade the pricing tier to a Standard, P10 Premium, or P20 Premium.

Thought experiment

In this thought experiment, apply what you've learned. You can find answers to these questions in the next section.

You are the architect for Contoso. Your Innovation team would like to deploy new services on Azure to support a new application Contoso is building. You get an email from the head of Innovation with the following request.

Letter from the Director of Innovation:

"As part of our new DevOps initiatives, we would like to deploy a new application project into the Azure cloud. We have one such application nearing completion, which is a multi-tier application with a .NET application front end and a SQL Server backend database. There are a number of different components, including a number of API applications that make up the system. The application will need to send and receive data from Contoso's network for various tasks both scheduled and on-demand. As we plan to deploy this application to Azure, can you help us understand how to design for high-availability, monitoring and alerting? This new application is critically important to the business. It is actually creating a new revenue stream for Contoso. I would not be surprised if 3 years from now it became our top flagship product. For some period of time, we will be giving away the high-end services for free to help us get all of our existing customers on the platform and to bring in a massive new pipeline of prospective customers. Let's have a meeting next week to discuss the architecture we should be using to monitor and manage the application. I will check our calendars and send you an invite.

Thanks so much for your help.

Dan"

With this in mind, think about following questions as you prepare for the meeting:

1. What services would you use to monitor and scale the application front end?
2. What services would you use to monitor and scale the SQL Database?
3. What alerts will need to be configured?
4. What automation should be put in place to make sure there is not configuration drift?
5. What foreseeable challenges do you think you need to discuss in your first meeting with Dan?

Thought experiment answers

1. Monitor Services: Azure Monitor, Activity Logs, Diagnostic Logs, Log Analytics, Azure Service Health, Azure Advisor, Application Insights, Network Watcher (Traffic & DNS Analytics, subscription limits, etc.), Azure Alerts, Azure Dashboards, Azure Security Center, Azure Scheduler, Azure auto scale using the web app platform & perhaps even Metrics Explorer to learn where bottlenecks may be occurring in the application.

   Scale: Platform application with auto scale enabled on many metrics including page load times. Other metrics should be evaluated as well especially in the beginning to determine if there are CPU, memory or other areas that could be a bottleneck.

2. Monitor: All of the above + Azure SQL Analytics Management Solution.

   Scale: SQL Database platform

3. Alerts for all application components availability and performance, platform availability, best practices, security alerts, log errors

4. Desired State Configuration

5. More information needed about: (many more answers could be correct)

   A. API apps and how they will run
   B. Background and scheduled tasks
   C. Application workflow
   D. SQL Architecture

E. System dependencies, authentication, etc.

F. What are the on-premises connections

Chapter summary

- Azure has many built-in monitoring tools. Some of these include: Azure Monitor, Azure Service Health, Azure Advisor, Azure Alerts, Azure Dashboards, and Metrics Explorer.

- Azure has many advanced monitoring services such as Applications Insights, Log Analytics, Service Map and Network Watcher as well as much extensibility through Microsoft and third-party management solutions.

- Azure Log Analytics ingests logs from Azure Monitor and on-premises or other systems. It can analyze the logs and send alerts.

- Log information can be shared, further analyzed or displayed to many destinations including through a REST API client, Management Solutions or exporting data to Excel or PowerBI.

- The Azure Activity Log is primarily for activities that occur in Azure Resource Manager. It does not track resources using the Classic/RDFE model.

- Operations Management Suite (OMS) is a service for pulling together data from any source including on-premises and Azure Log Analytics, acting on that data with alerts or executing automated actions. It has customizable dashboards and can execute configuration changes.

- All Azure resources provide metrics, and an Azure Monitoring Metrics section allows for consuming metrics telemetry to gain additional insights into your applications and systems. Based on metrics you can track performance, get notified via alerts, configure automated actions, perform advanced analytics, and archive performance or health history.

- Use Azure Performance Diagnostics VM extension for monitoring Azure virtual machines (both Linux and Windows).

- Azure Advisor will evaluate services you have running in your subscription and make recommendations for how you can improve: high availability, security, performance, and cost.

- Azure Health informs you of upcoming Azure platform planned maintenance through alerts.

- Network Watcher is built-in to the Azure platform, which performs scenario-based monitoring. It can do much deeper analysis such as IP flow, next hop, packet capture, and more. The capability of monitoring services including networking services such as VNET, load balancers, VPNs and more.

- Network Performance Monitor (NPM) is a scenario included with Network Watcher. NPM is a cloud-based network monitoring solution that monitors connectivity across public clouds, data centers and on-premises environments Azure.

- Security Center gives you the data you need to understand your security posture across on-premises and cloud workloads. It allows you to easily identify and mitigate risk limiting your exposure to security threats.

- Azure Automation is a method by which you can run Windows PowerShell commands to simplify and streamline long-running, error-prone or repetitive processes.

- A key tenet of Azure Automation is Desired State Configuration. This ensures that when a system is deployed, it conforms to the predefined state for this type of server. Additionally, the desired state can be enforced post-deployment, so if configuration changes are made, they are automatically set back to the desired state.

- Azure Automation uses "runbooks" as instructions. There are multiple types of runbooks including Graphical, Graphical PowerShell Workflow, PowerShell, PowerShell Workflow, and Python.

- There are several ways to perform deployment as well as post-deployment enforcement of Desired State Configuration. You can do this by using Azure Automation, Windows PowerShell, Puppet, or Chef. Puppet and Chef are the most popular methods and can perform desired state compliance across Azure as well as on-premises machines. You can use Puppet and Chef on Linux as well as Windows computers.

- Azure Automation and Windows PowerShell are the easiest automation components to set up and configure. They do not require additional server or host integration to manage. Both Chef and Puppet require a central management server to administer Desired State Configuration.

- Azure Logic apps are a serverless workflow in the cloud. Logic Apps allow you to build, schedule and automate processes as workflows. You can integrate apps, data, systems, and services from your own apps and almost countless other sources.

- Azure Event Grid is a service for managing message routing of all events from any source to any destination. It is a fully-managed intelligent event routing service that allows for uniform event consumption using a publish-subscribe model.

Index

Symbols

B